A Brit's Guide to Cruising

Simon Veness

foulsham

LONDON • NEW YORK • TORONTO • SYDNEY

foulsham

The Publishing House, Bennetts Close,
Cippenham, Berkshire, SL1 5AP, England.

While every effort has been made to ensure the accuracy of all the information contained within this book, neither the author nor the publisher can be liable for any errors. In particular, since laws change from time to time, it is vital that each individual should check relevant legal details for themselves.

ISBN 0-572-02394-4

Printed in Ireland by ColourBooks Ltd., Baldoyle Industrial Estate, Dublin

Contents

As an exciting new development in the British cruise world, we bring you this innovative joint venture that seeks to highlight the Best of the Best in each of the Brit's Guide categories, the first cruise 'Oscars'.

Awards 1998

The best-selling **Brit's Guide** series has teamed up with the dynamic new *What Cruise* magazine, with sponsorship from the Singapore Tourist Promotion Board, to produce this essential highlight of the UK travel world. With the aid of a panel of experts, we have created an extra element that will be prominently featured in both the book and magazine. Our 11 panellists, including **Brit's Guide** author Simon Veness and *What Cruise* insider Chris Coates, bring an unrivalled knowledge of the British cruise scene to bear on our 10 Awards, which we are proud to unveil for our readers. Here's how it works: the **Brit's Guide** identifies four categories of cruise style, Standard, Superior, Premier and Deluxe, and there are Awards for what we consider the best ship in each of those, plus Best Family Ship, Best Specialist, Best Cruise Innovation, Best Brochure and Special Service Award. We introduce the Panel on page 188, and you can read the results of our deliberations there. The **Brit's Guide**/*What Cruise* Awards made their official debut at a special presentation ceremony at World Travel Market in London on November 17th 1997, thanks to the sponsorship of the Singapore Tourist Promotion Board and we sincerely believe the **Brit's Guide**/*What Cruise* Awards will provide a valuable extra insight into this fascinating business. Don't forget to check out our section on the attractions of super Singapore on pages 236–238.

An annual subscription to the excellent bi-monthly What Cruise magazine, costs just £12.70 from: Cruise Travel Publications Ltd, Hitech House, Roebuck Road, Chessington, Surrey KT9 1LH, tel. 0181 287 0666.

Acknowledgements

A book as broad in scope as this could never be the work of just one person, and so, to that end, I am indebted to the help, research and advice of the following, and many others, who have all played a significant part in the creation of *A Brit's Guide to Cruising*.

The Passenger Shipping Association, The Passenger Shipping Association of Retail Agents, The Seatrade Organisation, Cruise Lines International Association, Cruise Europe, Pacific Asia Travel Association, The Guild of Professional Cruise Agents, Paul Mundy Cruising, Cruise Club International, Page & Moy, Going Places, Lunn Poly, Thomas Cook, P&O, Airtours, Crystal Cruises, Cunard, Thomson Holidays, Unijet, Virgin Holidays, Greater Miami Convention & Visitors Bureau, Port of Miami, Greater Fort Lauderdale Convention and Visitors Bureau, Port Everglades Port Authority, Cruise Industry News, the Port of Genoa and Genoa Tourism Promotion Office, Port Association of Eastern and Southern Africa, Singapore Tourist Promotion Board, Cruise New Zealand, Tourism Council for the South Pacific, Majorcan Tourist Office, Panama Canal Commission, Bermuda Tourism, Bahamas Tourist Office, Caribbean Tourist Association, Gibraltar Information Bureau, Hong Kong Tourist Association, Norwegian Tourist Board, Philippine Department of Tourism, Tourism Authority for Thailand, US Virgin Island Tourist Office, Vancouver Port Corporation, The Port of Southampton, Harwich International Port and Dover Harbour Board.

In particular, I would like to thank the following individuals for going out of their way to assist, usually on numerous occasions:

Bob Duffett (PSARA), Lynn Narraway (Carnival/Holland America UK), Graham Dullop (Cruise Club International), Edwina Lonsdale (Crystal/Radisson Seven Seas), David Dingle (P&O), Gloria Ward (Thomson), John Drysdale, Shaun Robinson (Airtours), Steve Odell (Celebrity Cruises), Eric Flounders and Robyn Griffith-Jones (Cunard), Peter Richardson (Costa Cruises), Paul Mundy (Paul Mundy Cruising), Ian Buckeridge (The Cruise Line Ltd), Peter Pate (Mediterranean Shipping Cruises), Nigel Lingard (Fred Olsen), Patrick Ryan (Royal Caribbean), Aris Zarpanely (Silversea), John Turgoose (Dover Harbour), Chris Hayman (Seatrade), Sarah Gibbins (Fleet PR), Debbie Hindle and Bronwen Griffiths (BGB & Associates), Deirdre Byrne (Barclay Stratton), Francine Mason (Fort Lauderdale), Alyce McDaniel (Miami), Bella Rangel Callan (Jebsens Travel), Mike Pawley (Anderson's Pacific Way) and Richard Bastow and Chris Coates (Cruise and Maritime Services).

Special thanks also go to my research team, Stephen Thorne, Carolyn White, Paul and Ruth Sherwood and Patricia Bell Piacente; plus my parents, John and Vera Veness, and my in-laws, Bernard and Beryl Lilly, for generously aiding my research in their own cruise time (!), and my wife, Karen, for continuing to be so supportive.

For another informative magazine on the cruise world, including up-to-the-minute news, ship reviews, ports of call articles and shopping tips, the American bi-monthly publication *Porthole* is well worth seeking out. An annual subscription from the UK costs $40. Write to: Porthole Magazine, 7100 West Commercial Boulevard, Suite 106, Fort Lauderdale, Florida, USA 33319-2124, or Fax on: 001 954 746 5244.

The author and publisher gratefully acknowledge the provision of photographic material by the following agencies:

Abercrombie & Kent (pp. 42, 90, 114, 257); Airtours (pp. 13, 63, 99, 116, 196); Australian Tourist Commission (pp. 190, 247, 249); Bermuda Tourism (pp. 19, 232); BGB & Associates (pp. 72, 220, 222, 224); Celebrity Cruises (pp. 50, 95, 121); Comité du Tourism Réunion (pp. 255, 256); Commodore Cruise Line (pp. 105, 125); Costa Cruise Line (pp. 79, 127); Crystal Cruises (pp. 40, 48, 54, 76, 81, 83, 91, 129, 203, 211, 225, 242); Cunard (pp. 39, 101, 132, 135); CTC (pp. 131, 227); Disney Cruise Line (p. 133); Equity Cruises (pp. 10, 15, 82, 106, 119, 141, 249, back cover); Festival Cruises (p. 137); Fred Olsen Cruise Lines (p. 150); Gibraltar Information Bureau (p. 195); Greater Fort Lauderdale Conventions and Visitors Bureau (front cover, pp. 217, 218); Greater Miami Convention and Visitors Bureau (front cover, pp. 215, 216); Hong Kong Tourist Association (p. 74); Hebridean Island Cruises (pp. 35–36); Indian Tourist Board (p. 253); Israeli Tourist Office (p. 205); Louis (UK) Ltd (p. 144); Majesty Cruise Line (pp. 32, 143); Mediterranean Shipping Cruises (pp. 67, 145); Norwegian Cruise Line (pp. 97, 147); Orient Cruise Line (p. 152); Philippine Department of Tourism (pp. 235, 239); Premier Cruise Line (pp. 80, 158); Princess Cruises (pp. 20, 45, 93, 102, 103, 160, 161, 198, 209, 228, 231); P&O (front cover, pp. 24, 47, 51–52, 104, 112, 153, 156, 157); Radisson Seven Seas (pp. 27, 57, 63, 68, 77, 96, 163, 164, 191, 194, 201, 238); Royal Caribbean Cruise Line (pp. 166, 168); Saga (p. 175); Silversea Cruises (pp. 107, 173); Singapore Tourist Promotion Board (pp. 177, 237); Star Clippers (pp. 112, 175, 244); Star Cruise Line (p. 241); Swan Hellenic (pp. 89, 178, 179); US Virgin Island Tourist Office (pp. 187, 213); Windstar Cruises (pp. 30, 181, 219).

Foreword

(or, How I Became Addicted to Cruising)

I GUESS I should blame my parents, really. After all, anyone who has done four Cape Town–Southampton voyages before their 17th birthday has little chance of avoiding the feeling later in life that cruising is somehow part of their life-blood, an essential requirement to well-being and happiness, a necessity.

Okay, so that may be a slight exaggeration, but there is definitely something about cruising that gets under your skin and makes itself a vital component of your way of life. Put simply, it is addictive. Whether it be a two-day "cruise to nowhere" or a luxury line voyage, life on the ocean wave is a heady mixture of excitement, enjoyment and, yes, even romance, that absolutely demands to be repeated.

Getting a taste for it so early in life (my parents, younger brother and I set sail for the first time from Durban in 1969 aboard the Union-Castle Line ship SA *Vaal*, when I was shortly past my ninth birthday) was without doubt a watershed experience, not least because I was heartily seasick before we had even lost sight of land! Although I obviously did not realise it at the time, it was a formative memory that would last long, strong and demanding.

So what is it that makes this form of travel, that has subsequently become one of the fastest-growing holiday types, so deliciously habit-forming?

First of all, there is still the misguided certainty you are doing something exclusive and selective, that somehow you have a social advantage over all those non-cruisers of the world. There is also the theory that, as an island race, we Brits have an unbreakable affinity for the sea, but, in these days of instantaneous world-wide communications and high-speed travel, it is not one to which I subscribe. It is more subtle than that. Cruising does still represent a bygone age of elegance, sophistication and romance, and it is that feeling of enjoying such a rich heritage of travel experience that instils a cruise holiday with much of its mystique.

And, make no mistake about it, despite the ultra-modern appeal of the new build of cruise ships and their facilities, there remains a mystique about cruising which no other holiday type can capture or recreate. There is nothing in the wide world of travel which can compare with the feeling of sailing into a new port first thing in the morning, of seeing the lights go down and the sun come up over the source of new adventure and new experience, a wonderful thrill of possibilities gradually unfolding in magnificent surroundings. (All right, I will admit not every port looks as if it is one of the scenic wonders of the world, but there are enough that do to make it an unforgettable event.)

On top of the mystique, there are many more tangible attractions to cruising, such as value for money, excellence of service, huge variety of appeal and the little-appreciated virtue of it being an ideal source of all-round family entertainment. This latter is something which all the major cruise companies are itching to exploit and, with few exceptions, is something they deliver with enormous success. I can certainly vouch for the inestimable youthful appeal of being in a world that caters specifically to kids' needs and delivers real excitement and facilities somehow divorced from adult life. I am equally sure my parents were similarly delighted that my brother and I were safely off their hands for large parts of the day!

Having therefore become convinced of cruising's lasting appeal from so early an age, it was only a small, logical step to want to rediscover those well-remembered delights as soon as I could afford to pay for them myself (this was admittedly not for a few years of being a humble journalist!). Almost inevitably, it was in researching all the wonderful options for a modern cruise holiday that I became fascinated in exploring this rapidly-expanding source of holiday appeal. So much so, in fact, that I have now spent more than three years recording countless interviews with cruise lines, travel agents, ship crew and passengers, as well as visiting ship after ship to get the full flavour of the differences and attractions of the main cruise lines (and at the same time thoroughly enjoying the occasional cruise!). During this process, the cruise lines and tour operators have co-operated fully in my research without once seeking to obtain a particular slant to a write-up or asking for the right to vet my material, which I believe speaks volumes for the quality of their service in general.

The days of line voyages and the Union-Castle Line are both firmly in the past, but in their place has sprung up a holiday industry that borrows heavily from cruising's elegant heritage while placing it firmly in a modern context. Gone are the days of the classic, class-structured cruise ships (with the one exception of the QE2), but instead has come a quickly-evolving new breed of vessels which can deliver the most flexible and varied experiences in some of the world's most beautiful holiday playgrounds. They retain their sense of style, but they have added a level of all-round comfort and sophistication (virtual reality gymnasiums, anyone?) that almost defies belief. And the huge diversity of the product, from the small, luxury cruisers to the modern, massive mega-liners means there is guaranteed to be something for everyone.

Happily, there remains, too, a sense of the industry's grand history. The debut in 1995 of P&O's new ship the *Oriana* brought a welcome sense of tradition and elegance back to the modern ship-builder and ensured, at least for my lifetime, that the memories of Union-Castle will remain proud and strong.

I therefore dedicate this book to my parents in the happy knowledge there is still a world of holiday enjoyment and romance awaiting a new generation of cruisers. I urge you to go out and explore it – but, be warned, it IS highly addictive.

*

CHAPTER ONE

Introduction

(or, Why Cruising? Isn't That for Fuddy-Duddies?)

WELCOME to the big, wide world of cruising! Whether you are a cruise novice or an old salt, you cannot have failed to notice that here is a holiday type that is rapidly becoming big business. The cruise lines of the world now have a high profile and a tantalising product – and they ALL believe Britain is a holiday market ripe to be exploited. To a large extent they are right – but, armed with this book, you can be safe in the knowledge you have all the facts at your fingertips.

Cruising is a wonderfully thrilling way to spend a week or more, but it is easy to go wrong in what is still a highly complex and specialised field. Just trying to work out the average cruise brochure can still be a forehead-creasing experience, and the variety on offer is becoming wider and more bewildering all the time. There are more than 30 major cruise lines dealing in the British market, with in excess of 120 ships to choose from. Newer, more dramatic and bigger vessels are being added all the time. It is a diverse, and multi-dimensional product. From the budget-priced basic cruise experience to the ultra luxury of the all-inclusive small specialist vessels, from the Caribbean super-liners to the individual adventure ships cruising the startling waters of the Antarctic, cruising is a breathtakingly broad experience.

So, let's start off with a few gentle facts to set the ball rolling (or the ship sailing, to be more precise). Britain is the second-largest cruise market in the world – a very distant second to that of America. Yet it is growing incredibly fast from a small base and is by far the most dynamically healthy segment of the UK holiday industry. Put simply, the secret of the cruise holiday has finally been let out of the bag, and an increasing number of people have decided it is for them. And, once they have sampled its delights, they are equally reluctant to return to their old land-based holidays. For this happy yet still relatively small band, the secret they have discovered is that of an intensely rewarding holiday offering really terrific value for money – and it is a holiday with the highest satisfaction ratio of any on offer. Once bitten, nearly always smitten.

However, it is also an inescapable fact that cruising has engendered more misconceived ideas and perceptions of its appeal than any other holiday type. To mangle a modern cliché, if I had a pound for every time someone asked me 'Why would you want to go cruising?' I would be a wealthy man (well, several hundred pounds better off, at least). Despite a veritable advertising barrage in the last three or four years, cruising STILL has an unfortunate image of being class- and age-conscious, not to mention it being something primarily for the well-to-do.

THIS IS NOT THE CASE!

Glamour and glitz aboard Holland America's Statendam

I am inclined to underline that statement as well, if only to get your attention from the outset. Henceforth, you will discard all pre-conceived notions of what cruising is and isn't, and you will be ready to enter a world of dramatic scale and appeal, not to mention magnificent value for money. Let me open up the world of cruising, therefore, with a detailed investigation of what it isn't.

For various reasons – and I will come to those shortly – cruising remains a bit of a mystery to the majority (a mystery formed from a bygone age of leisurely, long-distance travel peopled by the elderly, rich and titled), and its appeals are lost to the average holiday-seeker simply because it has yet to be properly explained. In the course of the next few chapters, this book will set out to destroy the myths, cut through the hype, explain the attractions and outline the wealth of opportunity that cruising really represents.

CHANGING THE IMAGE

To begin with, cruising's well-documented heritage, both in print and film, has helped to create this picture of it being exclusive and expensive. And, although the industry, particularly in this country, doesn't really like to be reminded, it is an image it has still not done enough to dispel. For many, the notion of taking a cruise holiday is one that just does not occur, hence the need to labour the point with all the subtlety of a cavalry charge. The modern face of cruising is so vastly different to the common perception as to make the comparison almost funny. Not only is it so *different*, it is also hugely *varied*. That means that, while there are still some bastions of cruising that remain staunchly faithful to past eras of bridge foursomes, ballroom dancing and high tea, there are equally up-to-date ships concentrating on totally youthful pursuits like video games, beer-drinking contests and teen discos. In between, you can enjoy bingo and art auctions, highbrow lectures and practical discussions on the best shopping, *cordon bleu* cuisine and all-you-can eat buffets, Las Vegas-style cabarets and ballet. And that is just a small sample. Hey, modern cruising can be FUN!

The other major area in which cruising has so dismally failed to sell itself in the past is through its travel agents. Until recently, your average high street multiple outlet of Thomas Cook, Lunn Poly, Going Places, AT Mays, Co-Op or whoever has been woefully ignorant of all the merits, intricacies and options involved in a cruise booking. To be fair, the cruise lines themselves have not helped by producing brochures that have made selecting your average cruise about as easy as planning an expedition to the North Pole. In simple terms, the amount of specialist knowledge required for even a relatively straightforward cruise inquiry is far in excess of that needed for your average two-week package holiday. Therefore, the travel agents have notably failed in the past to provide much impetus for the cruise industry, leaving the field clear for the growth of specialist agencies dealing only in cruises. This is now rapidly changing as the big retail outlets bring out their own cruise-dedicated brochures and operate Cruise Clubs for past passengers. Gradually, the high street outlets are catching up with the idea cruise holidays are good business for them and their customers alike and are training their staff in the necessary areas to understand and explain the product. I will return to this subject later as it has a number of implications when you sit down to debate the pros and cons of your cruise holiday.

IT'S BIGGER IN AMERICA

The basic truth remains, though, the British cruise industry as a whole is considerably under-developed when compared with America's. Herein lies the biggest contradiction, even allowing for the far greater numbers involved in the US tourist industry. To the average American, there is nothing prohibitive about going on a cruise, it is simply another holiday option. No drawbacks, no misconceptions, no problem. They do, of course, have the advantage of the world's biggest cruise playground, the Caribbean, virtually on their doorstep, but the essential idea of it being out of their reach for reasons of class or finance just would not occur to them. In Britain, on the other hand, it remains something for lottery winners, the retired or Lord and Lady Whoever. Joe Schmo from Chicago is FOUR TIMES more likely to take a cruising holiday than his counterpart in Birmingham or Manchester.

So let's knock this on the head once and for all – cruising is for absolutely EVERYONE, young or old, active or passive, wealthy or not-so-wealthy. Believe me, if you can afford two weeks on the Costa Blanca, you can afford a cruise – and you'll get far better value for your holiday peseta.

One of the most overlooked facts of a cruise holiday is that it is virtually *all-inclusive* once you have paid your initial costs. That means that all your food, entertainment, travel, transfers and, in some cases, even your shore excursions are paid for before you leave home. There are no hidden extras for unexpected meals, evenings out, discos, taxis or whatever. The only other expenses during your cruise are your drinks, ship-arranged shore excursions, beauty and health treatments, tips and, in a dwindling number of cases, port taxes. There are even a few of the deluxe lines that are totally all-inclusive – you do not need to spend a single penny extra once you step aboard.

FACTS AND FIGURES

The message may seem blindingly obvious to anyone amongst you who has already sampled cruise life, but the basic facts and statistics still suggest it is getting through only slowly.

Back in 1986, the number of Brits who took a cruise holiday was barely 90,000. The Magic Kingdom in Walt Disney World, Florida, can handle that number in a DAY! By 1990, Brits at sea had doubled to 186,000 and the rate of increase has grown since then to almost 25 per cent annually. In

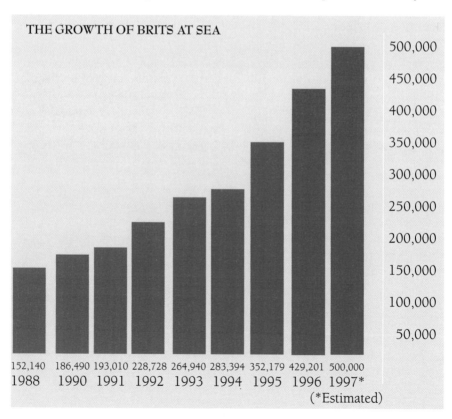

THE GROWTH OF BRITS AT SEA

	500,000
	450,000
	400,000
	350,000
	300,000
	250,000
	200,000
	150,000
	100,000
	50,000

152,140	186,490	193,010	228,728	264,940	283,394	352,179	429,201	500,000
1988	1990	1991	1992	1993	1994	1995	1996	1997*

(*Estimated)

1995, the total was up to 352,000, but that still represents only a small percentage of the holiday market in overall terms – some 21 million Brits holidayed abroad in 1995 – and suggests the message is not coming across loud and clear. By comparison, the American cruise market currently numbers almost 5 million.

The evolution of the modern cruise industry is perhaps partly to blame for this since the likes of Cunard and P&O were slow to catch on to the developments of the American cruise lines which seized this route in order to survive after the effective death of sea travel *per se* in the 1960s and 70s as Mr Boeing and his friends sent their jets further and faster around the world. Instead of selling off their liners at a fraction of their worth, the most go-ahead cruise companies experimented with turning their ships into floating vacation resorts, following the sun year-round and offering a taste of long-past class-orientated glories in modern, one-class comfort. The sunshine state of Florida became the centre of this burgeoning new tourist industry and Miami found itself the cruise capital of the world. Inevitably, America became the market leader. Fly-cruising became firmly established as the preferred method of holiday-making and, as the market became more sophisticated, California, Mexico, Alaska and the Far East quickly appeared on cruise itineraries. In the 1980s cruising was given another boost with the visionary strides made by the Carnival Corporation under the control of owner Ted Arison and his son Micky. Their massive input in new cruise ships and aggressive marketing in making it appealing (and affordable) have ensured continued growth, not only in America, but world-wide. The scheduled arrival of the Walt Disney company into cruising in 1998, with two massive ships, will enhance this process still further.

MEANWHILE, IN THE MED
In Europe, the Italian company Costa pioneered Mediterranean fly-cruising and the Greeks joined in, buying up old liners and turning them into island-hopping cruisers offering

Lavish buffets, like this one aboard the Airtours ship Seawing, are a notable feature of life at sea

guaranteed sunshine. Britain, by contrast, was slow to exploit these developments, partly because Cunard and P&O still had world-wide traditional shipping commitments, and partly because of the obvious drawbacks of cruising from UK ports. Any company wishing to sail year-round from Britain had to contend with the winter and Bay of Biscay factors: firstly, you needed a fast ship to get your passengers into the sunshine quickly in the winter months, and secondly, you had to cross the notoriously rough Bay of Biscay (between Brittany in north-western France and Cape Ortegal, at the tip of north-western Spain) to get there, and hence your vessels had more design restrictions than the fair-weather liners. A crossing of the Bay in heavy weather and high seas is also not for the faint-hearted, although many experienced cruise passengers do get a thrill from this sort of 'real' sailing!

The belated mass-market entry of Britain into the fly-cruise business in the 1980s, plus the advent of the *Oriana*, amazingly the first cruise ship purpose-built for the UK market, has finally given the British cruise industry the tools to expand its horizons. They are after YOU – and your family. For, make no mistake, the future of cruising is considered very much in family terms, with ships demonstrating a sophisticated array of children's facilities as well as baby-sitting and child-minding services.

The other significant development threatening to make Britain more cruise-conscious is the entry into the market of two of the biggest tour operators, Airtours and Thomson, and the possibility of more (Sunworld and First Choice have both been touted as potential cruise companies).

Airtours were first, in 1995, and, after sizing up what Carnival in particular were doing so well, they invested £52 million in buying up two existing ships and launching a new, mass-market product. Both they and Thomson, who chartered their own ship in 1996, make no bones about making cruising increasingly available for the budget-conscious as well as the traditional British package holiday-maker. It is a long-overdue development, but one eagerly greeted by (most) of the existing British cruise industry, who argue that it will attract a host of first-time passengers to the market, a welcome influx who will surely want to investigate all the attractions of cruising much further in future. The few critics are worried that the price-conscious nature of the new operations might devalue the product as a whole and actively discourage more people from cruising in future. There was certainly little sign of that happening in Airtours' first season of operation, but both they and Thomson do bear a significant responsibility for maintaining cruising's reputation for delivering a quality product. It is something the industry – and this author – will monitor closely in the next few years, although the fact American giants the Carnival Corporation took a 29 per cent stake in Airtours in 1996 helps to boost their level of technical expertise in the cruise field (not to mention making Carnival more popular on this side of the Atlantic).

LOOKING AHEAD

If that is the immediate past and present of the cruise industry, what of the future? Well, working on the theory that bigger is better, Carnival have unleashed the first 100,000-ton monster on the market, and Princess (the

American arm of P&O) will do the same in 1998, with an accompanying wealth of modernistic features that make the great liners of yesteryear look like closer relatives of the Ark than of these new ultra-megaships – there can be no other term for them. Prior to the 77,000-ton *Sun Princess* in 1995, the biggest previous passenger ship was the 84,000-ton *Queen Elizabeth*, launched in 1938. Typically, most modern cruise ships have weighed in around 70,000 tons, while, by contrast, the average cross-channel ferry is a tiddler at 25,000 (although the biggest ferries can handle 2,000 passengers). To put things further in perspective, P&O's new ship the *Oriana*, which carries more British passengers than any other, would more than fill Wembley Stadium if you dropped all its 69,153 tons in the middle.

It would comfortably span the full grassed area of the interior, some 408 feet in length, and it would extend over the running track at each end well up into the stands. In fact, the stadium's full length, from outer wall to wall, is officially 890 feet, and *Oriana* would come within 18 feet of those walls at each end. And, while the stadium's Twin Towers go up 126 feet in height, you would still be able to look down on them from the ship's topmost deck!

Carnival's Jubilee *is one of the new breed of cruise ships*

In fact, the trend is increasingly to build either very big or very small ships, working on economies of scale in the case of the former (where more cabins equals more people spending their money on board) and the attraction of all-inclusive, luxury service on the latter (where small scale means the epitome of the high-class, personal touch). There is also a tendency to build *faster* ships, which presents a fascinating throwback to the real glory days of the transatlantic crossings, when speed was everything, and the fastest ship was the best. The modern thinking behind faster ships, however, is not to win any particular award (as in the case of the Blue Riband, the cup awarded for the quickest transatlantic journey), but simply to get the ships to more ports of call in any one holiday, and for longer in each case.

Sadly for traditionalists such as myself, the tendency of the modern ship design is increasingly towards the large, slab-sided floating hotel type, which does detract slightly from the true aesthetic enjoyment of being at sea. The evolution of the modern design is quite straightforward. Whereas the classic ocean-going liners of the pre-1970 era were designed for long-distance travel, and therefore needed to sail quickly, efficiently and smoothly, modern cruise ships have more in common with the major land-based resorts. Their clients demand a full range of on-board facilities, a choice of things like bars, lounges, restaurants and entertainment centres and an unimpaired sea view no matter where they are. As a consequence, features like dining rooms, which on classic ships used to dwell lower down in the vessel's deck hierarchy (for smoother service), are now brought up to become more of a feature, with big picture windows. A greater number of cabins are also placed much higher up on the ship's profile to allow for modern additions like balconies. Long gone are the days when a ship had passenger cabins below or on the waterline (and had other authentic touches like portholes instead of windows!). The overall result is a demand to build ships with a vastly increased public capacity and with much of it above the mid-point rather than below it. Hence, in the quest to fulfil these new criteria, the designers arrive at a more high-rise, box-like profile rather than the sleek, well-proportioned look of ships like the QE2.

However, it is hard to argue that the modern liners do not cater for every conceivable activity in magnificent style – breathtaking, multi-storey lobbies, glass-sided lifts, state-of-the-art theatres, 24-hour restaurants, wide-ranging health and fitness facilities and even mini-golf courses are all regular features these days. And, while the outward appearance of a ship like *Sun Princess* is a touch monolithic, internally she is stunningly pretty.

The technology levels of the new build of ship are also a significant pointer to the way ahead. State-of-the-art sound systems (like Sony's link-up with Celebrity Cruise Line on their newest ships), ever more sophisticated theatres (witness *Oriana's* West End capability), interactive games (virtual reality golf and the rest) and service enhancements like in-cabin TV that can call up the day's menu, order your duty free goods and even play poker with you (for real money!) are all the marine order of the day. The variety of such entertainment options will continue to be the envy of the rest of the holiday world, and it is also not uncommon these days to find ships well fitted out for business users, with conference facilities, faxes, photocopiers and even, in the case of the QE2 and Celebrity's new ships, computer training facilities.

As if the massive level of hardware investment isn't enough (and there are something like 23 major new ships due to roll out of the world's ship-building yards before the end of the century), the cruise lines are also desperately seeking to develop new cruise areas for the mass market. Royal Caribbean have now put a ship year-round in the Far East for the first time, Mediterranean Shipping Cruises are opening up a regular link from the Med to South Africa, the Indian Ocean is seeing more cruise activity every year and South America, notably the Pacific coastline, is becoming the latest hot new destination.

The only real cloud on the world-wide cruise market is the steady growth of the industry's biggest players, often at the cost of some of the

THE WORLD'S LARGEST CRUISE LINERS

SHIP	CRUISE LINE	BUILT	TONNAGE
Carnival Destiny	Carnival Cruise Line	1996	101,353
Queen Elizabeth	Cunard	1938	83,673
Normandie	French Line	1932	82,799
Queen Mary	Cunard	1934	81,237
Galaxy	Celebrity Cruises	1996	77,750
Sun Princess	Princess	1995	77,441
Dawn Princess	Princess	1997	77,441
Norway (ex France)	Norwegian Cruise Line	1962	76,069
CostaVictoria	Costa Cruises	1996	75,200
Rhapsody of the Seas	Royal Caribbean	1997	75,000
Grandeur of the Seas	Royal Caribbean	1996	74,100
Enchantment of the Seas	Royal Caribbean	1997	74,100
Majesty of the Seas	Royal Caribbean	1992	73,941
Monarch of the Seas	Royal Caribbean	1991	73,941
Sovereign of the Seas	Royal Caribbean	1988	73,192
Century	Celebrity Cruises	1995	70,606
Fantasy	Carnival Cruise Line	1990	70,367
Ecstasy	Carnival Cruise Line	1991	70,367
Sensation	Carnival Cruise Line	1993	70,367
Fascination	Carnival Cruise Line	1994	70,367
Imagination	Carnival Cruise Line	1995	70,367
Inspiration	Carnival Cruise Line	1996	70,367
Queen Elizabeth 2	Cunard	1969	70,327
Crown Princess	Princess Cruises	1990	69,845
Regal Princess	Princess Cruises	1991	69,845
Oriana	P&O	1995	69,153
Legend of the Seas	Royal Caribbean	1995	69,130
Splendour of the Seas	Royal Caribbean	1996	69,130

NEW SHIPS FOR THE YEAR 2000

CRUISE LINE	SHIP NAME	TONNAGE	DELIVERY
Carnival	*Elation*	70,367	1998
Carnival	*Paradise*	70,367	1998
Carnival	*Carnival Triumph*	101,353	1999
Carnival	*Carnival Victory*	101,353	2000
Disney	*Disney Magic*	85,000	1998
Disney	*Disney Wonder*	85,000	1998
Holland America	Unnamed	65,000	1999
Holland America	Unnamed	65,000	1999
NCL	Unnamed	c.75,000	1999
P&O	Unnamed	76,000	2000
Princess	*Grand Princess*	109,000	1998
Princess	*Sea Princess*	77,000	1999
Princess	*Ocean Princess*	77,000	1999
Renaissance	Unnamed	30,200	1999
Renaissance	Unnamed	30,200	1999
Royal Caribbean	*Vision of the Seas*	75,000	1998
Royal Caribbean	*Project Eagle*	130,000	1999
Royal Caribbean	*Project Eagle*	130,000	2000
Silversea	Unnamed	22,000	1999
Silversea	Unnamed	22,000	2000
Star Cruise	*SuperStar Leo*	75,000	1998
Star Cruise	*SuperStar Virgo*	75,000	1999

smaller ones. Several lines have gone bust in recent years (notably Regency and Royal Cruise Lines in America), while others continue to struggle and face a rather uncertain future. Certain industry analysts can see this agglomeration of the most profitable companies (of which Carnival and, to a lesser extent, Royal Caribbean and P&O are the prime examples) only increasing through the rest of the decade, but there still seems a healthy market for the smaller, more focused lines like Crystal, Silversea and Orient.

Hopefully, by now, I will have answered the underlying question of this chapter and you will have cast off all pre-conceived notions of cruising's dated image and be prepared to explore more fully the delights and attractions it can offer. Over the course of the book I shall attempt to steer you through the full complexity of what a cruise holiday has to offer, with explanations of the bewildering variety of styles and ship types, how a typical cruise shapes up and how you should go about booking one, taking advantage of the welter of discounts on offer these days. We shall take a detailed look at the main cruise companies dealing in the British market, and their hardware, and there is also a unique *Brit's Guide* rating system that judges the cruise lines and their ships according to what they REALLY offer, and not what their brochures claim. Finally, to complete the picture, you can get an idea of all the different cruise areas in a chapter suitably sub-titled The World is Truly your Lobster.

Along the way, be prepared to be amazed and entertained by the trade-mark Brit Tips sprinkled through the book. They have quickly become a celebrated feature of the *Brit's Guide* series and help to mark out these books as specifically of use to a British audience – an idea unknown to most travel guides before now.

Hopefully, you are now in the mood to delve deeper into all the great attractions of A Life on the Ocean Wave . . .

✳

CHAPTER TWO

What's It All About?

(or, A Life on the Ocean Wave)

Having spent most of the opening chapter talking about what cruising *isn't*, it makes sense now to tell you more about what it *is*. To start with, it is a greater source of holiday excitement than any I have found, providing a much keener sense of anticipation and more wonderful reminiscences than anything else. But a full explanation of the modern cruise holiday also means identifying and dealing with the common objections to and misconceptions of it.

In basic terms, cruising is very much all things to all people. That is, it is so varied and flexible it can cater for all tastes and all types – providing you find the right ship and the right cruise line for you. That message cannot be emphasized enough, and is one of the essential reasons for reading this book. Even at budget level, a cruise still represents a significant expenditure, so it is vital you select the right one.

To that end, remember that cruising can be either the ultimate relaxation or the height of holiday frenzy. You can be as lazy or as active as you wish, and you will find plenty of facilities catering for both desires. You can also broaden the choice by selecting a cruise that is either port-intensive or which features a predominant amount of open-sea sailing.

Indeed, what other holiday type guarantees to transport you from place to place, from one superb vista to another in total comfort – and with the huge advantage of having to unpack only once!

It is perhaps therefore rather tempting to see the best value of a cruise in terms of the number of ports it visits, but BEWARE. A seven-day cruise that boasts seven (or more, in some cases) different ports of call can leave you in need of another holiday immediately afterwards! The itinerary of any ship is one of its most attractive features, but, if you have never cruised before, these port-intensive trips will not give you the best view of cruising, simply because they are so demanding. Of course, you can just stay on the ship, but it is difficult to ignore the charms of a new port of call completely, and you can quickly lose track of where you have been if you try to cram in too much. This is a particularly American affliction – our transatlantic cousins usually don't get as much holiday time as we do and therefore prefer itineraries that show them as much as possible in as short a time as possible. Hence, at the end of seven days and eight ports of call, it is not uncommon to find them debating among themselves: 'Honey, was that Antigua or Dominica on Monday?' Believe me, it happens. And, after all, your holiday is supposed to be a stress-free environment, so you need those sea days to be able to relax and get properly attuned to your nautical nature.

 BRIT TIP

It is a notable fact that British passengers DO prefer a higher number of days at sea to their American counterparts. The most comfortable ratio – especially for first-timers to cruising – is one day at sea for every port of call.

Ultimately, the amount of hectic port-visiting anyone can reasonably enjoy is obviously a matter of personal preference, but you do risk failing to take full advantage of your floating temporary home if you insist on a port-intensive itinerary, and, in most cases these days, you will be missing out on one of the primary attractions of your holiday. For, make no mistake, the modern cruise ship is indeed a wondrous vessel for the activity-conscious.

The vast range of facilities should destroy, well and truly, **Myth Number One:** I Will Get Bored On Board.

From early morning aerobics to late night discos, you are guaranteed a full daily programme of events, and there will always be a choice of things to do at any given time, be it organised deck sports and games, bridge, bingo, lectures, art auctions, karaoke or dance lessons.

The huge programmes of events (many of which are fairly common to all the main cruise lines) also hint at the vast array of on-board facilities with which modern ships are equipped – and they are becoming more sophisticated with the launch of every new vessel.

To illustrate both these points, I have taken the example of a typical day in the life of the cruise ship that carries more British passengers than any other, P&O's flagship mega-liner *Oriana*:

ORIANA TODAY

8.00am:	First Sitting Breakfast	2.45pm:	Dance Class – the Rumba
8.30am:	Fitness Centre – Gentle Stretch Class	3.30pm:	Laser Trapshooting
9.00am:	Second Sitting Breakfast	3.30pm:	Gymnasium Induction
9.15am:	Fitness Centre – Gentle Stretch Class	4.00pm:	Afternoon Tea
10.00am:	Promenade Deck Walk and Talk	4.00pm:	Short Tennis Competition
10.00am:	Port Enhancement Talk – Nauplia	4.00pm:	Golf Clinics
10.15am:	Bridge for Beginners	4.00pm:	Fitness Centre – Body Conditioning
10.30am:	Gymnasium Induction	4.15pm:	Jackpot Bingo
10.30am:	Deck Quoits Competition	5.30pm:	Individual Quiz
10.30am:	Coffee Chat with Entertainments Team	5.30pm:	Fitness Class – Legs, Tums and Bums
11.00am:	Antiques Chat – Victoriana	6.00pm:	Cocktail Music
11.00am:	Shuffleboard Competition	6.30pm:	First Sitting Dinner
11.15am:	Bridge Talk for Experienced Players	8.15pm:	Cinema Feature Film – Jerry Maguire
11.30am:	Pool Games	8.30pm:	Second Sitting Dinner
12 noon:	Buffet Luncheon	8.30 and 10.30pm:	Classical Concert
12.15pm:	First Sitting Luncheon	8.30 and 9.45pm:	Bridge Competitions
1.30pm:	Second Sitting Luncheon	9.30pm:	Evening Dancing Begins
2.30pm:	Board Games Handout	9.45pm:	Bridge Competition
2.45pm:	Cinema Feature Film – Independence Day	10.30pm:	Theatre Special: 'Buddy'
2.45pm:	Art Class	10.30pm:	Syndicate Quiz
2.45pm:	Bridge Competition	10.30pm:	Karaoke
2.45pm:	Whist Drive	11.30pm:	Late Night Music
2.45pm:	Shuffleboard Competition	11.30pm:	Late Night Snacks
2.45pm:	Organised Cricket Net	1.30am:	Nightclub Date

 **BRIT TIP**

For the best array of British sports and deck games, P&O take some beating. On my last cruise aboard *Oriana*, I barely had time to fit in my shore excursions around games of cricket, football, short tennis, shuffleboard, table tennis and deck quoits, plus visits to the gym (well, how else can you afford to fit in your fifth meal of the day?).

Typically, a cruise ship will consist of the following standard features, designed to further broaden your choice of what to do at any given time: a beauty salon, massage treatment rooms, sauna and steam room, modern gymnasium (with a full range of weight-training and exercise equipment), cinema, disco, observation lounge, a wide range of bars (as many as TWELVE on some of the larger ships), restaurant, buffet-service dining rooms (both inside and out), casino, swimming pool, jacuzzis, sun deck, deck sports, showlounge or theatre, library and video library, video games room, children's playroom, self-service launderette and medical centre.

Keep fit in style aboard P&O's Oriana

GET WITH THE THEME

As if all that is not enough, an increasing number of cruises now have sporting or other activity themes that provide extra attractions and incentives. Norwegian Cruise Line, for example, offer a fully-supervised Dive In programme which gives you the chance to learn snorkelling in some of the most idyllic spots for underwater activities. Other 'themed' cruises include scuba-diving (Princess, NCL, P&O, Club Med), bridge (P&O, Orient, Fred Olsen, Cunard), bird-watching (P&O), football (P&O), painting (P&O, Orient), cricket (P&O), baseball (NCL, Premier, Majesty), classical music (P&O, Swan Hellenic, Fred Olsen, Cunard), jazz (P&O, Seabourn, NCL, Mediterranean Shipping Cruises, Cunard), food and wine (Seabourn, Orient, Cunard, Mediterranean Shipping Cruises), Country and Western (NCL), golf (P&O, Seabourn, Royal Caribbean, NCL), enrichment lectures (Swan Hellenic, Seabourn, Orient, Fred Olsen, Cunard), old time, Latin and ballroom dancing (P&O), antiques (P&O), photography (Orient), fitness and beauty (NCL), American football (NCL), bowls (Orient), cinema (Holland America) and basketball (NCL).

Having set all that on the credit side **Myth Number Two** now rears its ugly head: I Won't Be Able To Relax If I'm Surrounded By The Hectic Hordes!

Okay, so relax. There are few better places to feel really at peace with the world than sitting on deck with no sight of land. The new build of cruise ship (notably the likes of *Oriana*, *Sun Princess*, Celebrity's most recent duo *Century* and *Galaxy*, Royal Caribbean vessels *Legend*, *Grandeur* and *Splendour of the Seas* and Costa Cruises' *CostaVictoria*) all feature huge expanses of open deck space with ample opportunity to find a quiet corner to read a book or just soak up some rays. Don't get the idea, either, that you are likely to be rail-roaded into joining in any of the deck sports or activities against your will – there is never any pressure to take part and there are no Redcoats at sea to make sure you have fun whether you like it or not (although on some of the more high-density, fun-orientated ships – notably the American Carnival Line vessels – it *is* sometimes hard to relax in the presence of so many dedicated, non-stop party-goers!). Equally, if the big-ship style doesn't take your fancy, there are a number of smaller, more exclusive vessels which are geared totally towards a more refined, laid-back approach, offering fewer facilities but more chance to unwind in a sophisticated environment.

GO WITH THE FLOW

Arguments of feeling confined on the modern cruise ship are similarly wide of the mark. Admittedly, the average cabin is still smaller than a typical hotel room or holiday apartment, but you actually spend so little time in it, it is more a question of the provision of public space around the ship and the way passenger flow is designed to prevent large numbers building up where they are not wanted. The latter has become a real art form in the 1990s, and you can be sure the newest ships will all have sophisticated design factors which prevent their 2,000-plus passengers arriving at the same place at the same time. Chapter Five, on the cruise lines and their ships, deals with these matters more specifically, looking at what is called the Passenger Space Ratio. This is a rather arbitrary figure that has no true meaning but does provide a sliding scale which helps to separate the good from the not-so-generous in on-board space terms. Basically, you divide a ship's gross registered tonnage by its maximum number of passengers and get a figure between 12 and 60. The nearer 60 you get, the better off you should be for space throughout the ship (although this doesn't take into account that a ship may be only half-full or the fact that its passenger flow may be poor).

The size of the ship, therefore, is not the paramount concern, it is the number of passengers it carries that defines the Space Ratio. For instance, Crystal Cruises' up-market 50,000-ton ship *Crystal Symphony* can carry as many as 960 passengers and has a Space Ratio figure of 52, while NCL's *Norway* (formerly the grand liner SS *France*) is much bigger at 76,000 tons but has a Space Ratio figure of 37.4 because it carries as many as 2,032. Similarly, Royal Caribbean's *Viking Serenade* is smaller at 40,132 tons but carries up to 1,961 customers, giving it a Space Ratio figure of only 20.5.

 **BRIT TIP**

Gross registered tonnage isn't actually a measurement of a ship's weight, but rather of the amount of enclosed space within a ship's hull and superstructure. One gross registered ton = 100 cubic feet of space. Fascinating, huh?

Still on the subject of relaxation, this is also, remember, a relatively hassle-free zone in terms of all your 'domestic' arrangements: your meals are laid on, transport is taken care of, there is rarely a rush to do anything and there is nearly always a *choice*. So, if it is relaxation you are after rather than an all-action holiday, cruising is still definitely for you.

 **BRIT TIP**

Be warned, however, the one area where all the large cruise liners fall down – and even some of the higher-density smaller ships – is when it comes to one-off activities. Embarkation and disembarkation are traditional bugbears of the megaships as long queues are common, and you can also have lengthy waits at the Shore Excursion Desk or Purser's Office.

Myth Number Three is rather more basic and simply insists: I Can't Go Cruising, I'll Get Seasick!

There are three main reasons why this is not the case. One: ships are getting increasingly larger in size, and that immediately makes for more stable sailing. Two: all passenger ships are equipped with stabilisers which take the edge off even the roughest seas. And Three: there are several ready remedies to seasickness which will be available on any ship (or which you can easily take with you). Dramamine is the most commonly-taken motion-sickness tablet, while the use of pressure bands worn on the wrists (called either Sea Bands or Aquastraps) is also quite widespread and comforting. Both are excellent protection against all but hurricane-force weather, and in extreme cases the ship's medical officer will be able to offer you a Dramamine injection that goes to work even faster. Quite often, the best cure for that slight nauseous feeling, which is simply your inner ear adjusting to the unusual motion of the ship, is just to get out on deck, put your face in the breeze and stare off to the horizon. Stroll the promenade deck to let your body get used to the new motion (it is called getting your sea-legs) and you will find the fresh air works wonders.

BRIT TIP

Don't be tempted to try to settle a slightly sea-upset stomach with a big meal. Eat a little, but stick to plainer foods. I have particularly vivid memories of being seduced by the aroma of a tempting Goan fish curry on one P&O cruise, only for my stomach to tell me it wasn't such a good idea an hour later!

There is even a new soft drink, called Smooth Sailing, which claims to Beat That Queasy Feeling, and several cruise lines have been so impressed they have started to stock it. However, one remedy that is universally frowned upon nowadays, is the use of the Transderm patch, which resembled a small, circular plaster and was stuck unobtrusively (yeah, right!) behind your ear. Available only on prescription from your doctor, this released a small amount of an anti-nausea drug into your system for up to three days, in theory thus allowing your body to adapt slowly to shipboard life. In practice, although it worked well for the majority, there were some unpleasant side-effects, including dizziness and disorientation, of which many of its users were unaware.

The bottom line remains, however, that seasickness is primarily a psychological worry, and it is really a thoroughly unneccessary concern for the vast majority of people, especially when

Radisson Seven Seas' ship Radisson Diamond *offers about the smoothest sailing of any vessel*

you remember the accuracy of modern weather forecasting allows ships to steer clear of any really nasty weather. And, to be honest, there are so few areas of cruising's mass market that stray out of calm waters, seasickness is really not a major issue in shipboard life these days. It may help to remember that according to the statisticians, it affects barely 3 per cent of all passengers on any cruise. The chances are you are more likely to be treated for sunburn than seasickness – it is amazing how many people think they can sit out in the Caribbean sun for a few hours without using a high-factor sun cream, especially when they are in and out of the pool.

BRIT TIP

The one exception to the rule, and a wildly unpredictable one at that, is the Caribbean during hurricane season, which lasts from July to October. A few notable storms have hit the headlines in the last couple of years, but it is only because they affect the cruise industry so rarely that they make headlines.

If, after all my consoling words, seasickness remains an issue, you should consider cruising aboard one of the classic, older vessels which offer a rock-steady ride (they have deeper drafts and are designed for the open seas), like NCL's *Norway* or the *QE2*, or the radically different, twin–hulled *Radisson Diamond* (one of the most stable craft ever built), and then opt for an area which doesn't stray into 'real' seas that much. The typical Alaskan Inside Passage cruise rarely encounters anything other than millpond waters, the eastern Mediterranean in summer offers dead calm sailing and the Caribbean in spring and early summer is similarly docile. Finally, if you select a cabin which is centrally situated and on one of the lower passenger decks, this reduces what little movement there is likely to be and should guarantee a worry-free voyage.

Myth Number Four has already been touched on in the opening chapter, but I might as well beat it to death here because some people still claim: Cruising Is Too Expensive.

It may well seem at first glance that your average cruise is likely to set you back as much as a week's wages for a Premiership footballer (okay, that may be a little extreme, no one spends THAT much on a cruise!), but the main mistake people tend to make in comparing a cruise to a normal land-based holiday is in looking at the price only as the starting point and imagining there will be much more to pay. The simple truth is that cruising represents much better value for money than most typical packages because you pay the vast majority of the cost straight away and there are no hidden extras once you are on board. You will also find the *quality* of shipboard life, whether it be in the facilities, food or service, of a much higher standard than the same type of holiday on land. In many cases, you would need to spend considerably more on a brochure package to the more expensive parts of the Mediterranean or the Caribbean than you would pay for the cruise equivalent. But don't take my word for it, consider this example drawn up for me by Jim Millward of NCL that lists a comparably priced Caribbean island holiday with one of their own cruise products:

BROCHURE:	LONG-HAUL TOUR OPERATOR	NORWEGIAN CRUISE LINE
Hotel/Ship:	Sandpiper Inn	MS *Dreamward*
Resort:	Barbados	Western Caribbean: Fort Lauderdale–Grand Cayman–Cozumel–Cancun–NCL's private island
Meal basis:	Accommodation only	Full board – seven meals per day
Flight supplement:	£35 (weekends)	None
Free connecting flights:	From 15 airports	From 18 airports
Duration:	7 nights	8 nights
Entertainment:	3 nights a week, live music	Every night, including Broadway shows, music, comedians, cabaret, casino and disco
Activities:	Watersports, sightseeing, tennis	Dive-In snorkelling programme, fitness programme, golf clinics, deck sports, dance classes, arts and crafts workshops, backgammon, bridge, fashion shows, art auctions, quizzes, films, beauty salon, sports talks, shore excursions, shopping, etc
Departing:	March 1997	March 1997
Adult price:	£1,647	From £1,292

In addition, it is easy to see where your expenses would mount up on the land-based example. Eating out is not usually a cheap option in Barbados, and then you would have extras like taxi or car hire, night club entrance fees and any kids' facilities or child-minding services. Start adding on the cost of a few drinks in the more up-market Caribbean resorts and your initial outlay can easily more than double, while your cruise ship, on the other hand, will generally charge usual bar prices for your drinks. Your only other outlay in the ship-board version is then how many organised shore excursions you take and your tips. And, in the Caribbean especially, there are few really unmissable excursions which will demand your money.

BRIT TIP

One of the biggest rip-offs in the cruise world is that of shore excursions which simply aren't worth the money. The best rule of thumb here is to consider only those options which you couldn't do on your own. E.g. submarine rides in Grand Cayman, and NOT a half-day tour of Nassau in the Bahamas (which you can easily walk around).

All the major cruise lines are currently desperate to ram home this message of price comparability and value for money, and the last couple of years have seen a near blood-bath in discounting, which is bad news for the industry but great news for the consumer in the short-term. With newer and bigger ships being added to the world cruising fleet all the time, capacity is still easily out-stripping demand in the mass market (mainly in the Caribbean and, to a lesser extent, the Mediterranean), and many operators have been forced to freeze or even lower their starting prices. This means there has never been a better time to take advantage of the numerous deals on offer by the likes of P&O, NCL,

Enjoy the Caribbean Windstar-style

Costa, Festival, Airtours, CTC and others. Airtours also made the whole business much more price-conscious when they entered the market in 1995 offering a seven-day cruise with a lead-in price (i.e. their lowest brochure price) of just £399. You need only look at the weekend travel sections or flick through the pages of teletex to see just how widespread cruise holiday discounting has become, and it is likely to last for another year or two yet as the big lines continue to slug out their price wars and some of the smaller ones inevitably sink out of sight. In the short term, therefore, it is a real bonus for anyone looking for a cruise bargain, especially in the family market. In addition, virtually every cruise line offers early-booking discounts and repeat-passenger special offers which often come on TOP of a discount you might get at one of the specialist Cruise Consultants that sell cruises (see Chapter Four).

 **BRIT TIP**

Don't expect to be able to pick up a cheap cruise anywhere in the world. Alaska and the Far East manage to sell well without discounting, but the real bargains can often be found in the Caribbean, especially if you can go out of the main holiday seasons.

The subject of children on holiday is another area where you can add to the value of a cruise, at the same time as removing some of the inevitable worry of keeping kids happy for the duration. Here's a question for all dads: How many times do you put your hand in your pocket for ice creams, sweets and other snacks for your brood? Just a few, I bet. Well, with so many ships now including complimentary ice cream bars and hot-dog or hamburger grills AS WELL AS the normal meal-times, you can blissfully wave goodbye to those pocket-tugging cries of 'Dad, can I have . . . ?' Add to this the amazing programme of organised children's activities on nearly all the main-stream cruise products (there are exceptions, but I'll go into those later), and you can quickly see how cruising represents outstanding value for the family market.

SAFETY FIRST

This leads on to the issue of general safety, and is just another area where cruising scores heavily over its rivals. There are few more secure environments than a modern cruise ship in the normal course of events, and, when you are travelling around potentially hazardous or troubled parts of the world (some areas of the Caribbean, like Jamaica, plus the Far East and South America spring to mind), the reliable sanctuary of your ship becomes that much more valuable to your peace of mind. A laughable minor myth believed by the totally uninitiated says something like: 'My kids will fall overboard or find some other way of hurting themselves on board.' And it is tempting to fall about laughing and answer 'Get real!' Instead, I will just say unless your children are total maniacs or you abandon all measure of parental control, your nearest and dearest are not likely to take a swallow dive off the nearest handrail. The big family cruise ships now all employ full-time children's counsellors (not to mention nurses and child-minders) to keep a watchful eye on the youngsters in their charge as well as master-minding a full programme of events and activities to keep them thoroughly occupied practically all day if you wish. Chalk up another success to the attraction of cruising. As an additional note on safety, all modern ships (dating back to the 1970s) are DESIGNED with children's safety in mind.

It should also be noted the international cruising industry has some of the strictest safety criteria to which it must adhere. The various maritime legislative bodies all demand the highest standards in passenger and crew safety, and regular checks are rigorously carried out, notably by the US Coastguard, who are real sticklers for detail (witness them detaining the QE2 in port in New York after the ship's disastrous 1994 Christmas transatlantic crossing with a repair programme still under way). Central to seagoing safety issues is the United Nations body, the International Maritime Organisation, which monitors a number of regulations, foremost among which is the SOLAS (Safety of Life at Sea) convention. A whole new array of measures

were brought into being in SOLAS 97 which ensured tough new criteria for fire protection measures. Any ship not conforming to these criteria is simply not allowed to sail, and this has meant many of the lines with 'veteran' ships have been looking closely at their viability.

It should also go without saying the industry just cannot afford the bad publicity that poor safety standards would bring. There has not been a single

Cocktail hour takes on a special atmosphere at sea

reported death on a cruise ship due to a marine incident in the last 11 years, enhancing cruising's reputation as one of the safest modes of transport.

This message was underlined at the Seatrade Cruise Shipping Convention in Miami where Peter Ratcliffe, the president of Princess Cruises, pointed out: 'A cruise ship is intrinsically a very safe place with a *substantially* (my italics) reduced threat of personal violence or loss of personal property. The ship is the maritime equivalent of a "gated community", third parties may not access the ship without authority, all members of the community (the crew) are known to each other and have been interviewed and recruited by the owner, a perpetrator of a crime has nowhere to hide and there is a disciplinary presence on the ship trained to supervise the security of the ship, its passengers and crew. A cruise ship is one of the most secure ways to visit the less developed countries of the world. There is limited exposure to airport or hotel crime, and shore excursions are undertaken in a controlled and super-vised environment.' Nuff said.

This discussion on personal safety and comfort leads neatly on to **Myth Number Five**, another familiar one, which states: Cruising Is For The Blue Rinse Brigade.

Now, it certainly isn't the aim of this publication to be in any way ageist, but there is little doubt that the world of the cruise liner was once the primary preserve of those folks who are slightly more advanced in years. Not any more. As you will surely have recognised by the emphasis on the family market, cruising is now a very different kettle of piscine creatures. The latest Passenger Shipping Association figures for the cruise market as a whole reveal the average age for passengers to the Caribbean is down to just 42 and, on some of the three- and four-day fun cruises, it can average 28. There are, of course, variations in the overall picture and so you will find many more families at sea during the school holidays than at other times, but the likes of P&O and Airtours have set their stall out firmly to attract the British family market and they are doing an impressive job of delivering the right product.

Naturally, if there are cruise lines offering great deals for the family market, there are equally others serving different areas of the market just as successfully, which is one of the reasons why studying the world of cruising is so fascinating and rewarding. The QE2, for example, remains a bastion of the bygone age of class-conscious cruising in the most stately of surroundings; the Holland America line caters in only a limited manner for children (on their Caribbean and Alaska sailings during school holidays, although all their cruises are slowly becoming more youth-friendly) and also retain the elegance of yesteryear; the Brit-popular Fred Olsen Line still averages between 50 and 60 years of age in its passenger profile and also handles children in only a limited fashion (although they are now encouraging more families); Saga, the over-50s tour operator, now has its own cruise ship; Swan Hellenic, with its smart new vessel *Minerva*, outwardly discourages young children on its voyages, which offer a rich cultural and heritage-orientated programme around the Mediterranean, Baltic and Red Seas and into the Far East; and dear old P&O, for all the fact that they cater so well for kids, still draw their passengers from ALL ranges of the age spectrum (and the average age definitely goes up out of season).

In addition to these general differences between the lines, there also tends

 BRIT TIP

P&O is possibly the best example of across-the-board social and age mixing, with *Oriana* in particular catering superbly for the full range of tastes, from classical concerts to teen discos and theatre to bingo.

to be a different age profile according to the *length* of the voyage. Hence, a seven-day cruise may attract a good number of families while a 10- or 14-day cruise would see the number of youngsters aboard reduced, quite drastically in some cases. And, when it comes to the major line voyages, the round-the-world trips which a few companies specialise in, you see an even greater preponderance of older folk aboard for the obvious reason that it is usually only the retired or very wealthy who can afford to spend a month or three at sea!

The following table, compiled by the PSA, serves to highlight these issues for the biggest cruise lines who deal in the British market:

PSA TABLE

Cruise Line	Typical age profile	Lower rate for sharing cabin with 2 adults?	Lower rate for sharing with 1 adult?
Airtours	Across the board	Yes (up to 15)	No
Carnival	20–50	Yes	No
Celebrity	Across the board	Yes (up to 17)	No
Costa	30–60	Yes (up to 11)	No
Crystal	Couples/ singles, 40–60+	Yes (up to 11)	No
Fred Olsen	Average 50–60	Yes	Yes
Holland America	40–60	Yes	No
NCL	30–60	Yes (up to 11)	No
Orient	40–60+	Yes	No
P&O	Across the board	Yes (up to 17)	Yes

Under 2s travel free?	Cots available	Kids facilities?	Other comments
£19 supplement (£39 to Caribbean)	Free	Yes	Three kids' clubs, 3–5s, 6–10s and 11–15s; special menus; fully-trained kids' staff and baby-sitters
No	Free	Yes	Four age groups, 2–4, 5–7, 8–12, 13–17; kids' menus, playroom, teen club, kids' pool, baby-sitting
Yes	Yes	Yes	Dedicated programme of events for 3–17s
No	Yes	Youth centre on all ships, teen centre also on *Classica* and *Victoria*	Kids' clubs for 5–12s and 13–17s; full-time youth counsellors; baby-sitting
No	No	Limited	Hostess during school holidays
Yes	Yes	Yes	Children's hosts on summer holiday cruises
No (£100 reduction for under 12s)	Yes	According to numbers	Playroom and supervised activities
No	Yes	Year-round on *Norway, Seaward,* seasonally on others	Fully supervised activities; free ice cream; child-minding in playrooms; baby-sitting
Yes	Yes	No	Not generally suitable for children
No (no babies under 6 months allowed)	Yes	Full youth programme and Junior Club	Kids' pool on *Oriana*; night nursery on *Canberra, Oriana* year-round, seasonal on *Victoria*

Princess	40–50 (50+ out of season)	Yes (up to 11)	No
Radisson/ Seven Seas	40–60+	Yes	No
Royal Caribbean	18–50+	Yes	No
Seabourn	40–60+	Yes (25% of per person fare)	No
Silversea	40–60+	Yes	No
Swan Hellenic	30–60+	No	50% for under 25s
Thomson	Across the board	Yes (2–16)	No

A different style of cruising – the charming little ship Hebridean Island Princess

No	Yes	Various according to ship; both children's and teens' centres	Daily activities on *Sun, Dawn, Regal, Sky* and *Crown Princess*; child-minding by hostesses during port calls; baby-sitting to midnight
No	No	No	Not suitable for children
No	Limited	Yes; year-round facilities and counsellors on most ships	Four kids' clubs in Adventure Ocean programme; 3–5s, 6–8s, 9–12s and 13–17s; special menus
No	By prior request	No	Children are tolerated rather than welcomed
No	No	No	Children are tolerated rather than welcomed
No	No	No	Not suitable for children
£15 supplement	Free, but in Superior and Premier cabins only	Children's playroom	Children's Clubs for 4–7s and 8–12s (provided a parent is on the ship); special menus

sails the coastal waters of Scotland

 **BRIT TIP**

Another easy way to gauge the level of formality on any given cruise is simply to weigh up the length of the cruise and the number of days at sea. More days at sea = greater formality, with cruises in excess of seven days becoming distinctly more formal than their shorter version options.

Of course, the age profile is intended only as a general guide, especially as it is one of the areas of biggest change in the cruise world as more and more people are sold on its appeal. There are also variations according to season of the year and even the location of the cruise (Alaska, for example, tends to attract an older customer than the Caribbean, while the Baltic Sea passenger is, on average, older than the Mediterranean variety), but it does serve to give you an indication of the huge variation on offer in this area, and about which there will be much more detail in Chapter Five. Once again, cruising can truly be said to offer something for everyone.

This is possibly the most-heard objection among the younger set, who

Everyone, that is, except those who still insist on **Myth Number Six:** Cruising Is Much Too Formal For My Holiday Taste.

envisage nights of black tie dinners, ballroom dancing and bridge foursomes. And yes, it is perfectly possible to find a cruise where formality of this type is still the order of the day, but the simple fact about the mass market is that it has moved miles away from its old image. Once again, the cruise companies themselves have been slow to deliver this message, but it is nonetheless true for all that. There is also another essential difference between the traditional British and American passengers here. As a general rule of thumb, Brits are keener to dust off their DJs and posh frocks for the occasional formal evenings on board, while our transatlantic cousins prefer a more relaxed style.

Of course, there are still people who are attracted to cruising just because it gives them a chance to dress up and show off, and the industry is just as happy to cater for them as well. On most seven-day cruises you will therefore find a pleasant mix of the formal and informal (and also what the cruise industry likes to call 'casual'). You will probably find that two nights of the seven are designated *Formal*, three or four are termed *Casual* (usually the days in port) and the other one or two are *Informal*. For practical purposes this means: *Formal*, a dinner jacket, tuxedo or dark business suit for men, and cocktail or evening dress for the women; *Informal* usually means jacket and tie for the men (although I often get away with just a smart shirt and trousers – I'm a bit of a rebel!) and most things for women (the Americans are keen on highlighting 'pant suits' for women on *Informal* nights for some reason); *Casual* means just about anything goes (except T-shirts and shorts in the dining room). I find the majority of people, even if they start off a bit reluctant, do actually enjoy wearing their glad rags occasionally, and the odd formal evening does add a really splendid appearance to the ship-board scene. Equally, you will NOT be keel-hauled for wearing the wrong attire on the wrong night or if you are really not comfortable to be fully suited up. The formal element is also less noticeable in the mass-market American cruise world (on lines such as Carnival, NCL, Commodore, Premier and Dolphin), as well as being more low profile on Thomson, Airtours and Fred Olsen than P&O and Cunard. A welcome new addition is that of themed or even fancy dress evenings. These can vary from obvious eras like the '50s and Rock 'n' Roll to more modern fads such as Country and Western and more geographical themes like the Caribbean (where the brightest, most flowery clothes suddenly become chic). P&O typically have a Black and White evening while the Italian line Costa now makes a feature of their final evening Toga Parties, with ready-made togas being handed out by the cruise staff and woe betide any party-poopers – when they say 'No sheet, no eat,' they mean it!

Elegant evenings are all part of the Cunard experience

CRUISING FOR NEWCOMERS

In addition to cutting down on the formality in a bid to attract the first-time cruiser, there are a few lines which also go out of their way to set up a cruise experience for beginners. These generally go under the heading of Newcomers' Cruises and can feature such pertinent extras as a special host to welcome first-timers and help them to settle in; a Newcomers' cocktail party to meet all your fellow rookies and ask any urgent questions (like, 'What time is the midnight buffet?' Don't laugh, it happens!); a bottle of Welcome Aboard champagne waiting in your cabin; a free shore excursion to get you in the swing of things; and sometimes a certain amount of free on-board credit (say, $50 per person) to encourage you to get involved with things like the beauty salon or health treatments. Princess Cruises are one of the most switched-on lines for newcomers, dedicating a number of attractive cruises to first-timers with all of the extra benefits mentioned above, while several *QE2* sailings offer free first class rail travel to Southampton or free car parking at the port, a first-timers' cocktail party, a newcomers' courier, free shore excursion and £100 of on-board credit per cabin. It is also now a feature of some P&O cruises.

Right, that should be the ground-rules for enjoying your cruise holiday established, let's see what else we can tempt you with . . .

CHAPTER THREE

The Indefinable Extras

(or, Adventure, Romance and Seven Meals a Day)

So, we should by now have established cruising as something that is both leisurely and up-tempo; that is highly safety-conscious and no longer a seasickness risk; that suits all budgets and all social types; that is for children as much as the retired; that is now cutting down on formality and raising the entertainment stakes; and that offers a really exciting alternative to land-based holidays. What more can it produce that satisfies our ideals of the perfect holiday?

FROM ALASKA TO ZANZIBAR

Well, how about the chance to visit some of the most remote and picturesque places on earth, the possibility of romance, the unquestionable air of mystique and the opportunity to eat yourself silly!

The fact that cruising has become so popular so quickly has inevitably led to the demand for more alternative itineraries and ports of call, and it is perfectly possible these days to sail just about anywhere in the comfort of your mobile home, from Alaska to Antarctica, Japan to the Galapagos Islands, Russia to Zanzibar, and nearly all points in between. Chapter Six will deal more fully with the various cruise areas of the world, but suffice it so say here that there is a mouth-watering choice, and there is an increasing demand to explore the more out-of-the-way places. The Far East, in particular, is seen as an area of up-and-coming cruise potential, while Alaska has experienced an incredible boom since the start of the 1990s and the Red Sea is just beginning to be explored by some of the main Mediterranean operators as an alternative for the winter months.

There is also a growing demand for adventure cruises, i.e. cruises that avoid the normal routes and levels of comfort and strike out to the more far-flung outposts of the world. Typically, there are even various different types of adventure options, from the 'soft' version of cruise lines like Orient, who operate the 22,000-ton *Marco Polo* in a fair degree of luxury to areas like Antarctica, to the real basic, close-up experience of purpose-built exploration vessels such as the 3,153-ton *World Discoverer* of Society Expeditions. Also, for those inclined to an even earlier age of cruising, there are a number of sailing vessels (Windstar and Star Clippers) where you can participate in the raising and lowering of the rigging (or just sit back and watch, if you want) and generally enjoy a more laid-back, leisurely approach to life at sea. These offer an outstandingly different cruise experience for the more discerning traveller and a much less structured atmosphere. The subject of the romance of sea travel is also close to my heart, in both general and specific terms, and I can heartily vouch for the extra appeal which this aspect of cruising can afford to both singles and couples alike.

The splendours of Antarctica with Abercrombie & Kent

THOSE WEDDING BELLS

Anyone familiar with the long-running but cringe-inducing American TV series *The Love Boat* (which actually did a major promotional job for Princess Cruises) may find this hard to believe, but there is a genuine romantic feel to many aspects of modern cruising. To start with it is one of the most popular and natural choices for honeymooners, and most of the cruise lines offer some really fantastic extras for newly-weds, from champagne, flowers and cake to more practical items like cabin up-grades, special portrait photographs and free on-board credit. There will usually be a special get-together for all the honeymoon couples aboard (upwards of 100 couples on some Caribbean cruises is not uncommon), and the staff often go out of their way to make you both feel extra-special at the start of your married life.

Equally, both established couples and mums and dads (with the kids safe in the hands of the ship's baby-sitters for the evening) can enjoy each other's company that much more just watching the sunset on deck, going for a late-night moonlit stroll or dancing the night away as they used to do in their courting days. It is also a far more civilised and tranquil setting in which to catch up on how much you really appreciate your partner. So much so, in fact, there is a similarly successful trade in anniversary packages and even the renewal of wedding vows at sea. Sadly, the captain of the ship can no longer perform the marriage ceremony itself, either in port or at sea, but several cruise lines (notably Carnival, Celebrity, Holland America, NCL, Princess and

Royal Caribbean) offer the chance of a wedding on board at the departure port before setting sail on honeymoon (with some of the wedding guests in many cases). The cruise company can coordinate the whole event for you, down to the provision of a cake, and I defy anyone to conjure up anything more romantic than sailing off into the sunset on your first wedded night together . . .

 BRIT TIP

Honeymooners take note. When you book that dream wedding holiday, make SURE with your travel agent that the cabin you choose has a double bed – some still have twin beds that do NOT convert into doubles!

All this may sound as if it precludes singles from getting the full benefit of their cruise, but that is most definitely not the case. Cruising is a genuinely easy and enjoyable way to make new friends, and it is certainly not unknown for people to meet that one special person in the wonderfully heady, almost tailor-made atmosphere of shipboard life. Many lines hold singles' parties to help break the ice, but the general run of events is usually sufficient to throw people together to find out if they enjoy each other's company.

 BRIT TIP

Quite often, it is the daytime events like organised sports and other social activities that can be as instrumental in sparking romance as the evening events. Singles' hang-outs are just as likely to be the gym as the bar.

Several lines (notably Cunard, Crystal, Fred Olsen and Orient) also offer a Gentleman Host programme for unaccompanied women, which provides company at meals, dances and other social occasions.

Once again, it all helps to add up to the general mystique of cruising that is ultimately hard to explain in plain language, but which, even in this age of the high-tech mega-liners, still adds an air of magic to the whole experience that is just impossible to reproduce on land.

 **BRIT TIP**

Girls, a quick word of advice from one of my female associates in the cruise research business – brief shipboard romances are all very well, but they are the product of a rather artificial environment and seldom transfer well to the real world (yet that shouldn't stop you trying)!

DINNER IS SERVED

Of course, an additional item that goes hand in hand with romance (well, sort of), is that of food. I am sure the majority of us enjoy the chance to dine out, and it is now a well-established legend of life at sea that mealtimes are an essential part of the experience – up to seven times a day if you have the capacity. Obviously, the standard does vary from cruise line to cruise line (even if every brochure does try to make out that every meal-time is a five-star gourmet experience), but there isn't a ship afloat that doesn't make a feature of every meal, and, in some cases, they can be hugely extravagant. Scarcely an hour goes by at sea without the chance to indulge yourself in some sort of gastronomic exercise or other, and the only real difficulty can be in deciding whether to dine out on deck or in the dining room, to enjoy a late breakfast or early lunch, or to see if you can fit in afternoon tea as well as dinner. It is even possible in many instances these days to enjoy 24-hour room service (at no extra cost, of course, on the majority of lines) or, on the more up-market ships, to take advantage of waiter-service dining in your own cabin. If your cabin also comes with its own balcony, you are back into seriously romantic territory once more with all the possibilities for moonlit dining *al fresco*.

 BRIT TIP

Beware. This is where your cruise can really take its toll – on your waistline. Typically, the average passenger puts on a pound a day in weight, and a quick turn around the Promenade deck will NOT be enough to stave off the danger of an expanding waistline. This is where those well-equipped gyms can come in handy!

CHECKING YOUR CRUISE ESSENTIALS

In all seriousness, however, food is just one of the FIVE essential principal elements of any cruise, all of which you need to study fairly closely to make sure you find the right cruise for YOU. All of the brochures proudly claim to have Luxury This, or Five-star That, but the reality is there are only a handful of lines which can truly claim to be at the Deluxe end of the market. And this will be reflected in these key areas of **Facilities** (essentially the ship's hardware), **Service** (or the software, the ship's crew), **Entertainment** (the mix of daytime activities and evening shows), **Food** (as outlined above) and the **Ports of Call** (their number, variety and the choice of shore excursions).

You will probably by now be aware of the vast differences that exist in the make-up of the 120-plus cruise ships operating in the British market. They can be anywhere from 3,000 tons (more of an overgrown yacht, really) right up to the new 101,000 tons of the futuristic *Carnival Destiny*; they they be anything up to 45 years old or the latest thing out of the ship-building yards of Europe; they can be high-density (in the mass market) or they can be immensely personal (with a high Space Ratio on the true Deluxe vessels); and they can offer a wealth of user-friendly facilities that put you in mind more of a small town than a mere ship.

I have already listed the standard array of on-board **Facilities** which you can expect from the modern cruise ship, but it also makes sense at this point to highlight some of the current developments in ship-building that are shaping the way forward and offering a continually changing emphasis of features.

The obvious main development is to build bigger and ever more impressively. The race to the first 100,000-ton monster has been won by Carnival with the launch of their *Carnival Destiny* in October 1996, and Princess will top that in 1998 with their *Grand Princess* which is due to weigh in at the little matter of 109,000 tons. Also, no new cruise ship is now complete without at least one multi-storey **atrium lobby** down the centre of the vessel, complete with glass-sided lifts, specially-commissioned artwork and cascading waterfalls. It almost seems in some cases as if ship designers are trying to compete more with the grand land-based hotel resorts than with their marine predecessors in terms of the amount of glittering, large-scale architecture they can incorporate in the newest examples of their work. The *Sun Princess*, launched in late 1995, possesses the most breathtaking four-storey central atrium, full of gleaming marble, bright chrome and bronze railings and ceilings, panoramic lifts, a stained-glass skylight and a magnificent sweeping, circular staircase. Costa's latest venture, the 75,000-ton *CostaVictoria*, includes a novel four-storey forward observation area that adds another new dimension, Royal Caribbean's most recent quintet of super-ships, the *Legend, Splendour, Rhapsody, Enchantment* and

Truly dazzling – the central atrium on board the Sun Princess

Grandeur of the Seas all feature a seven-storey atrium rising up to the ships' trademark Viking Crown Lounge at the very top of each vessel, and *Carnival Destiny* boasts a truly cavernous central atrium full of the line's characteristic bold neon designs.

One of the most recent innovations which has quickly been copied by others is *Oriana's* full-scale, West End-quality **theatre**, complete with revolving stage and full orchestra pit. Its detail includes excellent all-round sight-lines and individual air-conditioning on all the seats. Celebrity's newest offerings, the 70,000-ton-plus trio *Century, Galaxy* and *Mercury*, have also refined this theatre-at-sea concept, as has the *Sun Princess*, while the *Carnival Destiny* again goes one better with a three-level showlounge, revolving stage, hydraulic orchestra pit and even a scenery loft.

Celebrity have also pioneered the development of dramatic new sound systems for their ships, in partnership with the Japanese electronics firm Sony, and it is this willingness to embrace new techonology which will characterise much of future ship design. Notably, Celebrity have incorporated clever new facilities with their in-cabin TVs that allow you to order room service or duty free items on screen, peruse the day's menus and even read about and book shore excursions. Already, there are virtual reality exercise bikes aboard several of these new vessels, along with state-of-the-art golf simulators, and the advance publicity for *Grand Princess* promises a motion-based interactive cinema for virtual reality adventure rides and a Blue Screen room where passengers can be filmed alongside their favourite TV and cinema characters. The extent of this type of development seems limited only to the designers' imagination.

Alongside these twenty-first-century innovations, the enhancement of existing facilities is rather more mundane but nonetheless important for all that. **Health facilities** of the highest standard are now demanded on all ships as a matter of course as passengers become increasingly health-conscious (as a result, no doubt, of those seven meals a day). They expect exercise equipment incorporating all the latest in aerobic design as well as an increasing range of treatments like massage, hydrotherapy, reflexology, aromatherapy and even acupuncture, on top of the more common features like saunas and steam rooms. The average health centre's beauty salon will also be able to offer the latest in hair care and other treatments like manicures and facials.

 **BRIT TIP**

It is easy to get carried away with the enjoyable extras of massage and other beauty treatments, but remember they are EXTRAS on any cruise (although you shouldn't pay more for a cut or perm than you do at home).

As the average age of the cruise passenger comes down, so the demand for fitness facilities increases, and every ship now carries fully-trained gymnasium staff to supervise all these excellent facilities and to advise on and arrange comprehensive aerobic and other exercise programmes. These can be tailored to individual requirements in many cases (this could be the moment finally to knuckle down to that proper exercise routine you could never quite find time for), and there are usually programmes to analyse your aerobic capacity, fitness level and even body-fat content (for a small charge). For those happy just to do their own gym thing, there should be a full range of equipment like exercise bikes, rowing machines, stair-climbers and treadmills, plus the ever-popular multi-gyms and weights for weight training.

 BRIT TIP

Newcomers to the cruise world never cease to be amazed at how quickly a ship's beauty salon fills its appointments book. The trick is to get in EARLY and usually to book a visit to coincide with one of the formal evenings – experienced cruisers have got this off to a fine art.

From comprehensive health facilities, the demand increasingly is also for **children's facilities**, and the main cruise lines have not been slow to incorporate features especially for the youngsters. The *Oriana* is a typical example of this, with purpose-built rooms for 2- to 12-year-olds (Peter Pan's) and teenagers (Decibels), plus an outdoor kids' play area and paddling pool. The aft deck area on *Oriana* also becomes the exclusive preserve of the younger passenger on school holiday cruises, when up to 300 children on board is not unknown.

A feast of fun for kids in Peter Pan's playroom on Oriana

The incorporation of specialised areas like health and kids' facilities is also being extended in more general terms just to provide an increasing number of options throughout the modern cruise ship. The early days of the mega-liner were characterised by building along gargantuan lines when it came to public rooms. Nowadays, the tendency is towards providing an alternative as towards trying to be size-impressive, and you will find a greater variety of lounges and bars, many of which are designed to provide an intimacy that the early mega-liners lacked.

With this tendency towards high-tech, it is easy to overlook the appeal of more simple facilities like traditional **deck games**. Even on the newest ships, there is still an element of these and it will be a sad day for cruising if ship designers decide to do away with them altogether. Happily, that is certainly not the case yet as recent vessels like *Oriana*, *Sun Princess*, *Crystal Symphony* and Celebrity's *Century* have all continued to incorporate 'proper' deck sports. Indeed, the *Century* and sister ships *Galaxy* and *Mercury* all boast 62,000 square feet of open deck space to provide for table-tennis, basketball,

The deluxe Crystal line boasts the only Caesar's Palace casino at sea

volleyball and jogging as well as just lazing in the sun. *Oriana* boasts the best cricket nets at sea (I kid you not, and it is very popular), as well as short tennis, football and the usual array of traditional games like shuffleboard and quoits. And *Sun Princess* and *Crystal Symphony* both incorporate good-sized paddle-tennis courts that provide an excellent social focus as well as a chance to show off your sporting prowess. As I have already insisted, there is no way you will be bored at sea.

Of course, having extolled the virtues of cruising as one of the really great inclusive holidays, I have to say that more on-board variety means more opportunities for the cruise lines to try to persuade you to part with some extra money. And it is this area of on-board spending where lines attempt to recoup some of the money they have lost in the discounting wars. Therefore, you can expect all ships, particularly the newer ones, to include a dazzling array of **shopping opportunities**, including duty-free, to beguile you into running up your on-board credit.

On the subject of losing money (well, I always do, anyway), the **Casino** is now an absolutely fundamental requirement of all ships. The Americans in particular love to gamble because it is illegal in most of the USA, and you will frequently find this facility dedicated primarily to them. The casinos aboard Carnival ships in particular are massive affairs, and they are nearly always decorated in the best Las Vegas style with a major assault on the visual senses from flashing lights, neon signs, fruit machines (or 'slots' as the Americans

The cashless society

All cruise ships are operated on a cashless basis to make the day-to-day running that much simpler (and remove the hassle of having to carry money on board). You are given your own on-board 'credit card' or account as soon as you step aboard (usually in exchange for a swipe of your credit card at the Purser's Desk, although you can opt to pay by cash or cheque at the end of the cruise) and you then use this to sign for every purchase, whether it be in the bar, beauty salon or one of the shops. If you opt for the credit card method, you need only check the final itemised bill that is sent to your cabin on the last evening. If you have opted to pay by cash or cheque you will need to settle up in person at the Purser's Desk before you disembark – and, believe me, you won't be allowed off the ship unless you do!

call them) and other rather gaudy designs. A typical casino will offer roulette, poker, blackjack (or pontoon), standard fruit machines and machine poker and, on the American lines, a dice or craps table.

 **BRIT TIP**

The casino can be a daunting place for newcomers to the world of gambling, but don't be afraid to watch. They are frequently much more friendly than land-based varieties and some may even hold classes in the art of poker or blackjack playing.

In total contrast (and not, this time, a popular feature of American ships) is the still widespread provision of a **library** at sea. Quite often these days it is accompanied by a video library as well on the more up-market ships. This is a feature that really does hark back to the days of cruising's traditional style, of long voyages when there was often little else to do than settle down with a good book. Happily for British cruise passengers it is a tradition that is still keenly maintained by the likes of P&O, Fred Olsen and Swan Hellenic. The library aboard the *Oriana* is one of the most tastefully elegant public rooms on the ship, but, be warned – the first day or two of any voyage sees the book equivalent of a horde of locusts descend with the end result that the library's shelves can be seriously depleted before some passengers have even discovered it. By the same token, the **card room** is still a common feature of even the newest ships and some can also be quite elegant. However, they may also have to double up as a conference or business centre.

Every ship will also have its own **photographic services,** with a decent range of film and other equipment to buy or rent, plus several ship's photographers whose job it is to circulate regularly and take a variety of snaps of you enjoying the cruise.

 **BRIT TIP**

Another word of warning here. You may well want to collect the full set of ship-taken photographs ('This is us at embarkation,' 'This is us at the Captain's cocktail party,' 'This is us with a drink by the pool,' etc), but they are NOT a cheap alternative to using your own camera. A simple 5in × 7in can set you back as much as $6.50 (£4.20), and a portrait photo $20 (£14) or more. Also, a ship is just about the most expensive place in the WORLD to buy film. Stock up before you sail.

In a similar vein, all cruise ships carrying more than 36 passengers are required by maritime law to provide proper **medical facilities**, with at least one doctor of GP standard and a nurse. Typically, the newest vessels can boast better health care than some hospitals, with ships like *Oriana* having full surgery capability as well as more practical, common items like a pharmacy, X-ray machines and cardiac arrest units. Each medical centre will keep particular surgery hours, but the medical staff are on call 24 hours a day for any emergencies and cabin visits. Of course, medical treatment is neither free nor cheap, but provided you have proper travel insurance, you will be fully covered.

The final key area in this discussion of ship-board facilities and their development is **cabins**, and it is an area which causes most confusion and concern for cruise first-timers. The first concept to understand with a ship's accommodation is it is NOT like a hotel room, i.e. large and uniform. You do not specify a particular room when you book a hotel, but that is what you do with a ship.

A regal touch – the Royal Suite on Celebrity's ship the Zenith

To start with, unlike most hotels, there are different *categories* of cabin, which is a product of the evolution of the cruise ship and something which only the most modern of the larger ships are trying to standardise. On the classic old cruise ship, the categories were decided by the amount of space in the cabin and on which deck it was situated (another throwback to the old days of class-orientated cruising when the more you paid meant the higher the deck your accommodation was on – not very practical when it came to smooth sailings as the most stable cabins are invariably found on the decks lower down).

This profusion of cabin choice gives rise to an unfortunate side effect which is perpetuated for some reason best known only to the cruise lines themselves, and this is that the average cruise brochure can often resemble something akin to a page of algebra when it comes to trying to select your accommodation. A bewildering array of types, sizes and formats makes for a daunting task for the uninitiated, and even the average travel agent can find it tough sorting out this complexity of choice. On older ships in particular, the configuration of the decks lends itself to aiding this confusion, and it is only the modern way of ship-building that has helped to simplify matters. Instead of being built from the hull up and filled out accordingly in one homogenous build, the new cruise ship is constructed from pre-fabricated blocks, almost like a giant meccano kit, which allows for units like cabins to be 'bolted on' in a standardised fashion, so most cabins conform to much fewer types.

Using *Oriana* as a prime example, here's how a typical deck plan of a modern cruise ship will look, showing how the accommodation decks are kept largely separate from the public areas and how the different cabin categories are shown from the highest deck down:

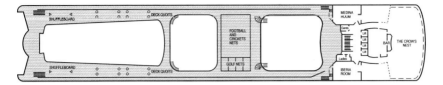

SUN DECK (Deck 13) Outdoor decks, deck sports, observation lounge

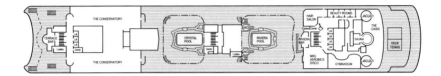

LIDO DECK (Deck 12) Outdoor decks, pools and health and fitness centres

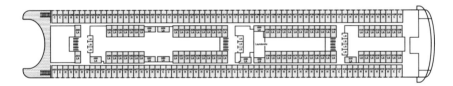

A DECK (Deck 11) Two-berth inside and outside cabins, 20 singles

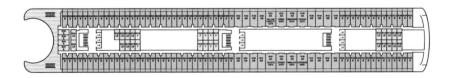

B DECK (Deck 10) Balconied staterooms, suites, a few inside singles and doubles

C DECK (Deck 9) Staterooms, inner and outer doubles, 42 singles

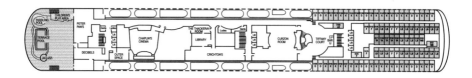

D DECK (Deck 8) Public rooms, children's facilities, one-, two- and four-berth cabins

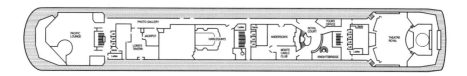

PROM DECK (Deck 7) Public rooms, including Theatre Royal and Harlequins nightclub

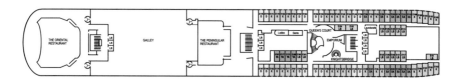

E DECK (Deck 6) Restaurants, one-, two- and four-berth cabins

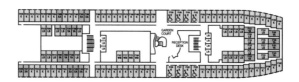

F DECK (Deck 5) Two-, three- and four-berth cabins, eight for disabled passengers

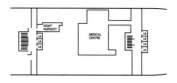

G DECK (Deck 4) Hospital and night nursery

BRIT TIP

Don't be fooled by the cruise lines who insist on calling cabins by the more grand title of Staterooms. There is rarely anything stately about them, it is just another case of brochure jargon.

As a general rule of thumb, your cabin will be notably SMALLER than a typical hotel room. The arrival of the mega-liner in the late 70s and early 80s increased this tendency as the emphasis was on squeezing in as many small, identically-built cabins as possible. Some cabins, particularly those on lower passenger decks, resembled little more than glorified cupboards as the then-current perception insisted that passengers spent only a limited amount of time in their cabin.

 BRIT TIP

Newcomers to cruising are often worried about the possibility of having a cabin down in the ship's bowels or even below the water-line. This is very rarely the case, but it can pay to pick a cabin on a lower deck if you are worried about sea-sickness as it minimises the effect of the ship's movement. The same also applies to cabins that are centrally located, i.e. away from both the bow and stern.

It is really only in post-1980s ship-building that designers have fully come round to the idea of providing passengers with a bit of elbow room in their cabins, as well as solving one of cruising's most ticklish problems, that of providing proper double beds! There is also, at long last, an increasing move towards standardisation of cabin design to reduce the unnecessary volume of variety. Usually, cabins can be arranged to accommodate two to four people with the use of convertible settees or fold down bunks, while several lines (notably Royal Caribbean) are experimenting successfully with purpose-built family cabins that have a second bedroom for the children. This should be the full range of extra choice beyond a standard two-berth (where berth is just ship-speak for bed), but check the small detail to see if those twin beds DO convert to a double as there are still instances where they don't.

INSIDE OR OUTSIDE?

So, just what should you expect from a typical cabin these days? Well, one of the most straightforward distinctions is that of either an inside or an outside cabin (and no, an outside or outer cabin DOESN'T mean outside the ship! That may sound absurd, but I can assure you it is a not uncommon query among those unfamiliar with ship terminology!). Thankfully, nowadays designers have gone a long way towards making this differentiation almost unnecessary by building cabins of identical size whether they are outer (i.e. with a window or porthole, though the latter, sadly, is becoming a rare feature) or inner (usually with a curtained mirror in place of the window). There is still, of course, a substantial difference in price between the two types, but, unless you suffer from claustrophobia, the inner cabin on a modern cruise ship represents excellent value for money – you pay less, yet you still benefit from ALL the facilities and public rooms outside your cabin door, you eat the same food and enjoy the same level of entertainment. The only other cabin distinction of note is the suite, which should have more than one room (i.e. a sitting room as well as a bedroom) and a higher level of facilities all round.

A second rule of thumb says you find steadily increased cabin space the higher up in the ship you go, and this holds true for nearly all but the most recent designs. This, of course, means you pay more on a higher deck than a lower one, but again, I would caution against automatically opting for the bigger cabin, especially if price is the most important factor to you. In many cases, the extra space is negligible and you should consider carefully if you will feel the benefit of, say, a two-seater settee – or an extra £200 to spend. Of

course, if money is not the prime consideration, the top levels of cabin CAN offer an attractive alternative to the standard varieties. A typical suite will provide a sitting room as well as a bedroom (and, more often than not, a queen-sized bed), more generous cupboard and drawer space (provision of these can be pretty limited lower down) and a proper bathroom. The latter should be stressed because standard cabins are usually equipped with a shower only and,

A 'room with a view' on the Paul Gauguin

while they are perfectly adequate, there is still no better way to relax in the bathroom than in a well-filled tub. Many up-market cruise lines (and the top level cabins on the middle-range ones) may also boast a whirlpool bath.

 BRIT TIP

Given the choice of a lower-rated ship and a higher category of cabin or a higher-rated ship and a lower cabin category, take the latter option. Your overall cruise experience will be much more rewarding.

In addition to the size and configuration, the facilities of the cabin may vary slightly as you go through the range, but once again this is something which is gradually being phased out. In the past, the standard cabin's extras may have amounted to little more than a coffee table or an additional chair. Any cruise ship launched today will include a TV (and occasionally a video recorder), a proper dressing-table, some sort of extra seating (be it an armchair or a settee), a hairdryer and a coffee or bedside table in even its lowest-grade cabins. The 'extras' at the other end of the scale now usually consist of refrigerators or mini-bars, video recorders, full seating area, and even a whirlpool bath. In-room safes have also become a common feature across the board, although they are a safety item which has little practical value on board except to provide peace of mind to the American passengers.

Other considerations to bear in mind when selecting your cabin are the proximity of the busier public rooms (you do not want to be near the night-club or casino if you are an early-to-bed type), the occurrence of jogging on the promenade or sun deck (you do not want to be directly underneath them when the early-morning fitness fanatics take to the deck), the position of the ship's lifeboats (which can obscure the view from your cabin window in some cases – typically, these cabins should come at a lower rate than those with unimpaired views) and location at one of the business ends of the ship: the stern is usually worst for a slightly enhanced vulnerability to engine vibration, while the bow houses the anchors – and there is nothing like the sound of a heavy-duty anchor being released as your ship docks in the early morning to act as an instant alarm call.

 **BRIT TIP**

No matter what the level of modern sound-proofing or the situation of the cabin itself, you are travelling on a MOVING object so there is bound to be some kind of background noise, some kind of creak or groan (and we're not talking about the honeymoon couples here!), usually low-scale but quite noticeable to cruise newcomers. This is not usually a reason to complain (as some newspapers might have you believe when relating stories of imaginary cruise horrors) but is simply the nature of the beast – and part of its charm.

TO BALCONY OR NOT TO BALCONY?

Finally (and this is a final Finally), comes the question of the feature which is beginning to dominate cabin design – that of whether or not to have a balcony.

In every ship that rolls off the production line these days, the percentage of cabins with this extra outdoor facility – however small – is increasing all the time. When the *Sun Princess* made her début in 1995, her owners proudly proclaimed almost three-quarters of her outside cabins as having balconies;

more than half of the up-market *Crystal Symphony*'s cabins come complete with balcony; the same proportion of outer cabins on *Carnival Destiny* will boast this feature; and no less than 710 cabins on *Grand Princess* will also offer the luxury of a balcony. Luxury? Well, yes and no. It usually adds a substantial amount to a standard cabin price and is therefore not something I would recommend to the price-conscious. But – and it is a fairly big But – if you can afford the step up, you really will feel the benefit.

If there is one thing the average cruise ship cannot guarantee it is your own *private* outdoor space. But, with a balcony, that dilemma is immediately solved. And, once you have tasted the sea air and watched the world sailing slowly by from your own little private enclave, you will wonder how you ever managed to stay in a normal, enclosed cabin. For all the fact that cruising is no longer the preserve of the privileged few, there is something wonderfully decadent and exclusive about sipping a pre-dinner drink on your own cabin balcony and luxuriating in your splendid, individual isolation!

SERVICE WITH A SMILE

If that gives you the lowdown on a ship's hardware, the second important element in your choice of cruise line concerns the **Service** you will receive on board and the people who provide it.

The most significant factor to bear in mind is the passenger/crew ratio, which provides a good indicator of the level of attention you can expect. The nearer 1:1 it approaches, the more pampering you can expect. At the luxury end of the scale, Cunard's *Sea Goddess* ships and both the up-scale Seabourn and Silversea vessels all boast this near-perfect ratio. The standard, mass-market ships all operate on ratios of upwards of 2:1. This has an inevitable effect on the quality of the service as well as the personal nature of it, yet there is rather more to the enjoyment of this aspect of your cruise than the simple logistics involved. For instance, the cruise lines take care of their crews in different ways, and often this is reflected in the style and friendliness of the service you receive; a happy crew makes for a happy cruise. Celebrity, Crystal, Orient and Seabourn all have excellent reputations for looking after their staff and consequently their care really does pay off in the attitude that is picked up by the passengers. By the same token, the older ships have fewer facilities for their crew, and therefore they have a higher staff turnover and lack that efficient edge which is noticeable only in its absence.

Equally, several lines go out of their way to ensure the service their passengers receive is that bit more memorable or special. All of the up-market lines guarantee this as standard, but it is noticeable in one or two others where they work wonderfully hard at producing an atmosphere that is efficient without being too formal and friendly without being too presumptuous. Swan Hellenic, Orient, Holland America, Fred Olsen, P&O and even the budget-priced Thomson and Airtours all excel at producing a level of service above and beyond the norm for their levels.

Indeed, in some cases the ship's 'software' can make for some of the most memorable cruise experiences and can be one of the primary reasons why people return again and again to that particular ship. The bar steward who always remembers your favourite drink, the friendly deck hand who somehow knows your name or the member of the entertainments staff who goes out of his way to ensure you feel involved, these are all regular examples of the personal touch which cruising does better than most hotels.

A ship's crew can be a pretty varied bunch, too, in both their country of origin and the function they perform on board. As the world's cruise fleet continues to expand, an ever-greater number of people are required to crew them and a typical

Having your own balcony is one of cruising's luxuries

nationality profile may encompass men and women from the Philippines, India, Pakistan, Europe (especially Eastern Europe these days), the Caribbean, USA, Canada and Latin America. It is a real United Nations at sea and often requires a degree in international diplomacy by the ship's hotel director, who is in charge of the majority of the service staff. The need for cruise lines to cast their nets ever further afield to find the necessary staff has meant something of a drop in the general service standards of the big, mass-market product as the lines struggle to train people up to the required level and encounter problems with language (for, although there may by a cosmopolitan atmosphere on board, the primary language on most cruise ships is still English). But, the industry insists, this is not expected to be a long-term problem.

There are six main groups who make up a cruise ship's staff complement, and they can be summed up as follows:

Cabin staff: usually, the steward or stewardess who is assigned to your cabin for the duration of the cruise. This is the individual you may well see most of, busily attending to a number of cabins on your deck and responsible for making sure each one is kept clean every day. He or she makes the beds, ensures the bathroom is kept stocked with the necessary toiletries and will attend to your extra requirements such as room service, laundry and shoe cleaning. Your steward or stewardess will almost certainly make contact with you soon after you have settled into your cabin for the first time and will appreciate being called by name, if only to make sure you know who to tip at the end of the cruise! Occasionally, there can be more than one steward/stewardess to each cabin and in the most up-market ships there may also be a butler.

 BRIT TIP

Unless you are used to having your own servants at home, the presence of a butler can be faintly embarrassing. It may sound like a quaint idea in theory, but, in practice, there isn't really a lot extra a butler can provide which your steward can't.

Deck staff: this is the most varied and multi-purpose staff group of all, combining the function of on-deck waiters and waitresses with that of general cleaners and tidiers. Very often they are assigned areas of the deck, and you will quickly become familiar with a particular face or two as you develop your own routine on board. It is sometimes baffling how they will cheerfully greet you by name when they must meet hundreds of passengers every day.

Restaurant staff: like your cabin steward, you will soon be familiar with your restaurant waiter and younger assistant waiter (usually referred to as the bus boy) who you will also see on a daily basis. This duo will play a vital role in your enjoyment of mealtimes, and cruise lines are now extremely adept at selecting some of the best characters for the dining room as well as those with a good understanding of the food itself. They will always be keen to discuss your day at the evening meal, offer advice for the next port of call and make sure you enjoy every course. I vividly recall a Costa Rican waiter on one ship who introduced himself as Earl the Pearl and who was, indeed, a real gem at mealtimes. And a Turkish duo called Attila and Ilhan who turned every meal into 'Showtime!' In addition to the waiters, you will also be looked after by the dining room's Maître d' and be able to order drinks from the omni-present wine waiter or waitress.

 BRIT TIP

When it comes to the end-of-cruise tipping, your waiter and bus boy should figure highly in your estimation. However, DON'T feel it necessary to tip the Maître d' unless he has arranged some special service for you, while the wine waiter/waitress will have benefitted from every order you have made during the cruise as drink orders usually carry an automatic service charge.

Take a tip from me

As a minor digression, having stumbled into the oft-misunderstood realms of on-board tipping, it is worth pointing out several things. Tipping is part and parcel of virtually every cruise, especially on the American ships where it is as natural as breathing. Brits, on the other hand, have a hard time with what is, after all, just a way of saying 'Thank You' for good, polite service. We are either embarrassed, ignorant or simply don't see the need for it. All of these reactions are easily overcome. There should certainly be no need for embarrassment these days as every cruise line makes it clear what the recommended daily gratuity rate is for the three main people who are most deserving of your cash – your steward, waiter and bus boy. You simply calculate the recommended rate (and more than 90 per cent of passengers DO adhere to the cruise line's recommendation) over the number of days of your cruise and then deposit the amount in the handy envelopes that will inevitably be left in your cabin on the final evening. The Purser's Desk will have spares or extras should you need them. As a general rule, American lines recommend $3-$3.50 (£2–£2.25) per person, per day for your waiter and steward, and half that for the bus boy. P&O put forward a slightly more pocket-friendly recommendation of £2.50 ($3.75) per person per day for all your tips.

The matter of ignorance of this ship-board custom is important to deal with as the stewards and waiters rely to a large degree on tipping for the bulk of their income. They work long contracts for a relatively low standard wage, and it is therefore up to them to provide the right level of service to encourage their passengers to be generous at the end of each cruise. Someone who simply forgets this custom at the conclusion of their holiday is unwittingly taking advantage of the individual workers concerned. Some people will argue the practice of tipping is rather objectionable and is only a way of allowing the cruise lines to keep their wages low. 'Why should I be required to help pay someone's salary?' is a typical objection I have heard. But it misses the point. Tipping is a perfectly respectable way of rewarding good service and it hurts only the innocent party if you decide not to. Of course, if you haven't received the right level of service you are perfectly at liberty to withhold your gratuity. But, if you experience that level of dissatisfaction it makes more sense to take it up with the Hotel Manager first.

However, having said all that, the cruise industry is aware tipping is not popular and is trying to change things. Firstly, an increasing number of lines now allow you to pre-pay all your tips at the time of your main payment. Then, instead of filling an envelope with cash at the end of the cruise, you are given a voucher to hand over instead. By far the better option – and something many cruise lines (notably Thomson and NCL) are considering is to abolish tipping altogether and actively discourage it on board.

You may end up paying slightly more to start with, but it does remove the one constant bugbear for many people.

As hinted at above, your bar staff and waiters are likely to benefit with every drink you order through a practice that is, to my mind, slightly more annoying. This is the American ship custom of adding an automatic 15 per cent service charge which you are expected to pay. In reality, it adds only a minor sum in the overall scheme of things, but it is a dubious automatic expectation. By far the better practice (and, I'm happy to say, a hallmark of British-run ships) is for the waiter or bar steward to leave the total blank on your bill and allow you to supply the tip which you think is warranted. That way you get to reward particularly good service, or your favourite waiter/waitress, in suitable fashion.

Bar staff: you will already have picked up the message that the bars and lounges are run by regular staff who will endeavour to have your drink ready before you have ordered it. Again, you will find some of the biggest characters responsible for dispensing the alcoholic beverages, and it is easy to be lulled into having that drink or three too many!

You will enjoy a drink or three with your favourite barman

Cruise staff: this is again a multi-purpose group of people who are those most immediately responsible for making sure you enjoy the cruise. They consist of the entertainers who put on the evening shows and, in some cases, organise the daily events; they man the Purser's Desk and they take the shore excursion bookings; they give talks on the ports of call and have titles like Port Lecturer and Social Hostess; they introduce the shows and are always there to make sure you Have A Nice Day; in short, they are the main interface between the ship and its passengers. The cruise staff DO get paid a decent wage and therefore do NOT get tipped.

The Officers: headed by the captain, these are the people who actually run the ship. It is their job to ensure it gets from place to place safely and on time, that the engines run smoothly, the air-conditioning works, the tele-communications links stay open, and, through the doctor and nursing staff, that everyone stays healthy.

The Captain is The Boss. In the overall chain of command he sits right at the top and oversees the running of the ship and its crew. His immediate aides are the Staff Captain and Chief Engineer, who between them oversee the day-to-day operation of the ship itself. Under the Staff Captain come the Chief Officer, the First, Second and Third Officers and the Radio Officers. The Chief Engineer runs the engine room and all the electrical facilities with a staff of Deputy, Second and Third Engineers, and the Chief Electrician and his Junior Electricians.

However, the running of a large, modern cruise ship is now such a specialised business in itself that further top staff are needed and so the Staff Captain and Chief Engineer are joined in their rank of responsibility by the Hotel Manager, or Director, and he oversees ALL the other groups of the crew. His chain of command also has five distinct links, and increasingly it is the Hotel Manager who is primarily responsible for a successful cruise (although the captain maintains the ultimate responsibility for the ship, crew and passengers – an important distinction). Under the Hotel Manager come: the Head Chef and his team of assistant chefs, galley staff and storekeepers; the Deputy Hotel Manager, who controls all the restaurant staff from the Maître d' to the bus boys; the Food and Beverage Manager, and his team of bar managers, barmen, waiters and waitresses; the Cruise Director, who fulfils another vital liaison role with the passengers, along with his Deputy Director, Social Hostess, Stage Manager, Cruise Staff, Entertainers and Childrens' Counsellors; and the Purser, the previous supervisor of 'domestic' matters before a Hotel Manager became necessary, with a staff of Assistant Pursers, Printers, Stewards, Stewardesses and, importantly, the outside operators or concessions who run the health and beauty facilities, shops, casino and photographers. It sounds like a cast of thousands but does in fact number only hundreds in most cases (the giant 101,000-ton *Carnival Destiny* is the first ship to break the 1,000-crew barrier).

 **BRIT TIP**

On board the American ships, if you find yourself yearning for a bit of British company and the rest of the passengers are all from Detroit or Chicago (unlikely, but possible), it is worth knowing that several ship concessions are staffed almost exclusively by Brits at sea. These usually include the photographers, the beauty salon staff (often a Steiner Transocean concession), casino staff and some of the entertainers.

THAT'S ENTERTAINMENT

The third vital component of an enjoyable cruise is the multi-faceted one of **Entertainment,** and this is an area where the larger, more up-market ships all score big marks.

From early-morning aerobics to the late-night disco or nightclub, a ship's entertainment staff are working almost non-stop to provide you with a range and quantity of attractions that often leave the cruise newcomer amazed. As already mentioned, the appeal can be as wide as bingo to antiques, napkin-folding to art auctions, karaoke to classical concerts, family variety shows and even adults-only comedians. In many cases the Entertainments staff are hire-contract professionals doing short-term bookings for just one or two cruises. These people will include singers, musicians, comedians, magicians and variety acts. The majority are not big TV or theatre names but have a solid background in live entertainment and can be more fun than some big-name stars (Bobby Davro is a notable exception – his live show is wonderfully funny).

 BRIT TIP

Two comedians to watch out for in particular are Mike Goddard, who worked closely with the late Frankie Howerd, and Scotsman Ron Dale, a genuine cruise enthusiast as well as a very funny man.

In addition to the imported entertainers, each ship will also have its own theatre company or dance group who will put on a series of ostentatious song and dance shows during the course of the voyage. On the new ships with big stage capability, these shows can be very elaborate indeed, drawing on material from the big West End productions or, in the case of the American ships, their Broadway equivalent. On the smaller or busier ships (notably Airtours and P&O), the dance company also help to organise a lot of the daytime activities and sports, and it is a nice way of getting to meet them as well. By the nature of this diversification they need to be more flexible and so they will often be good all-rounders rather than outstanding at any one type of performance.

With the growing development of the theatre-at-sea idea, it is true that the majority of lines are lavishing an increasing amount of attention on these big scale production shows to the point where they are now usually the main focus of the evening's entertainment. However, they may not be to everyone's taste and hence there will nearly always be an alternative form of evening entertainment in the ship's secondary lounge. The main show will also be repeated for the benefit of second-sitting diners on the larger ships, and so once again your only worry will be what to choose.

Another relatively recent addition, if only for the moment on the more up-market American lines, is that of art auctions. As a complete art duffer, I can assure even the most non art-minded people they will find these an unexpectedly satisfying source of entertainment, as well as providing an interesting insight into the art world. There is rarely any pressure to buy, and the patter of the auctioneer can be highly amusing (especially if he turns out to be Scotsman Gavin Watson, one of the busiest art auction men at sea and a very humorous guy as well).

Obviously, the actual programme of entertainment varies from cruise line to cruise line and some do things better than others, but the overall quantity and quality should not leave you without amusement, especially when you add in the omnipresent events such as port lectures, bingo sessions, bridge competitions, dance classes, films, quizzes, singalongs, and board games. Once again, I defy anyone to get bored.

IT'S MEAL-TIME (AGAIN!)

Without wishing to over-stress the importance to a good cruise of the **Food**, it is quite instructive to examine just why it features so prominently in the brochures and advertisements (and in passengers' memories).

To start with, meal-times are one of the principal social occasions of ship-board life and the likelihood for couples is that you will find yourself sharing a table with two or more people you haven't met before. Some find this thought a little off-putting, but it is true in nearly all cases that it is a wonderful way of making friends, discussing the day's events and other cruise experiences, and the chances are you will want to keep in touch with your new-found companions once the cruise is over.

Entertainment at sea is a truly glamorous affair

Occasionally it is possible that two couples really do not get along together, and then you are perfectly at liberty to seek a change of table, or even of sitting, with the restaurant's Maître d'.

 BRIT TIP

If you are offered a table for six or more, take it. It both reduces the chances of being stuck with the Cruise Bores and enhances the social ambience which a ship's restaurant creates, making every meal a real occasion. Tables for two are relatively rare.

The standard practice, when you first join your ship, is to be offered the option of first or second sitting in the dining room (unless you are on one of the handful of truly up-market ships which offer open-seating dining at your convenience). Traditionally, first sitting will be 8am for breakfast, 12 noon or

12.15pm for lunch, and 6.30pm for dinner, with second sitting at 9am, 1.30pm and 8.30pm. On some ships, breakfast and lunch will be open seating due to the reduced demand, and this will often be the case all round when a ship is in port. Alternatively, there will always be a buffet option away from the main restaurant for both breakfast and lunch, with the chance to experience one of life's real pleasures – cruise ship dining *al fresco*. Your choice may be slightly reduced in the buffet option, but the added bonus of enjoying your meal on deck more than compensates. There will also usually be at least one featured buffet lunch, with a regional food theme such as Italian or Chinese, where the ship's chefs really go to town with visual as well as culinary style.

For those just wishing to pig out and get the maximum value for their cruise pound, here is a typical example of the full run-down of how your Seven Meals a Day line up: from 6am, Early Riser's Breakfast (usually pastries, fruit juice and coffee on deck); 8–10am, Full Breakfast (in the restaurant or the buffet alternative); 10.30–11.30am Bouillon (not literally broth, but a savoury mid-morning snack comfortably eclipsing elevenses!); 12 noon–2pm Lunch (again in either the restaurant or buffet); 3.30–4.30pm Afternoon Tea (and a chance to snack up on sandwiches and cakes in the best British traditions); 6.30–8.30pm Dinner (up to seven courses in many cases); and finally, a Midnight Buffet for those who can take it.

Dining is always an experience at sea

Having detailed the culinary experience in deliberately general terms, it should be fairly evident that the quality of the food and service DOES vary from line to line according to the individual style (and the price) of that line. At its most basic, you are likely to miss out on some of the finer points of content and service and the accent will be on hearty portions rather than finesse. At its best, the top cruise lines can rival the best restaurants in the world for their quality and presentation and you can expect a meal fit to grace the table of any top London chef.

These differences will be discussed in more detail in the next couple of chapters under the subject of rating the cruise lines, but it serves here to highlight two particular examples of the type of menu you can expect, using P&O's mass-market *Oriana* and the top-of-the-range *Crystal Harmony*.

ORIANA DINNER MENU

Appetisers

Smoked Scottish Salmon with Lemon and Brown Bread

Half Avocado filled with strips of Parma Ham, Celeriac and Apple Mayonnaise

Spinach Risotto with Masala and Parmesan

****

Soups

Cream of Asparagus Soup with Chive Cream

Consommé of Beef Jardinière

****

Main Courses

Fillet of Cod with Champagne and Saffron Sauce

Roast Sirloin of Scottish Beef with Yorkshire Pudding and Rosemary Gravy

Steamed Breast of Chicken with Winter Vegetables and an Arran Mustard Sauce

Stir-fried Fragrant Pork with Shi-take Mushrooms, Water Chestnuts and
Soft Noodles

Fusilli Pasta and Winter Vegetable Bake

Today's Cold Cuts served with a selection of Salads and Dressings

Side Orders

Selection of Market Vegetables

****

Desserts

Sticky Toffee Pudding with Butterscotch Sauce

Traditional Sherry Trifle

Rich Dark Chocolate Terrine with Grand Marnier Sauce

Fresh Fruit Salad

Vanilla, Strawbery and Peach Ice Creams

Passion Fruit Sorbet

****

Selected British and Continental Cheeses with Biscuits and Fruit

Espresso/Decaffeinated/Filter Coffee

After Dinner Mints

Fresh from the Bakery: White, Wholemeal, Granary and Garlic Rolls

CRYSTAL HARMONY DINNER MENU

Appetisers

Iced Caspian Sea Sevruga Malossol Caviar with Traditional Trimmings, Melba Toast

Blackened Fresh Sea Scallops with Tropical Fruit Relish

Truffled Chicken Liver Parfait with Warm Brioche

Chilled Assorted Fruit in a Half Coconut Perfumed with Honeydew Melon Liqueur

****

Soups

Fresh Mushroom Soup 'Cappuccino Style' with Whipped Cream and Paprika

Clear Oxtail Soup with Barley and Chester-sesame Sticks

****

Salad

Captain's Salad

Medley of Selected Crunchy Field Lettuce with Cherry Tomatoes and Eggplant Chips

Dressings available in the tradional favourites plus today's specials:

Fat-free Honey-lime or Low-calorie Carrot-cucumber Yoghurt

****

Sherbet (Sorbet)

Refreshing Peach Champagne Sherbet

****

Main Courses

Broiled Lobster Tail 'Madame Butterfly'

Served with Light, Creamy Lobster Sauce, Steamed Baby Vegetables and Truffled Pilaf Rice

Grilled Fresh Halibut Fillet

With Fennel Vinaigrette, Assorted Baby Vegetables and New Potatoes

Chateaubriand

Sliced Black Angus Beef Tenderloin with Port Wine Sauce
Baby Vegetable Mix with Asparagus Spears and Stuffed Baked Potato

Sautéed Medallions of Veal Loin

With Light Tarragon Sauce, Steamed Green Asparagus and Angel Hair Pasta with Tomato Confit

****

Side Orders

Garden Fresh Baby Vegetables   Green Asparagus Spears   Truffled Pilaf Rice
Stuffed Baked Potato   New Potatoes   Angel Hair Pasta with Tomato Sauce
****

Desserts

Chocolate Fantasy - Crunchy Chocolate-almond Sticks with Grand Marnier and
Fresh Berries; Tartelette Pavlova - Meringue Shell with Lemon Cream; Sugar-free
Tiramisu; Freshly Frozen Non-fat Hazelnut-Amaretto Yoghurt; Plantation Truffles
and Petits Fours from the Chocolate Treasure Chest; Assortment of Seasonal fruit
and Selection of International Cheeses with Crackers and Biscuits

 BRIT TIP

To get the maximum enjoyment from your meal, opt for second sitting if given the choice because you will rarely be hurried to finish and you will get more chance to make the most of the social setting, something which British passengers are much keener on than their American counterparts.

Increasingly, too, cruise lines are concerned with providing a full-time alternative to the main restaurant, be it only a hot-dog or burger bar or a small, specialist restaurant, again all at NO extra charge (apart from the occasional tip). Princess Cruises feature pleasant, well-serviced (and highly popular) pizzerias, while NCL ships each offer a bistro dining experience and an afternoon chocoholic's buffet (not for the faint-hearted – the Americans take meal-times seriously at the best of times, and there is a positive stampede for this). Crystal's claim to fame in this department is the addition of two intimate, themed restaurants (Japanese and Italian on the *Crystal Harmony*, Chinese and Italian on the *Crystal Symphony*), and Holland America can boast outdoor taco, pasta and ice cream bars. A further feature of every cruise ship is the Midnight Buffet, one last chance to indulge your taste buds. Watch out in particular for the Grand or International Midnight Buffet where the chefs serve up a positive extravaganza of culinary temptation, complete with set-piece displays of magnificent ice and butter carvings.

It may come as something of a relief to the more dimensionally well-endowed among us (myself included) after all this emphasis on quantity to know that most lines also now cater for the health-conscious. A lean or low-fat option will usually be highlighted on the menu, along with low sodium, vegetarian and even kosher offerings.

YOUR PORTS OF CALL

The final key element in weighing up the cruise product on offer is, of course, where your ship takes you, how many **Ports of Call** it visits and your options for **Shore Excursions** while you are there. The actual areas the main cruise lines visit will be discussed in detail later in the book in Chapter Six, but here it is a good idea to make yourself familiar with the kinds of standard itinerary on offer.

First of all, it is another fairly basic difference between ourselves and our American cousins at sea that we take rather more interest in the ports of call once we are there. We want to be well-informed on the sights to see, the local culture and the people we are going to meet ashore, as well as knowing all about the shopping opportunities (which often seems to be an American's *raison d'être* on a cruise). Therefore, we take more care over our choice of itinerary and, as a result, the predominantly British cruise lines tend to put together more packages that have those tastes in mind. Fred Olsen have realised this trend and now offer trips to the Far East, South America and even a transatlantic crossing via Greenland in addition to their more traditional Scandinavian and Canary Island itineraries.

Santorini is the picture-perfect Greek port of call

Having said that, it is now an established fact of modern cruising that there is an increasing demand to get off the beaten track, to explore new itineraries and new areas . . . to boldly go where no cruiser has gone before! Well, almost. The Caribbean remains the Number One cruise destination world-wide, with the Mediterranean still a strong second, but the fastest-growing area of cruise interest over the last few years has been Alaska, and most of the main companies now offer some very attractive packages to America's largest yet most natural state.

The Far East is seen as the next big area of growth, while there are also increasing amounts of cruise traffic to the Red Sea, South Africa, South America and Australasia. In fact, with the emergence of the adventure cruise ships, there are now few areas which cannot be explored by sea.

 **BRIT TIP**

Something of which the majority of cruisers are unaware but which is in the small print of EVERY brochure, is the cruise line's right to change a given itinerary at little or no notice for operating reasons. The two big Caribbean hurricanes of 1995 are the best case in point as they gave rise to some hysterical newspaper stories – passengers complained bitterly of missing out on ports of call simply because they were being trashed at the time by 120mph winds! The captain of the *Oriana* even had the audacity to put the safety of his ship before his passengers' wishes to go ashore – such impertinence. Be warned, therefore, a ship's itinerary is not set in stone and, if you have your heart set on one particular port, double-check it for adverse weather conditions before you book.

As the mass market increasingly switches on to the potential and excitement of cruising, there is an inevitable standardisation of the main products, and these can be summed up in several ways.

Most significant for the UK market is the huge predominance of seven-day cruises. In most cases these are geared for the American market because the US does not enjoy as much holiday time as Europe and so they will rarely devote more than a week at a time to their 'vacations'. This means on the majority of fly-cruise trips (the Caribbean being the prime example) we are travelling a long way just for a week's holiday when we are far more used to taking two weeks at a time. A typical American seven-day cruise can also be pretty port-intensive due to their taste for cramming in as much as possible in their vacation time. This can leave the average Brit at sea just a little bit breathless after such a long-distance but short-duration dash. Happily, the cruise companies have quickly realised they have a wider audience to appeal to, and so there are now plenty of packages that offer cruising as just half or part of your overall holiday. There is a wealth of wonderful opportunities for a week's stay on one of the Caribbean islands in addition to your seven-day cruise, and several lines also offer an individual tailor-made packaging service which can fix you up with several possibilities – NCL, for example, can marry up any of their Caribbean cruises with visits to most resorts in the region or the USA through their Cruise Plus service – in addition to the ship-board half of your holiday.

WALT DISNEY WORLD AND ALL THAT

As Florida is still the biggest long-haul market for British holiday-makers, the main tour operators have also cottoned on to the possibilities of offering a week's cruising as well as a week in the theme park wonderland of Orlando or one of the coastal resorts of the sunshine state. This is potentially one of the biggest growth areas of the UK fly-cruise holiday business, and it will soon be common procedure for Caribbean cruising to be featured quite prominently in Florida brochures, the theory being that so many Brits going there are now repeat visitors they are likely to be looking for something slightly different to do, and cruising does offer a terrific value add-on to a week's theme-parking in many cases. The Walt Disney company themselves also expect to be able to exploit this with their two mega-ships which are due for launch in 1998. Bookings for the 85,000-ton *Disney Magic* and *Disney Wonder* are already being taken, but, crucially, a cruise can be taken ONLY with a package to Walt Disney World as well, which highlights how these two markets will continue to go hand in hand.

In Miami, don't miss a visit to the Venetian Pool at Coral Gables

First-timers will also be tempted into the cruise world in this area by the increasingly well-advertised prospect of only a three- or four-day cruise in addition to their land-based week or 10 days. Now, these shorter cruises are an excellent way of finding out if cruising is really for you without going to the full expense of the whole cruise experience, and Florida is the centre of this particular cruise activity, again focusing on the vast numbers of holiday visitors there. The only comparable British cruise activity of this kind are a handful of three- or four-day cruises out of Southampton with P&O or Cunard. The three- and four-day cruise market is BIG business with the Americans, but somehow it has more limited appeal to the British market, perhaps because we are not comfortable with the idea of going all that way for such a short cruise. But it WILL become a regular feature of our holiday brochures, and it is certainly worth considering if you don't fancy going the whole hog straight away.

CHOOSE YOUR TYPE OF CRUISE

A discussion of this short-duration style of cruising leads on to a breakdown of the FOUR main types of cruise which are the staple fare of any cruise brochure. Every cruise will conform to one of these formats, and they all affect the ship's itinerary in different ways.

Circular cruises: these are the most common in the mass market. They start and finish at the same point (in the case of the mass-market Caribbean, usually Miami or Fort Lauderdale in Florida or San Juan in Puerto Rico) and visit the same ports of call every week or 10 days. The ports are always ready for the ship when it arrives, the facilities will be guaranteed and the shore-side organisation is well-grooved to the point of being hum-drum. The chances are you will be in port with at least one other sizeable ship and, in some cases like the US Virgin Islands, it is not uncommon for there to be four or more liners in at once, meaning BIG crowds in all the main shore-side tourist spots. The seven-day cruise is absolutely tailor-made for the circular style and it usually runs like clockwork. The three- and four-day versions are similarly of the circular variety, and are run even more on bus-like lines. They are the most *informal* types of cruise and nearly always have the youngest age profiles, with plenty of couples and plenty of children and teenagers. In many cases, if you feel seven days is just not enough, a circular cruise can also be taken back-to-back with a complementary itinerary that turns it into a figure-of-eight cruise. For example, Celebrity Cruises offer a 16-night package that takes in first a seven-day circuit of the Western Caribbean and then, after returning to the home port, a seven-day circuit of the Eastern Caribbean. This can also be done with Costa, NCL, Princess, Holland America and Royal Caribbean or by changing ships at the end of seven days with Carnival. You should also get a decent mix of sea days and port days, remembering that you don't want a surfeit of ports of call unless you are REALLY keen to see every island.

 BRIT TIP

Cruising remains the best way of sampling the Caribbean because many of the islands would not keep you actively interested for a full two weeks, while a day's visit is just enough to give you a good taste of what's on offer (plus, there is a school of thought that says one island paradise looks much like another after a while).

P&O operate the best example of circular cruises out of the UK (along with Fred Olsen) but the very nature of sailing out of British waters demands a longer voyage, hence you will not find any seven-day cruises in this area. Airtours and Thomson are both in the process of creating Britain's first mass market in circular cruising, with summer itineraries out of Palma in Majorca, but the Italian firm Costa were the pioneers of Mediterranean fly-cruising and they still have some of the best itineraries in this field, sailing out of Genoa and Venice.

Linear cruises: these tend to operate on a back-and-forth basis and are as well-grooved as the circular variety. The best example is the trans-Panama Canal route, which sees ships sail from Miami, Fort Lauderdale or San Juan through the magnificent Canal to Acapulco or Los Angeles, and then retrace their steps eastbound with a new set of passengers. The minimum length of time for a linear cruise is seven days, and 10- to 14-day varieties are not uncommon. The latter will have more days at sea and will therefore tend towards the more *formal*, with a slightly older passenger profile (say, 50-plus) and fewer children. Linear cruises also include transatlantic crossings on a regular basis, which used to be the real essence of life at sea. The *QE2* is now the only ship offering a regular transatlantic service, and, as there are no ports of call as such (Southampton at one end to New York at the other) the formality is high, but although tending towards the older, the age range can be quite broad.

Irregular cruises: the more up-market lines all operate on a less bus-like

basis and, therefore, offer more intriguing itineraries that are rarely repeated. These work solely for cruises of at least seven days, and usually longer, and so are likely to be more *formal*. A typical example is the way the Crystal ships work their way around the world, offering various segments as they move around South America, the Panama Canal and Caribbean, Alaska and Canada, the Far East and then back to Europe to start the whole slow cycle over again. Usually, these provide the most fascinating itineraries as they specialise in getting off the beaten track, although they do also feature some of the world's main ports, like Sydney, Hong Kong, Rio de Janeiro and San Francisco. The length of the cruise (upwards of seven days) means the passenger profile will again tend towards the older (50-plus) range with few children and fewer children's facilities. An alternative version of the irregular cruise is the repositioning cruise, where one of the mass-market lines moves one of their ships from one main cruise area, for example the Caribbean, to another like Alaska or Europe. This will be a once or twice a year occur-

The Concorde Waterfall in Grenada

rence and offers the chance to sample the ship for longer (and more *formally* therefore than is usual) and through more varied ports of call. There is an extra spontaneity about repositioning cruises which makes them highly popular, and they also often represent especially good value for money.

World cruises: these were an all-but-dying breed until the up-market lines managed to create a new market for the ultimate in ship-borne extravagance in recent years. Cunard's *QE2*, P&O's *Canberra* and a couple of similar classic liners of equal maturity were virtually the sole representatives of the round-the-world fraternity until the likes of Crystal, Holland America, Cunard's *Royal Viking Sun,* and, most recently, Saga rediscovered the demand for a leisurely month or three. They represent the last word in ocean-going formality because of the length of time you spend at sea and it is almost unknown to encounter children on a world cruise (well, could your kids afford to take three months off school?). World cruises specialise in the grand destinations and offer an extra level of glamour that goes with the huge expense which spending this long at sea represents. Increasingly, they can also be purchased in smaller segments, from two weeks to a month, and these are another growth area in the cruise world.

The facet of a cruise that goes hand-in-hand with your ports of call is that of the **Shore Excursions** which your ship will offer. This is an area that can make or break your cruise, particularly on a port-intensive one. In theory, every cruise ship should have a qualified Port Lecturer on board to give you the full run-down on your next port of call the day before you get there. In conjunction with the daily lectures, there should also be a full explanation of the range, nature and cost of the shore excursion options open to you right at the start of the cruise. It is easy to miss the shore excursion talk (I know from bitter experience), so try to make a note of it as soon as you board and make sure that at least one member of your party attends. It is usually better to attend *en masse* as that makes it easier for you to formulate a coherent plan of campaign for your excursions – and in most cases you will need a plan.

Your shore excursions will take the form of three or four possibilities for each port of call, with the cruise line or their land-based agent providing all the necessary transport, transfers, tickets and guides. You simply buy each excursion as a package from the ship's Excursion Desk and the total cost is added on to your ship-board account. If the cruise line supplies a brochure of the excursion options with your tickets before you board, study it carefully and draw up a provisional list of what appeals to you. The ship should also provide on-board literature on all the ports of call, highlighting the most interesting tourist points. Once you have digested as much of the written information as possible, go along and listen to the shore excursion talk aboard the ship, fill in the form you will be given with your choices and hand it in at the Excursion Desk in person or post it through their letter box. Be warned also, the Shore Excursion Desk frequently has the longest queues (or lines, as the Americans call them).

 BRIT TIP

Try to get in as early as possible with your excursion requests. Many are on a limited number basis and it is easy to miss out on the best tours by leaving it too late. It is occasionally possible to pre-book excursions when you get your cruise tickets, and this is an even better solution.

It is quite easy to get carried away with the number of excursion options you will be offered and end up with a huge bill on top of your other cruise costs. The best advice is to stick to no more than one excursion per port of call and try to weigh up what you are really getting: if the half-day island tour of Barbados costs £30 per person and includes a rum punch lunch, you can probably get better value by doing your own tour of the port of Bridgetown first, calling in at one of the island's own information points for a list of any comparable tours and prices, return to the ship for lunch (it's already paid for – why pay for an extra meal you don't really need?) and then see if one of the local excursions takes your fancy. In nearly all cases, it will be cheaper to take the local option providing you are confident enough to deal with the local agents or taxi-drivers. Your daily port talks should give you an idea of how safe it is to venture off on your own, and don't hesitate to ask for up-to-date safety advice or other local travel tips. The only real benefits of taking the ship-bought excursions are that they occasionally come up with tours you would not be able to do on your own (like white-water rafting in Alaska – this is not

to be missed!), they allow you to budget in advance and they should provide an in-built element of extra safety which is important to some people. As a general rule, all shore excursions are designed for people completely new to the area, so, if you have been before, you are likely to be better off on your own.

It is hard to be more specific about the excursions themselves, other than to say that the Caribbean has the fewest examples of the Must

A Star Cruise ship is welcomed to Hong Kong

Try excursion. They tend to be unimaginative and rarely anything you couldn't do on your own, especially as English is widely spoken nearly everywhere.

 BRIT TIP

In ports where English is not the first language and you want to go off on your own, make sure you have the name and address of the ship and the port written down to be able to show a taxi driver to get you back to the right place and on time. I very nearly came unstuck in Turkey without that essential information!

Greece and Turkey frequently offer the best guides with ship-bought shore excursions, while parts of the Far East and South America are also best done in large groups for safety reasons.

In Russia and other parts of the former Soviet Union, you need to apply for a separate visa in advance if you wish to go exploring on your own as the ship's visa covers only the organised excursions.

Just keep your common sense with you at all times when you leave the ship and you should be fine.

As an additional note on the Caribbean, the Port Lecturer is your best friend for local shopping. The main cruise lines now take in advertising from the bigger and better stores ashore, and these will be recommended by the lecturer as they carry a guarantee for all your purchases. By all means shop around to compare prices, but rest assured that the days when the port lecturer (or more likely the Cruise Director) got a kick-back for shop recommendations are long gone.

 BRIT TIP

Sadly, you are unlikely to unearth any real bargains in the well-trodden paths of the Caribbean ports. There will be plenty of claims of the Best Price for this or that, but the chances are you will get just as good value from the airport duty-free shop on the return home (Hong Kong, Singapore and other parts of the Far East are the exception to this rule).

Finally, when it comes to buying things ashore, the US dollar is an almost universal unit of currency. The majority of ships (the major British lines being the main exceptions) all run on the dollar and, while they will offer a *bureau de change* on board (usually with the rate of exchange heavily weighted in their favour) to allow you to collect some local currency for Jamaica, Curaçao or wherever, you can usually rely on the power of the dollar to do most for you in the main towns and ports of call. If you do want to take some local change with you (a good idea, in particular, for taxis) change only a limited amount as it can be difficult to re-convert to dollars or sterling. Major credit cards – Visa, Mastercard and American Express – are also widely accepted and also offer their own built-in safeguards, too.

Now, that concludes this review of the principal features of your everyday cruise, let us look closely at some of the more specific aspects of cruise ships, including who the main players are, how their ships rate and what a typical cruise experience is all about . . .

*

CHAPTER FOUR

Making Sense of the Variety

(or, Some Like It Hot – and Some Don't)

Up until now, I have been dealing with cruising largely in general terms. Now it is time to start talking in specifics and discuss some of the more practical issues, like how to choose the *right* cruise for you. This involves rating the main cruise lines, how a typical cruise shapes up, how to book it and the main considerations involved.

Tropical splendour and technical excellence – Radisson Diamond in the Caribbean

Having frequently mentioned various lines and some of their ships in the opening chapters, it makes sense at this point to take a more detailed look at the ways in which the cruise companies differ, and to formulate an easy-to-understand guide to the main types. Now, just the merest perusal of your average cruise brochure might lead you to think everyone is offering the same luxurious standard of holiday indulgence, the level of pampering you will receive will be uniformly high and the five key elements of the cruise experience (Facilities, Service, Entertainment, Food and Ports of Call) will be of guaranteed five-star standard. There is just one word for that idea – balderdash (I had thought of something more pithy and down to earth, but balderdash will suffice in this instance). Along with the Six Big Myths listed in Chapter Two, it is also wide of the mark to imagine all cruise products as largely equal. They might want to make you believe that is the case, and the cruise industry is certainly one of the worst for the over-use of such terms as Luxurious, Top Class, Five-star Plus and Supreme Quality, but in reality things are extremely different.

Basically, there are FOUR distinct levels of the cruise experience and once you have grasped the essential requirements of each you will be in a much better position to make your choice. **Here is the fundamental and unique *Brit's Guide* formula to the different standards of cruising.**

1   STANDARD

This is the budget-minded entry level of all modern-day cruising. The product will basically be a no-frills operation where the accent is on value for money rather than finesse. The ships will tend to be high-density (i.e. with a low Space Ratio figure, nearer the 20 mark than the 50 which represents the true benchmark for a spacious ship) and of the older variety (pre-1980). Therefore some facilities, like modern gyms, theatres and fancy lounges may be missing; service will still be with a smile but will lack the personal touch; on-board entertainment will be broad-based rather than star quality and choice will be more limited; food will tend towards the hearty rather than the gourmet; and the ports of call will be the more standard, well-known destinations rather than anything particularly exotic. It is very much the mass-market version of cruising, but it is also the youngest part of the market and the area which most seeks to break down all those tired, old mis-conceptions of the cruise world and make it more exciting, interesting and fun for the newcomer. In short, it is a great introduction to all that cruising has to offer – and usually at an excellent price. Family packages are big business here, but there are rarely any big discounts to be had at this level because the starting price is already cut to the bone. The advent of operators like Airtours and Thomson has ensured it will have a high-profile future.

2   SUPERIOR

The next level up sees some of the biggest operators and some of the newest, glitziest ships as the cruise companies look to tempt the first-timer into something rather more extravagant, and the repeat passenger into a new, more quality-conscious experience. The mass market is also firmly involved in this level through the sheer size of the ships (rarely anything below 30,000 tons), and so you can expect the full range of facilities, a friendly if occasionally less than totally efficient service (simply because of the large numbers involved), a varied package of entertainments with some high-

Ready for a work-out? CostaClassica *boasts a large aerobics room*

powered main shows, a more extensive menu, but still the more tried and trusted ports of call. The average age profile is showing the biggest change in this area through the efforts of the big operators like Royal Caribbean, NCL, Costa, Princess and P&O to attract the family market. Discounts are at their most common at this level as the cruise companies find themselves directly in competition with the cost-conscious **Standard** level lines and with the other lines competing for a larger slice of the huge volume which there now is in **Superior** cruising.

3   PREMIER

Here you find the widest range of cruise options in terms of the hardware, from the small sailing vessels, through the niche products like Hebridean Island Cruises to some extremely grand new designs that offer the latest in cruise technology. Size therefore varies enormously, but the Space Ratio figure should still be good, at least 35 if not better. This is also the more classic, stylish version of cruising, hence some of the more mass-market facilities like video games, kids' rooms, multi-gyms and multiple lounges may be missing. Service will always be attentive and personal, albeit with a slightly more formal style than on **Standard** or **Superior** lines. Entertainments will be less the likes of bingo, karaoke and organised sports and more lectures, art

auctions and so forth, with the occasional ballet show or classical concert in place of the Broadway-style spectacular. The food will be more varied, with the smaller ships of this type able to score heavily for quality. Your fellow passengers will be widely travelled and the itineraries will consist of some truly outstanding ports of call. In some instances the age profile can be wide here, with **Premier** cruising attracting the wealthy, retired types as well as the younger go-getters and jet-setters, but the cruise experience will be primarily a formal one. Discounts are rare but not unknown and can therefore provide some of the best value for money. In some cases all your gratuities and drinks are included.

4 DELUXE

There are more claims for this particular distinction than any other, but few lines and their vessels truly match up to the proper definition of the word. Consequently, with few exceptions, the **Deluxe** ships are small, boutique-type vessels, catering with supreme style of service and food to the most discerning passenger. The Space Ratio figure will be at least 50 and cabins will be particularly spacious, with a high proportion having balconies. In many cases it is not so much cruising as pampering of

Setting sail on one of the Big Red Boats of Premier Cruise Line

the highest quality that just happens to be at sea. Competition in this part of the market is therefore as much with the top land-based resorts and hotels as with the rest of the cruise world. By the nature of the ships being smaller and more exclusive, the level of facilities will therefore be fewer (although there are a couple of notable exceptions – see the tables pp. 84–7), but everything is maintained to the highest standards. Service will be of the white glove, silver service variety and the food as good as anything you can get in the best restaurants of the world, with the great benefit in most cases of open-seating dining (i.e. the chance to eat when you want with who you want).

Entertainments are distinctly low-key, with the accent more on social discourse than big-production shows. These ships also operate only Irregular or World-type cruises, hence the ports of call are the most exotic you will find. The level of formality is high (but not stiflingly so) and the age profile older than most. Extras like gratuities, drinks and shore excursions are often included, and the **Deluxe** cruise therefore attracts some seriously wealthy passengers. Discounting is virtually unheard of by the necessity of keeping this level exclusive. The one real exception here is Crystal Cruises, which operates the two largest **Deluxe** ships in the world, which are both 50,000 tons and therefore, to my mind, more versatile. They DON'T offer single-seating dining (which some claim knocks them out of this category) or any fully-inclusive packages, but they do offer big-ship facilities with small-ship quality of service. Very occasionally they discount – if you see one, snatch their arms off!

Alternative dining is a key feature of the Crystal Ships

MIX 'N MATCH

In some cases, it is possible for a cruise line to have ships in more than one of the four classes as they try to cater for as wide an audience as possible or as they introduce newer ships which knock their older stock down a peg or two. A typical example of this is the Italian line Costa Crociere, where their older ships are definitely in the **Standard** bracket but their newest ones are most certainly of **Superior** quality.

It should also go without saying, that the price scale increases steadily through each of these four levels. A week's cruise on a **Standard** ship may cost as little as £500 and seven days on a **Superior** product might set you back only £800, but a week on board a **Premier** vessel will surely take you into the four-figure region and the **Deluxe** class, well, you are into really big money.

The other essential difference between the main lines has been hinted at in several places already but should also be dealt with in its entirety here, and that is the fundamental distinction between the American companies when compared with the British ones (hence the need for the *Brit's Guide* in the first place). With almost 5 million Americans at sea compared with barely 500,000 UK passengers, it stands to reason the majority of cruise lines cater primarily for US tastes and styles. This can be slightly off-putting for someone who has never travelled on a ship full of Americans (and there can be more than 2,000 of them at a time, remember), but the reality is they are no better or worse than 2,000 of any other English-speaking nationality. The American tourist abroad tends to get a rather unfortunate press, and, while it is true there will always be one or two who will conform to the loud, garishly-dressed, camera-bedecked stereotype, the vast majority are of a different type altogether. I have made many transatlantic friends in the course of my cruises and have never had any worries about being surrounded by American accents. There is always the fact, of course, that cruising tends to attract the more cosmopolitan, thoughtful tourist in the first place, rather than the brash variety. It also, therefore, tends to attract like-minded souls who enjoy similar social tastes, and so there is usually nothing to be gained or lost in social terms by opting for the all-American variety of cruising.

Showtime is always a lavish affair at sea

The differences in style should be fairly obvious, and it is the matter of your own personal taste in these areas that will lead you to decide whether the American way is more appealing than the British way (even allowing for people who prefer simply to travel among their own). The American style is, of course, slightly more ostentatious and showy, and this can be easily seen in the elaborate design of many of their ships where they tend to go for immediate visual impact. The British (and European) way is to be rather more restrained, almost formal, and to hark back to the more traditional era (hence the preference for proper promenade decks). The Americans make no bones about their lack of any class differentiation, while British cruises still tend to have an element of class-consciousness. Equally, the typical British cruise profile will show a more broad social mix while the American is more even. When it comes to entertainment, the US tendency is for the big, glitzy production shows while the British version is somehow just that bit more reserved (although this difference is diminishing all the time). American tastes in comedy are definitely different (but don't ask me to define how), and so if the likes of *Cheers!*, *The Golden Girls* and *Seinfeld* leave you cold, then you are probably going to be better off with British entertainment. By the same token, if you are a meat and two veg type of eater, you will probably yearn for a proper meal by the end of an American cruise. Once again, US tastes are for quantity in terms of courses (a salad course is ever-present, for example), a glamorous touch in presentation and, ultimately, a kind of universal blandness in their treatment of anything spicy. It is no coincidence that the menus displayed in the brochures for Thomson and Airtours both feature a good old roast, while the typical American version would highlight lobster thermidor or *filet mignon*. For some reason, however, Baked Alaska is a universal dessert on *every* cruise ship.

 **BRIT TIP**

As a final note on Anglo-American differences, it remains true the average US cruiser is more adept at complaining than his British counterpart. We tend to keep our niggles and worries to ourselves and whinge about it to each other. An American will tell the person in charge straight up – 'This isn't right and I want it changed!'.

But, if that is the broad picture of the different types, how does this work in real terms? Well here, in true *Brit's Guide* fashion, is the most honest *Who's Who* appraisal of the main lines in the main cruising areas of the world:

Dining Japanese-style in Crystal Harmony's *Kyoto resaurant*

WHO'S WHO IN THE CRUISE WORLD

Line	Ships	Rating	Passenger profile	Caribbean (inc the Bahamas)	East Coast USA (inc Bermuda)	The Med
Abercrombie & Kent	1	Standard	American-European	N	N	N
African Safari Club	1	Standard	European	N	N	N
Airtours	3	Standard	British	Y	N	Y
Arcalia	2	Standard	British	N	N	Y
Carnival	11	Standard-Superior	American	Y	N	N
Celebrity	5	Premier	American	Y	Y	N
Commodore	1	Standard	American	Y	N	N
Costa	7	Standard-Superior	American-European	Y	N	Y
Crystal	2	Deluxe	American	Y	N	Y
Cunard	5	Premier-Deluxe	American-British	Y	Y	Y
Disney	2	Premier (expected)	American-British	Y	N	N
Dolphin	3	Standard	American	Y	N	N
Festival	3	Standard	British-European	Y	N	Y
Hapag-Lloyd	4	Premier-Deluxe	German–European	N	N	Y
Hebridean Island Cruises	1	Premier	British	N	N	N
Holland America	8	Premier	American	Y	Y	Y

...st Coast A c Alaska d Mexican /iera)	Northern Europe (inc Britain)	The Atlantic (inc the Canaries)	Indian Ocean	Far East	Australasia (inc the South Pacific)	Others
	N	N	N	N	Y	Antarctica, S America
	N	N	Y	N	N	N
	N	Y	N	N	N	N
	Y	Y	N	N	N	N
	N	N	N	N	N	N
	N	N	N	N	N	S America
	N	N	N	N	N	N
	Y	Y	N	N	N	S America
	Y	Y	Y	Y	Y	World cruise
	Y	Y	Y	Y	Y	World cruise & S America
	N	N	N	N	N	N
	N	N	N	N	N	N
	Y	Y	N	N	N	Black Sea, transatlantic
	Y	N	Y	Y	Y	Antarctica, S America
	Y	N	N	N	N	N
	Y	Y	N	Y	N	World cruise

Line	Ships	Style	Passenger	Caribbean	E. Coast USA	W. USA
MSC*	4	Standard	European-British	N	N	N
NCL*	9	Superior	American	Y	Y	Y
Fred Olsen	2	Standard-Superior	British	Y	N	N
Orient	1	Premier	American-British	N	N	N
P&O	3	Standard-Superior	British	Y	N	N
Premier	1	Standard	American	Y	N	N
Princess	9	Superior-Premier	American-British	Y	Y	Y
Radisson/Seven Seas	3	Premier-Deluxe	American-European	Y	N	Y
Renaissance	4	Premier	American-European	Y	N	N
RCI*	12	Standard-Superior	American	Y	Y	Y
Royal Olympic	6	Standard	American-British	N	N	N
Saga	1	Premier	British	Y	N	N
Seabourn	3	Deluxe	American	Y	Y	Y
Silversea	2	Deluxe	American-European	N	Y	N
Star Clippers	2	Superior	American-European	Y	N	N
Star Cruise	6	Superior	Asian-American	N	N	N
Swan Hellenic	1	Superior	British	N	N	N
Thomson	4	Standard	British	Y	N	N
Windstar	4	Premier	American-European	Y	N	N

*MSC = Mediterranean Shipping Cruises

The Med	Northern Europe	The Atlantic	Indian Ocean	Far East	Australasia	Others
Y	N	Y	Y	N	N	Red Sea, South Africa & S America
Y	Y	Y	Y	N	N	Transatlantic
Y	Y	Y	Y	Y	N	Round-Africa
Y	N	N	Y	Y	Y	Antarctica
Y	Y	Y	N	Y	Y	World cruise
N	N	N	N	N	N	N
Y	Y	Y	N	Y	Y	Amazon
Y	Y	Y	Y	Y	Y	S America, Red Sea
Y	Y	N	Y	Y	N	N
Y	Y	N	N	Y	N	N
Y	N	N	N	N	N	Red Sea, S America
Y	Y	Y	Y	Y	Y	World Cruise
Y	Y	N	N	Y	Y	S America
Y	Y	Y	Y	Y	Y	S America
Y	N	Y	N	Y	N	N
N	N	N	N	Y	N	N
Y	Y	Y	Y	Y	N	Red Sea
Y	N	N	N	N	N	N
Y	N	Y	N	N	N	N

L = Norwegian Cruise Line   *RCI = Royal Caribbean International

If that is the full run-down of the main cruise lines working in the British market, it is also informative (not to mention quite an amusing game with which to annoy party guests) to try to list the Top Ten lines world-wide in order of their size. Obviously, this is a fairly inexact process at the best of times because of the continual changes occurring in the cruise market, with companies selling off old stock, acquiring new ships or simply going bust. But, with the main ones, it is at least possible to come up with a table something like this:

THE TOP 10

SHIPPING LINE	NO. OF SHIPS	TONNAGE
Carnival Corporation:	31	1,432,688
Carnival	11	687,050
Holland America	8	405,896
Seabourn	3	29,925
Windstar	4	31,854
Costa (with Airtours)	7	277,963
Royal Caribbean International:	17	1,027,241
Royal Caribbean	12	709,525
Celebrity	5	317,716
P&O:	11	586,506
Princess	8	424,938
P&O	3	161,568
Norwegian Cruise Line:	9	338,874
Cunard:	5	141,319
Star Cruise:	6	133,743
Cruise Holdings:	5	112,045
Dolphin:	3	68,434
Premier:	1	19,500
Seawind:	1	24,111
Crystal:	2	100,404
Mediterranean Shipping:	4	84,711
Royal Olympic:	6	77,238

It is fairly clear three lines dominate, with Carnival now owning around 40 per cent of the world's total cruise capacity. Royal Caribbean have kept pace with the surprise acquisition of Celebrity in June 1997, and P&O remain the other mega-line, with the 109,000-ton *Grand Princess* due to join in 1998. Carnival continue to lead the cruise world in simple profit terms though, with annual income of $566 million in 1996.

The picture for the Mediterranean – where the majority of British passengers can still be found – is slightly different. Italian line Costa, now jointly owned by Carnival and Airtours after a takeover in 1997, is the biggest carrier, followed by P&O, the Greek line Royal Olympic (which was formed in late 1995 from a merger of Epirotiki and Sun Line), new boys Thomson, Airtours and Royal Caribbean, who made a significant jump up the cruise charts with the arrival of their 70,000-ton mega-liner *Splendour of the Seas* in the spring of 1996. Mediterranean Shipping and Festival are also making significant progress.

When it comes to identifying the major *British* carriers the picture is rather harder to make out, however, as most of the lines are pretty cagey about the figures they release for UK passengers. Still, you can be reasonably certain P&O will be top of this particular hit parade, followed by Airtours and Thomson (once again making a big impact on their arrival on the cruise scene), Cunard, Norwegian Cruise Line, Princess, Fred Olsen, Costa, Royal Caribbean, Carnival, Festival, Mediterranean Shipping, Celebrity and Swan Hellenic. The likes of the more up-market lines Holland America, Crystal and

Dramatic entrance: Swan Hellenic's new ship the Minerva *passes Tower Bridge in London*

Silversea all aim to claim more of the UK market in 1998. Even allowing for the vagaries of the cruise lines' figures (and my dubious mathematics), that should give you a solid idea of where the British passengers will be thickest on the ground if you are set on sticking with your fellow-countrymen (and women). Incidentally, the figures for Carnival's British passenger carry could well increase dramatically over the next couple of years as they take advantage of their commercial links with Airtours, in whom they now hold a 29 per cent stake. Airtours have already started to market the glitzy Carnival product through their own brochures and their big high street travel agent chain Going Places, and it could be a significant breakthrough in getting the cruise message across to the holiday mass market. Watch this space!

BIG SHIP v SMALL SHIP

As well as the inherent differences between the lines, there is also a fair bit of variety to choose from when it comes to the size of the ships themselves, and so it is possible to set out some additional criteria which further help to focus your choice.

Big is not necessarily always best for some folks, even allowing for the fact the mega-liners now have excellent passenger flow designs and will seldom make you feel you are at sea with as many as 3,000 fellow cruise devotees. The statistics show you can pick a ship as small as 3,000 tons (Star Clippers,

Smaller ships can explore little-seen corners of the world, like Antarctica

Abercrombie & Kent) with as few as 96 passengers aboard, while you can go up to the new *Carnival Destiny's* 101,000 tons and 3,300 passengers. As I have already pointed out the need to study a ship's Space Ratio figure in order to assess its relative level of comfort, the other aspects of ship size are relatively obvious but worth pointing out nonetheless.

The most basic difference is in the facilities on offer, and to a lesser extent the style of the ship as a consequence. Small ships in the sub-20,000-ton category seldom offer a large range of sporting activities, apart from water sports, and so if you are of an active persuasion and enjoy the social aspect of the likes of paddle tennis, shuffleboard and modern gymnasiums, then the larger ships will be more your cup of marine tea. However, the smaller ships score higher marks for a more personal level of service, greater relaxation potential and a more unstructured approach to life at sea. They also have the potential (sometimes overlooked) to get into the intimate nooks and crannies of the cruise world where their bigger brethren cannot squeeze in. This means more imaginative itineraries, greater variety and the bonus of usually being able to dock alongside a pier rather than having to ferry passengers ashore by tender, which is common practice with the bigger ships in some ports of call and is a minor nuisance because of the extra time it can take to get ashore as well as the question of accessibility it poses. The latter is of more concern to older passengers who may feel disinclined to tackle steep ladders and moving decks, as well as disabled passengers, but I will say more about those aspects later on.

Perfect Harmony – life at sea on Crystal Harmony

In cruise terms, bigger (in the 50,000-ton-plus range) also tends to mean more modern, so you can be sure of state-of-the-art technology on offer in equipment like in-cabin TV, health facilities and video games, as well as much greater emphasis on children's activities, even to the provision of kids' swimming pools and on-deck play areas.

FLY-CRUISE v EX-UK CRUISE

Another key area where your cruise selection is important is that of *where* you cruise from. This may sound like a lecture in the absurdly obvious, but many people do not take the opportunity to consider the advantages of sailing out of a British port rather than flying to pick up your ship, and vice versa.

The choice is straightforward: **Fly-cruising** is the big area of growth in the British cruise market and offers far more variety and possibilities. The 1995 PSA figures for British passengers showed a ratio of 2.3 to 1 in favour of fly-cruising. The world is genuinely your lobster (to quote TV's Arthur Daley) and the full range of cruise line and ship choice is yours. The likes of Airtours and Thomson also have an extensive choice of regional airports in use with their Mediterranean cruises, which adds to the flexibility of their packages. If you live in Newcastle, say, you have a much closer gateway to the ports of Palma (Majorca) and Limassol (Cyprus) than you have by travelling down to Southampton. However, it does not appeal to everyone simply because not everyone is happy with the idea of flying, and there is inherently more hassle involved in a fly-cruise than with the ex-UK variety. You are more limited in the luggage you can take (flight allowances tend to be 20–25 kilos per person) and there is more of a let-down if you have a long journey home from, say, San Juan or Vancouver, than if you sail back into Southampton or Dover. The real beauty of **ex-UK cruising**, which gives you the choice of

Southampton, Dover, Tilbury, London, Harwich (in the case of Royal Caribbean), Liverpool and Greenock (the new Direct Cruises) and Oban in Scotland (in the case of Hebridean Island Cruises), is that you have to make only one journey to the docks – and both Southampton and Dover now have excellent road links – so you avoid all the hassle of getting through an airport and you can carry as much on board as, well, as you can carry. In many cases, cruise lines like P&O (and big cruise agents Page & Moy) also have a well-organised coach transport system that picks up regionally, with the added bonus that you put your cases on the coach at your starting point and pick them up again outside your cabin – it is all done for you. The down side of ex-UK cruises is twofold – it takes longer to get to the areas you really want to see (with often the added drawback of losing out on a couple of days of good weather), and all Mediterranean-bound cruises have to negotiate the Bay of Biscay, which can be a mean stretch of water. There is also the option of mixing both varieties, i.e. by cruising out of Britain and then flying back either at the mid-point of the cruise or its final destination somewhere further on, or the other way round by flying out and cruising back. Somehow this option lacks the appeal of either, but P&O are still adept at matching you up with your car back in Britain either way.

 **BRIT TIP**

Having insisted that most modern ships take rough seas very well, the Bay is usually an exception and can catch out even the most seasoned travellers – I know from bitter intestinal experience!

SHORT v LONG

The question of how long to cruise for is probably the final all-important consideration at this stage, especially for first-timers to the cruise world. With this in mind, many cruise lines (notably Airtours, Carnival, Dolphin, Louis Cruise Lines, NCL, Premier, Royal Caribbean and, to a certain extent, Cunard) offer a selection of three- and four-day cruises specifically designed to attract the younger, new element interested in cruising, and much of the hardware used on these routes has been significantly up-graded by many lines from the rather tired, older ships that used to concentrate on this part of the business. The basic product is a rather more intense version of longer cruises, with more crammed into the available time, but is still a fairly accurate reflection of what it is all about and can make for a thoroughly worthwhile introduction, especially as an add-on to a land-based holiday. The main markets for the three- and four-day cruise are Cyprus and the Greek islands, the Bahamas and Mexico (out of Miami, Fort Lauderdale or Port Canaveral) and the Mexican Riviera (out of Los Angeles). My personal feeling is three days is not really long enough to appreciate fully the delights of being at sea, and, seeing as all the shorter options are fly-cruises only, it is quite an effort for such a limited experience. But there is no denying the short-cruise option has gained significantly in popularity in the last five years, so I am probably in the minority here.

Having said all that, a week's cruise is generally regarded as the mass-market standard these days and is the area that has experienced most growth in the modern era. Seven days is obviously the ideal length of time to fit in with most holidays, especially as a cruise-and-stay option; and, if you pick the right cruise, you can enjoy the perfect cruise balance of days at sea and ports of call. It is still primarily a fly-cruise experience (there are few seven-day cruises out of Britain simply because you cannot get far enough in that time for a worthwhile, interesting cruise), and so, with the exception of Airtours and Thomson, Brits are more likely to be in the minority. Also, several of the American-designed week-long varieties in the Caribbean and even the Mediterranean are pretty port-intensive, which does not necessarily make for a relaxing experience. In addition, a week is the ideal length of time for you just to be getting the hang of it – and then it is time to get off!

Once you look beyond the fairly standardised three-, four- and seven-day products, you find a much more eye-catching array of longer cruises which are designed in particular to appeal to the repeat passenger. They can be anything from 10 days up to the marathon World cruises of three months or more and will usually boast more exotic itineraries. As a general rule, they will also offer more days at sea (which is of direct interest to British cruisers I find) and a slight increase in the formality of the experience that goes with it (i.e. more dinners that demand a jacket and tie or DJ).

That really concludes this look at the specific reasons for choosing a particular type of cruise, but there are two other areas that require more specialised advice, and those are for singles and the disabled.

CRUISING FOR SINGLES

The attractions of cruising should, by now, be absolutely clear, but its viability does have limitations, and this is especially true for people travelling alone. Even though cruise figures show almost 25 per cent of cruisers are going solo, singles at sea consistently get the worst deals in terms of price with surcharges of up to 200 per cent on standard double-occupancy cabin rates. This is palpably unfair, but the majority of cruise lines argue they have to include a surcharge simply because their figures are all worked out on the basis of two sharing a cabin. There are, however, two ways around this for those who object to paying the extra.

Firstly, there ARE a handful of ships that offer genuine **single cabins**, although these tend to be the cabins that are most difficult to sell or are otherwise the least popular on board, such as the smallest inside ones. Several older liners (notably Fred Olsen's *Black Prince*) plus an occasional new one (the *CostaClassica* and *Romantica,* Fred Olsen's *Black Watch* and P&O's *Oriana*) offer single cabins, but they tend to be extremely limited in number and still work out slightly more expensive than double cabin rates.

BRIT TIP

Sadly, as single cabins are usually at a premium, you are not likely to find them discounted in the same way as many others. The key is to book as EARLY as possible and take advantage of any early-booking incentives that many lines offer.

The second alternative to paying the single-occupancy surcharge is to take advantage of the quite common offers of a **guaranteed share cabin,** whereby the cruise line will attempt to find you a fellow passenger of the same sex and smoking preference. This way you pay only the normal double occupancy rate, and, if the company fails to find you a match, you get the whole cabin to yourself. Even if a cruise line does not show cabin-sharing in its brochure, it often pays to ask as they may well feel it necessary to compromise if that cruise is selling slowly.

 BRIT TIP

Obviously, sharing a cabin with someone you have never met can have its drawbacks. Try making a guaranteed share booking either out of season or on a repositioning cruise to increase your chance of getting the cabin to yourself.

If you can't avail yourself of either of these, you will find the alternative of a **guaranteed single rate,** where the cruise line guarantees the standard of your cabin (or possibly higher) but assigns the actual cabin to you only when you board, or a straightforward **single supplement,** which can be as low as only 110 per cent of the double occupancy fare (notably some Seabourn, Silversea and Holland America cruises); however, it can also vary to twice the standard rate if it is a popular cruise. Once you are on board ship, there are obviously no limitations on singles enjoying the full range of facilities and activities, while there are several lines that go out of their way to make singles feel welcome with special parties, notably Carnival, Celebrity, Costa, Holland America, NCL, Orient, P&O, Princess and Seabourn. The romantic implications of travelling on your own have already been detailed in Chapter Three.

THE DISABLED AT SEA

It remains an awkward facet of holiday life that people with disabilities are regularly discriminated against, often thoughtlessly, but always to the point of their being excluded or their enjoyment of a particular activity being drastically reduced. This is especially true, as a general rule, at sea. Until the modern build of cruise ships, little or no thought was given to disabled passengers, either in providing specially-adapted cabins or in making the ship generally accessible. So, if someone tries to tell you a ship built in the 1960s or 70s will happily accommodate anyone who relies on a wheelchair for their mobility, take your custom somewhere else. The very nature of sea-life makes the use of wheelchairs extremely difficult unless special provision is made or design factors are built in, as they are in newer ships. Smaller ships (i.e. under 20,000 tons) also generally have narrower aisles and companionways which make access awkward, while the older liners tend to have corridors within corridors on the main accommodation decks that again make negotiating them in a wheelchair almost impossible.

Having said all that, there is no reason why the physically challenged shouldn't enjoy a cruise as much as, or even more, than anyone else. Every new cruise ship now contains at least a

New ships like Celebrity's Century have highly elaborate theatre facilities

handful of cabins designed for wheelchair users, with extra-width doorways (most cabin doors are only two feet wide and hence completely inaccessible to most wheelchairs), conveniently-placed lights and shelves and bathrooms with stool-showers or grip bars.

 **BRIT TIP**

If there is no available disabled-adapted cabin, opt for the largest grade cabin you can afford and check the deck plan to pick one close to a lift and as near to the middle of the ship as possible to reduce any movement caused by the sea.

Modern-build ships will also have plenty of lifts (the Americans call them elevators) and ramps rather than stairs into the public rooms and out on to the decks, with electric-eye doors. You MUST be sure to let the cruise line know of your disability in advance, and once again the specially adapted cabins do tend to be at a premium, so try to book early. Most lines will also insist that a disabled person should bring their own wheelchair along (some ships do have them, but they are few and far between) and should be accompanied by an assistant or companion to help out in case of an emergency; however, it is sometimes wise to double-check the exact arrangements if a ship claims to have special facilities for the disabled. Ask especially about whether the ship docks or uses tenders at each port of call. The latter may well be completely impossible for wheelchair-users.

BRIT TIP

Even if a cabin is specifically labelled in the brochure as for wheelchair access, get your travel agent to double-check the extent of the cabin design. It is no good if it has extra-width doors but there is still a storm-seal (a raised lip of several inches in height) on the door into the bathroom.

Not every cruise line will accept guide dogs for the visually impaired, and so it is even more important to be able to take along an able-bodied companion. In addition, it is also wise to let your cabin steward or stewardess know

Cocktail hour has a special appeal at sea

of any disability you may have, especially in case of hearing impairment, as they may have to make arrangements to enter your cabin in an emergency.

Common sense should also be your guide to enjoying the full cruise experience – don't try to do anything you wouldn't normally attempt at home, and don't feel you have to try everything just because it is there! For more information or advice on this subject, you can contact the Royal Association for Disability and Rehabilitation (RADAR) in London, who publish several brochures on cruising, on 0171 250 3222.

TRAVEL AGENTS v CRUISE CONSULTANTS

Now, once you have a good idea of what type of cruise you fancy, the next thing you will want to know is where to go to book it. Once again, your choice is quite varied, although, unlike the majority of holidays of the package variety, cruising does not readily conform to the type of standard retailing you encounter in your average high street travel agent. It is more complicated, booking information is not usually accessible on their main computer terminals (although Royal Caribbean in particular are changing this aspect of the business for travel agents), it requires more specialist knowledge – and it is initially more expensive than a two-week package to the Mediterranean. The latter is crucial for two reasons. One, because the customer is spending more, they will demand a much higher level of service from the travel agent to ensure the booking is done correctly. And two, because the big multiple travel agents (the main five previously mentioned, Thomas Cook, Lunn Poly, Going Places, AT Mays and Co-Op Travel) realise there is a boom in the British cruise business, they don't want to miss out on their slice of the pie and so are training up their sales agents to be more knowledgeable about cruising holidays in general and about selling cruises in particular. This in turn means the service does vary from each branch of the Big Five according to their level of training. Lunn Poly are the latest to implement a Cruise Club for their existing cruise customers and have a number of key staff trained to offer a much higher level of advice and service, as well as producing specialised literature in all their travel shops

Cruising into a new port on NCL's Windward

aimed at explaining all the advantages of cruising and highlighting its attractions (ask for the Cruise Welcome Aboard Directory which contains some useful at-a-glance information on the main lines as well as general cruise advice). Going Places have a well-organised cruise agent network, while Thomas Cook also have cruise consultants in some branches. But it remains true, for all their efforts, that the average high street holiday sales agent is still on the young side (average age early 20s) and there is a high turnover of staff, so some of the main misconceptions on cruising can still be perpetuated and you will not necessarily get the most comprehensive advice in this specialist area.

Thankfully, there is an organisation that has helped to make the business of selling cruises more reliable, and there is also an alternative to the big retail outlets.

An important qualification to look out for when booking your cruise is if your travel agent is a member of PSARA, or the **Passenger Shipping Association of Retail Agents**. This body effectively tests and 'approves' all the responsible agents who sell cruises and runs training programmes and ship visits to try to ensure they really know their stuff. The trained agents will have a certificate from PSARA indicating their level of training and you can be reasonably confident they will be well clued up on recent developments as well as having a much better grasp of the complexities and varying aspects of cruising generally. In addition, if your cruise package is registered with the PSA (of which PSARA is the training arm), you can be sure your holiday will be fully protected against the possibility of the line cancelling your cruise, going bankrupt or otherwise ruining your holiday (although a full ABTA bonding is still the best protection for you and your holiday).

In addition to the PSARA qualification, the business of cruising is also unique in having its own specialist travel agents, or **cruise consultants**, who have grown up in response to the traditionally poor level of service provided by the high street multiples. One of the prime movers in the development of cruise consultants in Britain is London-based **Paul Mundy Cruising**, which celebrated a 25th anniversary in 1995. As well as being the Harrods of cruise selling, PMC produces its own brochures and newsletters with plenty of up-to-date information on the cruise world. Paul Mundy himself was also instrumental in setting up the **Guild of Professional Cruise Agents**, who go even further than PSARA in their cruise training and the upmarket service they offer as a result. The other benefit of a PSARA or GPCA travel shop is they also work closely with the main cruise lines to produce their own special deals, discounts and other incentives which are not always available at the multiples, and the chances are their sales agents will have sailed on many of the ships they are dealing with and so will have *first-hand* knowledge of the product.

 BRIT TIP

A quick perusal of Teletext should give you a choice of several PSARA-qualified cruise consultants and their latest offers (ITV, Page 228 the last time I looked). But, always check their ABTA or PSARA qualifications for your peace of mind. It is a fast-changing section and some offers come and go suspiciously fast. If in doubt, a cruise line will always be able to recommend a list of reputable agents.

The largest British cruise consultants are **Page & Moy** who frequently charter whole ships or block-book large numbers of cabins and then sell them at their own, usually discounted, rates. They publish their own Cruise Hot List (call 0116 250 7722 for a copy) with the latest deals and special offers, and arrange notable extras like coach transfers on many ex-UK sailings.

What the travel agent said

Page & Moy director David Short – another cruise addict like myself – once told me: 'Very often when I meet people after they have just come off their first cruise, the first thing they say to me is "If only I had discovered cruising when I was younger!" That is the single biggest message the industry needs to get across, how enjoyable it is for people of ALL ages. This is especially true for people with families. It is an ideal kind of holiday. From the age of three or so upwards, it just gets better and better for kids as they get older. And, if you create a happy child, you create happy parents!' So, you see, you don't have to take just my word for it.

Another GPCA cruise agent worth knowing about for their expertise are **The Cruise Line Ltd**, especially as they also publish their own glossy brochure, *World of Cruising*, which contains a wealth of useful and up-to-date information for both the first-timer and experienced cruiser alike. Call 01273 835252 for more details.

Take the plunge on Airtours' ship the Carousel

The essential advice here is to shop around before taking the plunge. A cruise still represents a significant outlay of money and it makes sense to have a good idea of all your options. Don't be afraid to ask questions, no matter how basic they may seem to you, and don't be forced into accepting something which is not totally to your taste just because there is a bigger discount, and, if the advice on offer does not seem quite up to the mark, go elsewhere. Beware in particular of an agent who insists that so and so is 'The best cruise line in the world,' or such and such a ship is 'The ultimate in luxury.' There are no such definitive designations and these claims are usually a sign of a major discount

BRIT TIP

It is still possible (and I stress the 'possible' as it is gradually being eliminated by the cruise lines) to reduce your cruise cost further by flying out to Miami or Fort Lauderdale and ringing the lines *direct* to see if they have any last-minute availability (called distressed stock in the trade), usually at knockdown prices. These walk-up cruises are not something the lines like to advertise, but you *can* pick up some bargains, especially as the likes of Florida-based Laker Airways now have well-priced, scheduled services to both destinations. However, it should be stressed there are no guarantees and many sailings are now fully booked well in advance. But, if you are flexible enough to give it a try, here are the local numbers to call: Carnival, 1 800 CARNIVAL; Celebrity, 305 262 6677; Costa, 1 800 462 6782; Dolphin, 305 358 5122; Norwegian Cruise Line, 305 436 0866 (in Miami) or 1 800 327 7030 elsewhere in Florida; and Royal Caribbean, 305 379 4731 (in Miami) or 1 800 432 6559 elsewhere in Florida. Alternatively, in the Miami area try South Beach Cruises on 305 538 3020 for any last-minute deals. For details of Laker flights to Miami or Fort Lauderdale, call 01293 789000. Nearly all cruises depart on Saturday or Sunday and, obviously, you are taking a chance, but there are savings to be had and you are handily placed for a pleasant holiday even if you don't get on.

Don't mention the 'D' word!

When it comes to booking a cruise, the price you see in the brochure often bears little relation to what you finally pay, except as a starting point from which to work down. It is an unfortunate fact of life for the cruise lines (but something of their own creating) that passengers have grown to expect some form of discount whenever they are booking. These discounts come in various forms (and sometimes are called anything BUT a discount simply because the industry has become so averse to the term), but are always worth checking on. The most common incentives are the last-minute bookings where a cruise is likely to sail less than full and so the line advertises significant late discounts or two-for-one offers to try to fill the spare capacity. You may have limited choice of cabins, but, if you can travel at short notice, you can snap up some real bargains, especially in the Caribbean out of the main holiday periods. However, the industry as a whole has become a little wary of this practice and so now often tries to do things in reverse by offering significant savings for EARLY bookings. In the case of Royal Caribbean, they promise early-bookers will get the BEST price possible and, if anything, on popular cruises discounts will DECREASE as the sailing date approaches. Alternatively, Costa Cruises offer a retrospective-discount policy to encourage early bookings by promising, if they subsequently drop the rates for late-bookers on a less-than-full sailing, those who have already booked by a certain date will also benefit from that last-minute discount. On top of early-booking discounts, look out for additional discount rates with some of the Cruise Consultants (which the cruise lines pass on as an incentive for good business or for taking out block-bookings) which come ON TOP of the early booking savings. Finally, you can also make substantial savings where a third or fourth person shares a cabin with two full-fare-paying adults, although you need to be very good friends as this can make for a crowded cabin in most cases.

on an unpopular cruise. While cruising does genuinely represent great holiday excitement and value, you will NOT enjoy being put on the wrong ship for your tastes.

There are more than 1,800 PSARA travel agents, all identifiable by the bright red and blue window sticker which announces them as an 'Official Travel Agent for the Cruise Industry'. For more help and advice on these matters, and for the nearest PSARA cruise agent to you, contact PSARA on 0171 436 2449. For more information on the Guild of Professional Cruise Agents call Paul Mundy Cruising on 0171 734 4404. And, for examples of the independent cruise consultant for whom I can personally vouch, try Cruise Club International in Bromley, Kent on 0181 466 7000 or the Cruise Advisory Service in Salisbury, Wiltshire on 01722 335505.

WHAT I DID ON MY HOLIDAY!

Now, once you have booked your cruise, what sort of experience should you expect (apart from one that's fun, relaxing, exciting, family-orientated and value for money)?

Here, especially for cruise newcomers, is a typical example of what cruising is all about, from start to finish.

BRIT TIP

I always try to embark at the earliest possible opportunity. The queues may well be at their longest, but you will still be on board before the majority and will have the chance to explore the ship before it starts to get busy, which is a wonderful experience.

Embarkation: Your anticipation should be at its highest for the moment of boarding your chosen vessel. In most main ports, embarkation is now a process similar to an airport check-in. On American ships you will have to surrender your passport (you're a foreigner, remember) and in return you will receive your Boarding Card, which in most cases you will keep with you at all times, especially when re-boarding the ship at its ports of call. It will also be your on-board credit card and ID.

If you still have your cases at this point, they will be taken away from you for delivery to your cabin, so make sure they are properly marked with your deck and cabin number. On fly-cruises, the chances are your luggage will be carried after the baggage hall by the cruise line's local ground agents to the ship and aboard without you having to reclaim it.

The Welcome Aboard photo is an early obligation

BRIT TIP

As you are standing in the queue at the embarkation desk, try to get one of your party to make sure you have received, and filled in, the necessary paperwork which will usually consist of an embarkation form and a customs declaration. It is so annoying to get to the front of the queue and find out there is another form to fill in.

Once checked in, you will usually meet the Maître d' who will show you the dining room's seating plan and your choice of First or Second Sitting.

First impressions count – like the impressive foyer of Regal Princess

Check if your dining arrangements are as per your booking as this will be your best chance to change them. Before you are allowed aboard, you will have to endure the obligatory Welcome Aboard photo session with the ship's photographers. You are NOT obliged to buy anything (you may not be at your best if you've just had a long flight, after all), so it is churlish to be unco-operative. This will also be the first of many official photo opportunities that can be a bit irksome after a while, but they will always be on display at the ship's photo shop before you have to decide whether to buy.

 **BRIT TIP**

Your luggage should be waiting for you outside your cabin, or arrive shortly after you do. If it has not arrived an hour before you are due to sail, contact the Purser's Desk urgently.

Boarding: Again, this is a moment to savour as you make your way up the gangway and into (usually) the ship's main reception area or foyer. If you are lucky enough to be walking into the *Sun Princess* for the first time (or one of the other mega-liners who specialise in impressive atrium lobbies), prepare to have your breath taken away by the awe-inspiring splendour of the initial view. This will be your first confirmation you have made the Right Choice.

You should immediately be met by one of the Purser's or Hotel Director's staff who will ask for your cabin number and assign a steward to show you the way.

Your cabin: The steward will usually leave you at your cabin to allow your full-time steward to welcome you officially and show you how everything works (if it isn't immediately obvious. I still have nightmares about trying to use the pen in one particular cabin, only for the steward to demonstrate with

Get in the swing with a golf lesson

great tact I was trying to open the wrong end!). Check straight away that the cabin's facilities are exactly as you ordered, especially whether those twin beds do REALLY convert into a double. Any queries or errors should be reported immediately to your steward or the Purser's Desk and, while it may take a little more time on the busiest day of the cruise, you should receive relatively prompt attention. Whether you unpack straight away is obviously up to you. First, however, cast an eye over your *Cruise News* as this is the single most important piece of literature you will receive. The *Cruise News* (or other variations on that name) is your daily shipboard newspaper which lists all the various activities, their times and locations, dining times, opening hours of the bars, health centre and beauty salon, and the entertainment programme for the evening. It will be delivered to your cabin every evening so you can study the next day's schedule of events and plan your campaign accordingly.

Exploring your ship: If, like me, you have been studying the brochure layout of the ship avidly in advance of the cruise, you will now find it bears little or no relation to the reality! This is because, no matter how well versed you are or how many other ships you have been on, you can never get your bearings straight away, even to the point sometimes of not knowing which deck you are on. Stop just for a second and make sure of two key points: one, whether you are facing forward or aft, and two, if you are on the left or right hand side (port or starboard, see below). Try to establish some key landmarks that will enable you to orientate yourself along these two lines and you will be half way to being able to tell your fellow passengers smugly: 'The Crow's Nest Bar? Ah yes, that's forward and up three decks.' Obviously, the way you progress after that is up to you, but I find it best to work my way systematically up through the decks before taking a turn around the topmost deck (this is usually the Sun Deck) and then retiring to the nearest bar to congratulate myself on my choice. You can also visit the Purser's Desk to arrange your on-board credit, but you will not be hassled to do this straight

BRIT TIP

The best advice for booking any alternative dining arrangement is to avoid the formal nights as these are best enjoyed in the main dining room. A port day may be a better choice, especially as you can probably leave the time a little later than normal to allow yourself maximum time ashore.

Dinner is always a special occasion

away as you can still start signing things to your cabin providing you have your Boarding Card handy. This is also your opportunity to get ahead of the rest by booking your visit to the hair salon for the optimum time for you and, if the ship has an alternative dining room, to book a visit there while you have the most choice.

In most cases, before you sail (and certainly within 24 hours of being underway) there will be the Lifeboat Drill, which you are required to attend, with your life-jacket. These days it is little more than the type of safety advice everyone ignores before a plane takes off, but it is compulsory and it doesn't take too long. It is also important, especially with children, to know such details as your Muster Station and how your life-jacket does up. And, please, don't walk along with your life-jacket tapes undone and trailing behind you – the number of people that trip over them is just amazing.

The First Evening: This will probably be a fairly casual affair with people boarding at different times, and it is possible you may not meet all your dinner table companions straight away. The dining room staff should be at their keenest to welcome you aboard, however, and you will be introduced in quick succession to your wine waiter/ waitress, the Head Waiter for your section of the dining room and the Maître d', if you have not already met. The rest of the evening will be relatively low key as the entertainments staff keep their powder dry to impress you later in the cruise and the majority will opt for an early-ish night in preparation for the first full day (unless you are on a three- or four-day cruise, in which case it is party time from the moment you step aboard).

 **BRIT TIP**

If you are one of those people who hate doing Christmas shopping for fear of finding everything you buy reduced in the New Year sales, don't use the first day aboard as an opportunity to do all your souvenir shopping in the ship's boutiques. Apart from the fact you may want to avoid looking like several hundred others in your MS *Whatever* T-shirt, you will probably find the shop has various special offers during the cruise, especially on the last few days, when standard items are seriously reduced in price.

The First Day: If you have chosen your itinerary carefully, you will have the enjoyment of a full day at sea to start with, thus giving you a proper and leisurely introduction to the ship. You can get an early taste of the daytime events and facilities, like the deck games, and get a feel for which areas of the deck are most likely to be crowded, and where those quiet little spots are. There may also be a 'Question and Answer' session in the morning for any queries about ship-board life you may have at this stage. Watch out in your *Cruise News* for the Shore Excursions presentation (mentioned in Chapter Three) as this will probably be your first chance to book those organised shore-side jvisits.

The evening is likely to be a formal one, with a Welcome Aboard reception for each sitting, hosted by the captain, which offers you the chance to sip a complimentary glass of champagne and meet the rest of the ship's crew in a brief *Who's Who* parade presented by the captain.

Water sports are now a regular feature of your shore-side excursions

The First Port of Call: This gives the ship a chance to slip into a different gear as the majority of events are orientated towards going ashore rather than staying on board (although there's nothing to stop you just putting your feet up by the pool all day – it's a good time to enjoy a larger amount of deck space to yourself). If you have never sailed into a new port before, it is worth being up early to enjoy that unique, heady experience as the ship takes on board the local pilot and almost imperceptibly drifts into the harbour ready for the start of a new adventure. Quite often, there will be something of an undignified stampede for the disembarkation station (which may well be lower down in the ship

Enjoying a stroll on deck is a wonderful experience

than the reception area where you came on) as everyone tries to get off at the same time in order to take full advantage of their port time. This is one of the few areas where the larger ships really struggle to cope with their passenger volume, and it can take a little while to get everyone sorted out and off the ship. People booked on the first shore excursions will have right of way as they are running to a well-organised schedule and need to be first off, then it is every man (and woman) for themselves. If you are just wandering ashore under your own steam, make a good note of where the ship is docked (get a written address if you take a local taxi) and how long it takes to walk into the main town area. Sometimes the harbour is not immediately adjacent to the town and the ship will lay on shuttle buses to do the round trip. Again, make a good mental note of where they pick you up and drop you off. Finally, the ship will ask you to be back on board half an hour before sailing again, so try to leave 30 minutes on top of that to be on the safe side. There is no more doomed feeling than racing back to the ship thinking you might miss it – I speak from personal experience! It's not like missing a plane, either. There WON'T be another one along soon.

FOOD AND DRINK

Here's a typical shopping-list for a 14-day cruise aboard the *Oriana* – more than a few trips to Sainsburys.

On an average 14-day voyage, the 1,975 passengers and 760 crew will eat no less than 116,550 meals, prepared from:

Meat	14.4 tons	Shellfish	1.7 tons
Fish	3.6 tons	Poultry and game	6.8 tons
Bacon, ham and gammon	3.4 tons	Butter, fats and cheese	4.5 tons
Fresh fruit and vegetables	28.0 tons	Flour	8.4 tons
Potatoes	17.7 tons	Coffee	0.6 tons
Sugar	1.9 tons	Fresh eggs	51,000
Milk and cream	2,775 gallons	Ice cream	1,050 gallons
Champagne, sparkling & white wine	2,600 bottles	Red wine	1,200 bottles
Whisky	1,600 litres	Gin, rum and vodka	1,200 litres
Cognac	400 litres	Beer	33,000 bottles/cans
Minerals	28,000 bottles		

The Final Evening: Cries of 'Where did the last week/10 days/two weeks go?' abound as you realise you have arrived at the penultimate day of your cruise and have to prepare on the final evening for disembarkation the next morning (cruise ships invariably dock at the most inhospitable times, around 6–7am, in order to be able to get one load off and the next load on the same day). There is something of an art form to preparing your cases, hand luggage and what to wear as most cruise lines will insist on having your suitcases loaded and outside your cabin door before midnight (some insist on

Your dinner wines are included in the price on Silversea ships

8pm which is patently absurd when you have not even been to dinner by that time. It pays to be 'forgetful' in that instance – as long as your cases are ready to go by midnight there should be ample time for the crew to sort them out). You will probably be given a series of colour-coded tags to put on all your luggage so it can be readily identified on the quayside. If you are on a fly-cruise and have a flight to catch that day, you shouldn't need to do any toting of your own cases, you simply identify it as yours and it will be put on the coach to the airport for you. The colour-coding system also allows for passengers to be disembarked by flights, so that if you have an earlier plane to catch you will be among the first off. Other disembarkation details will include a final statement of your ship-board credit account which you should always check to make sure it tallies with your recollections of your own spending (this can be a frightening moment when the awful truth of enjoying those daily rounds of cocktails finally catches up with you). In most cases, if you have left a credit card imprint with the Purser's Desk and the account adds up correctly, you need do nothing else. If you are paying by cheque or cash, you must obviously visit the Desk in person to pay up. The other last evening ritual is tipping, and you will find at least three empty envelopes have mysteriously appeared in your cabin, usually marked 'Steward', 'Waiter' and 'Bus-boy'. At this stage you have to work out the recommended daily tipping rate (every line should make this clear either in their brochure or in the *Cruise News*). It generally works out at $3–$3.50 (or £2–£2.30) per person per day for your cabin steward and waiter, and half that for the bus-boy and any assistant steward. If the Head Waiter or Maître d' has been of particular help, $10–$15 (£7–£10) is the going rate for tipping them. The end of the last evening's meal then usually sees a mass exchange of envelopes like some secret society! Once the dining room staff have received their gratuities, it is a rare but not totally unknown occurrence for them to be less than their fully co-operative and friendly selves on the next morning. Should you run into this attitude you should report it to the Hotel Director.

Disembarkation: Remember all those queues to get off at the ports of call? Well, this is worse. The final ritual of disembarking is an unavoidable pain in most cases simply because the vast majority of passengers have little alternative but to hang around in the main lounges with their hand luggage waiting to be called off. The effects can be lessened by breakfasting as late as possible (there should still be a buffet choice to avoid having to suffer first sitting in the main dining room at 5am or some similarly ridiculous hour) and taking a final stroll around deck (a surprising number of people seem to neglect this), but you will not be able to wait in your cabin as the steward will be wanting to get it ready for the next passengers, and they are on a strict timetable. Make sure you know your luggage tag colour code and try to be patient. Even allowing for a full passenger load, disembarkation rarely takes more than two hours and the whole process is pretty well organised to minimise any hassle once you are off the ship. I'm afraid there is no known antidote for that sad, end-of-cruise feeling, but you can console yourself with the thought of planning your next cruise. You see, I TOLD you it was addictive!

LEARNING SHIP-SPEAK

No explanation of the world of cruising would be complete at this stage without an explanation of what all those nautical terms really mean. And here, to help you be able to speak like an old salt, is the unique *Brit's Guide* to that wonderful world of marine language.

SHIP-SPEAK	WHAT IT REALLY MEANS
Aft	Toward the stern or blunt end of the ship
Amidships	In the middle
Astern (as in, to go astern)	Reverse gear (or, a very serious look)
Avast there!	There's something rather large over there
Beam	Width of the ship (or, what you do to the ship's photographer)
Bow	The pointy bit at the front
Bridge	Where the captain watches the computers running the ship
Bulkhead	The main 'walls' that divide the ship into compartments (see, a sensible one!)
Companionway	The ship's narrow corridor where people can't avoid being friendly
Course	Where you play golf (Eh? – Ed.)
Crew	The ship's staff (Cue the question: 'Do the crew sleep aboard?' I kid you not)
Crow's nest	A hair-do in rough seas
Disembark	Everybody Off!
Embark	Everybody On!
First sitting	The chance to digest your evening meal in time for the Midnight Buffet
Fly-cruise	A really fast cruise
Forward	Towards the pointy bit (or, the right attitude at the Singles' Party)
Funnel	A yellow-flowered aniseed-flavoured herb (Er... – Ed.)

Galley	The source of every cruise passenger putting on about 1lb a day
Gangway	What you shout when disembarking
Gross registered tonnage	The opposite of civilised registered tonnage
Hull	A shortened greeting
Inside cabin	An obscure tailoring measurement
Knot	A nautical mile per hour that frequently gets land-lubbers in a tangle (see below)
Maitre d'	The person in the dining room you will see only on the first night (to ingratiate himself) and the last (to hope for a tip)
Nautical mile	A 60th of one degree of the earth's circumference, equal to 6,080 feet, and 800 feet longer than a land mile (so there!)
Open seating	The cruise version of Open Sesame
Port	1) The left-hand side; port = left because it has the same number of letters in 2) Where the ship visits; hence, 'We *left* the *port* well alone'
Port tax	1) Left-handed drawing pins 2) A sneaky add-on charge that is gradually being phased out
Quay	What you use to unlock the door
Rudder	An alternative; as in, 'I'd rudder be on anudder cruise'
Ship	Never, NEVER a Boat
Space Ratio	The bigger the ship, the more space it takes up in port
Stabiliser	The first drink of the next day
Starboard	1) An uninspired guest star

Starboard (*cont.*)	2) The right-hand side; right = starboard because it has, er, more letters in
Stateroom	Cabin, as in, look at the state of this room
Stern	The blunt end
Tender	The BOATS which the SHIP carries to get you ashore where the SHIP can't dock (or, what you are without a stabiliser)
Tips	'Look both ways before crossing the road" 'Neither a borrower nor a lender be', etc
'Weigh anchor!'	'23lb 4ozs!' (My mum's favourite nautical joke, apart from her son)

To complete this rather irreverent finale, I'm going to borrow a few famous cruise quotes, as asked by some of the (American, I hope) passengers of Celebrity, and a few others.

'Does the elevator go to the front of the ship?' 'Why does the ship rock only when we are at sea?' 'Does the ship generate its own electricity?' (You can just imagine the answer: 'No madam, can't you see the cable we're running all way back to Miami?') 'Will I get wet if I go snorkelling?' 'What do you do with the ice carvings after they melt?' (Have you ever heard of water carvings?) 'Does the crew sleep on board?' (No, they swim ashore every night.) 'Is there water all around the island?' 'What time is the midnight buffet?' (The oldest and most often-repeated saying) 'Will the trap-shooting be held outside?' ('No sir, we thought we'd use your cabin') 'How will we know which photos are ours?' And my current favourite – to one of the deck staff, 'Is that sea water in the pool?' 'Yes sir, it is.' 'Ah, that would explain why there are so many waves in it.' All additions gratefully received.

Now, it is time to delve deeper into the specifics and ask the vitally important question, Who do I cruise with . . .?

*

CHAPTER FIVE

The Cruise Lines and their Ships

(or, Knowing your RCI from your NCL and P&O)

Having discussed the generalities of cruising and then tried to put them into perspective with Chapter Four's look at how and why to make your booking, it now seems logical to make a more in-depth examination of the cruise lines themselves, how they differ, the ships they offer and what to expect of the different cruise experiences.

At the last count there were 42 major cruise lines all selling directly to the great British public, 43 if you count the new Disney Cruise operations which are not even scheduled to begin until 1998. With the aid of the *Brit's Guide* ratings, you should be able to draw a comprehensive picture of the style and appeal of each one and decide which is the one for you. It should also be fairly evident where a cruise line deals more heavily in the British market (like the predominantly Brit-filled ships of P&O, Airtours, Thomson, Swan Hellenic and Fred Olsen), and I make no apologies for concentrating more of my attention and therefore more of this book's space on them for obvious reasons. No other travel guide attempts to do this, but I am convinced it is a worthwhile exercise and you can be sure, therefore, of the best possible attention to detail in the British area of the market.

To that end, several of the ships have been marked out as **Brit's Guide Favourites** due to their innate Brit appeal. Some are obvious (where they cater specifically for British passengers), others not so obvious (where they have yet to be discovered in great numbers by UK passengers), but all possess an extra element that makes them a bit special for the British market.

Look out at the end of the chapter for the 1998 **Brit's Guide/What Cruise Awards**, a celebrated new feature in the cruise world, put together by an eminent panel of experts, which has really given the industry a new dimension.

When it comes to the technical terminology, the Space Ratio figure, remember, is the rather arbitrary figure derived by dividing the ship's Gross Registered Tonnage by its full passenger load to give you a general idea of spaciousness. Anything 20 or less is poor, 30 is average, 40 very good and 50 or above is excellent. The average price range (with 1997 brochure prices) is included only as a *general* guide to a cruise line's costs – it is impossible to be specific as prices change all the time, especially with the amount of discounting that goes on. Where brochures are unlikely to be found in your average travel agent, I have included a 'phone number for the cruise line.

Ship prefixes: these merely denote the type of engines which drive the vessel. Hence, MS = motor ship, MTS = motor twin screw (or motor turbine ship), MV = motor vessel, MSY = motor sailing yacht, RMS = Royal Mail Ship, SS = steam ship, SSC = semi-submersible craft (in the case of the Radisson Diamond because of its small waterplane area twin hull design, or SWATH), TES = turbo electric ship, TS = turbine steamer, TSMV = twin screw motor vessel, YS = yacht ship.

ABERCROMBIE & KENT

Ships	Tonnage	Passengers	Space Ratio	Built/ Refurbished	Cruise Area	Rating
MS *Explorer*	2,398	Max 104	23.0	1969/1993	Antarctica, Australasia, S America	Standard

Cruise line notes: This up-market company specialise in world-wide tours, particularly safaris and other off-the-beaten-track adventures, and their one-ship cruise operation has been running since 1990 with a high degree of expedition-type flavour. Of special interest are their spring voyages along the Amazon River, a full 2,000 miles and further than any other cruise ship.

Antarctica is an A&K speciality

Ship notes: The cruise rating is of little real importance to this unique little adventurer, which primarily offers the chance to get right up close with the landscape you have come to see. She is not exactly built for creature comforts, hence the Standard rating, but she is serviceable enough, although her lack of space (and some tiny cabins) means she is definitely NOT for the disabled or people with children. She features a comprehensive and sophisticated lecture programme to back up her itineraries and rubber Zodiac boats for shore excursions. There are few on-board facilities as the emphasis is on shore-side activities, lectures and films. Her usual passenger complement consists of Americans and Germans, with a few other European nationalities. Brits are rather scarce, except when the whole ship is chartered by Saga Holidays around Europe. Age profile tends to be a healthy and adventurous 50-plus.

Extras: All tips and shore excursions are included in the basic price; large, well-stocked library (with big National Geographic input); single-seating dining and hearty, well-presented food. They also collaborate on Royal Geographical Society Tours, a special association of operators who share the Society's belief in the value and enjoyment of geography and environmental matters. For brochures phone 0171 730 9600.

Average price range: From £4,777 on an 18-night Antarctic cruise, £2,387 on the Amazon Rainforest Experience.

AFRICAN SAFARI CLUB

Ships	Tonnage	Passengers	Space Ratio	Built/ Refurbished	Cruise Area	Rating
MV *Royal Star*	5,600	Max 200	28.0	1956/1994	Indian Ocean	Standard

Cruise line notes: African Safari Club is a Swiss-owned hotel group offering specialist tours to Kenya and running its one cruise ship in conjunction with land-based holidays and safaris. It flies British customers from Heathrow, Gatwick or Manchester to Mombasa via Frankfurt or Basel and offers a combination stay at one of its resorts with a cruise varying in duration from 7–18 nights.

Ship notes: Charming small-ship style is allied with some wonderful itineraries, taking in the Seychelles, Madagascar, the Maldives, Mauritius and the Comores. Limited facilities and daytime events, plus smallish cabins (and even smaller 'bathrooms') add up to a Standard rating, but service comes with a ready smile and the atmosphere is always relaxed and friendly. International cuisine style reflects fully European passenger profile, mainly couples of 40-plus. Again, not recommended for children or the disabled.

Extras: A minimum of six nights full board at ASC's Flamingo Beach Hotel is included with every package, along with your port taxes. Single supplement is only 30 per cent on the majority of cabins and shipboard currency is, unusually, the German mark. Excellent value for money at these prices. For brochures, phone 0181 466 0014.

Average price range: £1,790–£7,600 for a 7-night Spice Island cruise with 6-night hotel stay.

AIRTOURS

Ships	Tonnage	Passengers	Space Ratio	Built/ Refurbished	Cruise Area	Rating
MS *Carousel*	23,200	Max 1,200	19.3	1971/1995	Mediterranean, Caribbean	Standard
MS *Seawing*	16,607	Max 976	17.0	1971/1995	Mediterranean	Standard
MS *Sundream*	22,945	Max 1,146	20.0	1971/1994	Mediterranean, Caribbean	Standard

Cruise line notes: One of Britain's Big Three tour operators, Airtours, effectively broke the mould of budget-level cruising when they bought two ships to enter the market in 1995. Suddenly, here was cruising offered to the

Keeping fit the Airtours way on Seawing

British package holiday market at a hugely tempting price and without too much compromising on quality. Airtours were so successful, they sold out their summer seasons in both 1995 and 1996 in double-quick time and effectively opened up the cruise world to a whole new clientèle, adding a third ship in 1997. Airtours' existing tour infra-structure means they can cut down on traditional cruise overheads like flights, ground agents and shore excursions and pass on the savings to their passengers, hence terrific value for money in the Standard level of cruising. Their company tie-up with American giants Carnival in 1996 gave them access to much of Carnival's hugely-successful know-how, while their joint venture to buy Costa Cruise Line in 1997 promises to spread the mass-market message still further. Airtours' Scandinavian, US and Canadian travel company links mean you will find Norwegian and Danish passengers on many of their Mediterranean sailings and Americans and Canadians on the Caribbean ones, but this is essentially a British operation from top to bottom and will appeal to anyone who has enjoyed a land-based Airtours holiday as well as those cruisers on a budget. A full age profile is highlighted by large numbers of families during the holiday periods and busy kids' programmes, but the ships are not well suited for disabled passengers. Airtours also tried to introduce non-specific cabin booking (i.e. you book just a grade of cabin rather than a cabin in particular) but this proved unpopular with regular cruisers and the policy is currently under review. Lack of formality is a strong Airtours policy, and they also offer a full programme of one- and two-week stays at their land resorts in Palma and Cyprus in the Med and Barbados and the Dominican Republic in the Caribbean. *Seawing* is also destined for year-round operations from Cyprus in 1998, with a new series of cruises to Egypt, Israel and the Greek Islands.

 **BRIT TIP**

Airtours' standard product is 7-day fly-cruising in both the Mediterranean and Caribbean, but they also offer several cruises up to 28 days long as *Sundream* and *Carousel* position across the Atlantic twice a year.

Ship notes: Airtours started by buying the *Southward* from Norwegian Cruise Line (now the *Seawing*) and quickly found they needed another after selling out, so they immediately added Royal Caribbean's *Nordic Prince* (now the *Carousel*) to their stable. A further Royal Caribbean vessel, *Song of Norway*, sister ship to *Nordic Prince*, soon followed. All three are 1970s vintage, and so, despite being thoroughly refurbished before sailing under the colours of Airtours' cruise arm Sun Cruise, they lack some of the sophisticated touches of modern ships, but the hardware is nonetheless sound for all that. Standard cabins are a little on the cramped side (especially for wardrobe and drawer space), but they all make good use of some pleasant artwork and tasteful soft furnishings. Unobtrusive service and average food are offset by keen and eager-to-please entertainment staff, friendly waiters and a full programme of daily events. The ships can feel a little crowded when full and deck space is then at a premium (these are originally American-market vessels, and hence open deck space was not a priority to them), and you may not find the overall experience relaxing if you are looking for a quiet holiday. The virtually identical *Carousel* and *Sundream* are slightly the better-equipped of the three ships, with a choice of three lounges to *Seawing's* two, but the latter has the snazzier Crow's Nest Nightclub. The gyms are all rather small and could be better equipped.

Extras: Apart from Airtours' general value for money, on-board drink prices are very reasonable and shore excursions well-organised, as you would expect from a package holiday outfit. No frills or glitz, and the overall product could do with a bit of polishing, but staff help to make it a fun experience and the appeal is quite broad-based. No special provision for disabled passengers, but huge choice in the number of UK airports that link up with the cruises and good number of reduced-price offers for children.

Opposition to the usual tipping culture is high from Airtours passengers and the company has considered making them all-inclusive, although no final decision had been reached as we went to press. There is, surprisingly, a charge for room service, but it still represents great value at these prices, especially for families. For a free Airtours video, call 01235 824428.

Average price range: £499–£1,059 for a week's Mediterranean cruise, £939–£1,699 on a 14-night Caribbean cruise-and-stay.

CARNIVAL

Ships	Tonnage	Passengers	Space Ratio	Built/ Refurbished	Cruise Area	Rating
MS Tropicale	23,200	Max 1,400	26.1	1981/1989	Far East	Standard
MS Holiday	46,052	Max 1,800	25.5	1985/1994	California, Mexico	Standard
MS Jubilee	47,262	Max 1,896	24.9	1986	Caribbean, Alaska	Standard
MS Celebration	47,262	Max 1,896	24.9	1987	Caribbean	Standard
MS Fantasy	70,367	Max 2,634	26.7	1990	Bahamas	Superior
MS Ecstasy	70,367	Max 2.634	26.7	1992	Caribbean, Bahamas	Superior
MS Sensation	70,367	Max 2,634	26.7	1993	Caribbean	Superior
MS Fascination	70,367	Max 2,634	26.7	1994	Caribbean	Superior
MS Imagination	70,367	Max 2,634	26.7	1995	Caribbean	Superior
MS Inspiration	70,367	Max 2,634	26.7	1996	Caribbean	Superior
MS Carnival Destiny	101,353	Max 3,350	30.2	1996	Caribbean	Superior

Cruise line notes: Carnival is the mass-market arm of the giant American Carnival Corporation, the largest cruise operation in the world (incorporating the traditional style of Holland America, the majestic sailing ships of Windstar and a financial interest in the Deluxe Seabourn Line, plus the recent buy-out of big Italian line Costa in partnership with Airtours). And, if Airtours have rather rocked the traditional boat with their new operating style, Carnival have staged a full-scale mutiny, dragging the cruise idea kicking and screaming into the late twentieth century. Not for nothing are their vessels dubbed the Fun Ships, and they typically feature the youngest age profile anywhere at sea, with large numbers of children and college-age teens during the main holidays. That is only a small part of the story, however, as Carnival have revolutionised the US cruise industry through the 1980s and 1990s, opening it up to a much wider audience, from the teeny-boppers right through to their parents and even their grandparents. There is an overwhelming sense of glitz and glitter about all the ships, but the one drawback with their wild neon colour schemes and fun-style décor is that it tends to date rather quickly, hence the older ships in the line are starting to look in need of a new image. It is very much a budget cruise experience in modern surroundings, hence there is less attention to making the food and cabins look appetising than to creating fabulous evening shows and non-stop entertainment. You don't ever take a Carnival cruise for a

Carnival's huge pool slides are a trademark of the line

rest cure! The ship names alone tell you they are a long way removed from the cruise formality of yesteryear. The itineraries are all standard fare and the shore excursions pretty ordinary since the ships are as much a destination in themselves as the ports of call. You'll find every possible amenity and facility aboard, especially when it comes to activities for the kids, and, if the service is a little utilitarian (down to the unfortunate practice of waiters roaming the decks selling tray after tray of identikit cocktails), the value for money, especially for the younger set, is unarguable. Carnival has not been a big player in the British cruise market in the past, but they are likely to be far more visible and attractive as a result of their tie-up with Airtours.

Ship notes: Almost the ultimate in slab-sided, floating hotel-block appearance, Carnival ships are subdivided into the oldest of their ships still operating, the 1981-built *Tropicale* (which is being sent to the Far East to start a new service for Carnival-Hyundai Line in 1998), the three Holiday-class ships (*Holiday*, *Jubilee* and *Celebration*) which also fall into the Standard category and were originally dubbed 'Disney World for adults', the six mega-liner Fantasy-class vessels (*Fantasy, Ecstasy, Sensation, Inspiration, Fascination* and *Imagination*) which all take the line up to the Superior rating through the quality and modern styling of their facilities, and the ultra-new *Carnival Destiny*, the world's first 100,000-ton cruise ship. Carnival designer Joe Farcus has really let his imagination run riot, with a huge retractable glass dome over one of the three outdoor pools, the world's longest water-slide at sea (all of 200 feet long and adding visually to the line's trademark winged funnel), a glass-domed nine-storey atrium, a three-level, 1,000-seater showlounge, 418 cabins with balconies (more than half of the outside ones), a massive spa and gymnasium and a pair of two-storey dining rooms. The Fantasy-class ships all feature individual design themes running throughout the vessel, such as a Metropolis theme on *Ecstasy*, with some quite outrageous use of bold, in-your-face architecture on the first four. Farcus has rather toned this down a touch on the *Imagination*, while the *Inspiration* shows some almost elegant features, such as the classically-themed Chopin Bar, the French-accented principal promenade and the art nouveau décor throughout, notably in the Grand Atrium. The Shakespeare Library is a bit tacky for anyone acquainted with genuine period style, but the Rock and Roll Dance Club, the ship's disco, is a positive riot of lights, TV screens and pulsating imagery that is sure to go down well with the younger set. Amazingly, Carnival will début no less than three new ships in 1998, adding 8,848 berths to their already vast capacity. The *Elation* and *Paradise* are both additions to the Fantasy class, in February and November respectively, while the *Carnival Triumph* will be a sister ship for the Destiny in December.

 **BRIT TIP**

Carnival's three- and four-day cruises aboard the *Fantasy* out of Port Canaveral, only an hour's drive from Orlando, are an excellent add-on to a holiday in Walt Disney World.

Extras: Cabins are surprisingly spacious and well-equipped for this sector of the market, while the public rooms are all imaginatively themed and styled, if your senses can get past the vivid neon lights and the bright, clashing colours of the décor. Indoor promenades promote the image of being in a typical American shopping mall, but, while the emphasis is on the non-stop glitter of places like the garish Diamonds Are Forever disco (on *Fascination*), there are quieter, more subtle retreats on each ship, as in the classy Chinatown Lounge (on *Ecstasy*). On-board entertainment is high-energy, glamorous and quite diverse, from Country and Western duos to magicians, jugglers and full-scale Las Vegas revues. Health and spa facilities on all ships are excellent, and Carnival also offers a well-organised and well-priced wedding service. There are well-tried shore excursions on *Jubilee's*

Alaska run due to company tie-up with Holland America. Reasonable wheelchair access features on all but *Tropicale*. For Carnival's UK office, phone 0171 729 1929.

Average price range: £499–£1,665 on seven-day Caribbean cruises.

CELEBRITY

Ships	Tonnage	Passengers	Space Ratio	Built/ Refurbished	Cruise Area	Rating
MV *Horizon*	46,811	Max 1,660	28.1	1990	Caribbean, Alaska	Premier, *Brit's Guide Favourite*
MV *Zenith*	47,255	Max 1,796	26.3	1992	Caribbean, Bermuda, Panama Canal	Premier *Brit's Guide Favourite*
MS *Century*	70,000	Max 2,150	32.5	1995	Caribbean	Premier *Brit's Guide Favourite*
MS *Galaxy*	77,713	Max 2,150	36.1	1996	Caribbean, Alaska	Premier *Brit's Guide Favourite*
MS *Mercury*	76,000	Max 2,150	36.1	1997	Caribbean	Premier (expected)

Cruise line notes: The takeover of Celebrity by Royal Caribbean International in June 1997 took many industry observers by surprise and raised a few questions over the viability of two major lines operating together. But RCI are adamant Celebrity will continue as a separate brand – as Carnival have managed with Holland

Zenith highlights the Caribbean scene

America – and the early signs are that this will, happily, be the case. Greek-based but American-run, Celebrity was formed as an upmarket version of the mass Caribbean cruise experience by the owners of Chandris Cruises (who were one of the originators of fly-cruising) and effectively delivers a Premier experience at a Superior price. Touches of the traditional cruise atmosphere and style mix with ultra-modern design but in a more refined way. Their newest ships, *Century* and *Galaxy*, incorporate some of the most sophisticated marine design, like state-of-the-art theatres, wonderfully inviting central atriums and virtual reality gymnasiums, and also have far more open deck space than is common in the American market. The passenger profile tends to be slightly older (and so more formal) than some of the Caribbean competition, but Celebrity still run some busy and popular children's programmes in the holiday periods, including their trademark Slumber Parties, where youngsters eat and play games from 8pm until as late as 2am under the careful supervision of the children's counsellors, while their kids' menus are also well above average. Daytime activities are fairly routine, as are the shore excursions, but they are paying more attention to the evening entertainment these days.

 BRIT TIP

The best value aboard Celebrity ships, as on most of the upmarket lines, is with the standard range of cabins and especially the inside ones (although you might want to avoid those aft on *Zenith's* Europa Deck on prime holiday sailings as the children's playroom is situated there).

Ship notes: *Horizon* and *Zenith* were purpose-built for the Celebrity style in the early 1990s and have been beautifully maintained, still looking nearly new in keeping with the line's upmarket touch. They lack a proper, wrap-around promenade deck, but both feature elegant décor that is easy on the eye and doesn't make the common American mistake of equating class with glitz. The two newer ships, *Century* and *Galaxy*, take Celebrity's appeal a step further forward with a huge range of sumptuous public rooms, cleverly designed to play down the ships' overall size. Newest arrival *Mercury*, due out in October 1997, should build on the fabulously imaginative style they have created, while they also boast acres of open deck space, superb health and fitness facilities and an increased range of children's activities, including junior discos and video games rooms. The advent of *Galaxy* in particular marked out Celebrity as one of the brightest thinkers in modern cruise ship design. Her two-storey restaurant, eye-catching theatre and quite startling Savoy Nightclub are all outstanding features in the cruise world. The combination makes for a ship overflowing with the 'wow' factor and also one that is even quite sexy.

Extras: The cuisine has been Celebrity's watchword from the start and is among the best at sea, comparing even with some of the Deluxe range. It is designed by famous French chef Michel Roux who remains a consultant on all things food-orientated and ensures a consistently high standard. A special 'elegant' high tea is also a feature of every cruise, while the service is just the right blend of friendly and efficient. Celebrity takes good care of its staff on board, and that extra attention pays dividends in their attitude towards the passengers. Cabins throughout the line are above average in space terms and are all elegantly finished. Butler service is also available with all suites and *Galaxy, Mercury* and *Century* boast the largest suites at sea, a massive 1,100 square feet of space. The line is one of the prime operators to the popular island of Bermuda and benefits from special docking concessions. Celebrity also offer an excellent range of land-based add-ons, plus a tailor-made service to increase their overall appeal. Watch out, though, for some of their on-board prices – drinks and extras like photos are a bit steep compared with the competition. For Celebrity's UK brochure phoneline, call 0990 902901.

 BRIT TIP

The Fleet Bar (*Zenith*) and America's Cup Club (*Horizon*) are two of the most inviting and relaxing places at sea to sit and enjoy a drink and watch the world sail by.

Average price range: £1,149–£3,319 for a nine-night Caribbean trip.

COMMODORE CRUISES

Ships	Tonnage	Passengers	Space Ratio	Built/ Refurbished	Cruise Area	Rating
SS Enchanted Isle	23,395	Max 729	32.0	1958/1995	Caribbean	Standard

Cruise line notes: This American line does not sell directly in Britain, but does pick up a few Brits holidaying in Florida or New Orleans, which is its home port. It is a basic, budget-priced operation on a long-serving veteran of the cruise world which has been around a lot, seen slightly better days but still provides a consistent level of service. Commodore are a million miles removed from Carnival's Fun Ships, but their keen pricing still attracts large numbers of first-time younger cruisers (especially families) as well as the 45–60 age bracket. It's informal, lively and friendly, with the service earning high marks from repeat passengers and first-timers alike.

Ship notes: *Enchanted Isle* is starting to show her age a little and is short of some of the facilities taken for granted on more modern vessels (notably for fitness and spa treatments), but there is still a good range of bars and lounges and plenty of energetic day-time activities and evening shows. Food is decent

if a little limited in choice. As befits a ship of her vintage, cabins come in a great mix of sizes and shapes and tend to be fairly down-to-earth. Finesse is not this company's middle name, but, like Airtours, they do offer outstanding value for money as long as your expectations aren't unrealistic.

Extras: Children's counsellors are on board during summer cruises, and themed music cruises

Enjoy the fun, friendly style with Commodore

(Country and Western, Jazz, Mardi Gras) are popular. Sailing out of New Orleans on *Enchanted Isle* is a novelty. Good value honeymoon and anniversary packages, but there is no room service.

Average price range: $498–$1,598 for a week's Caribbean cruise WITHOUT air fare. For details phone 1-800 854 3835 in the US.

COSTA CRUISES

Ships	Tonnage	Passengers	Space Ratio	Built/ Refurbished	Cruise Area	Rating
SS CostaRiviera	31,500	Max 974	32.3	1963/1996	Mediterranean, Canaries	Standard
MS CostaPlaya	12,475	Max 480	25.9	1967/1995	Caribbean	Standard
MC CostaMarina	25,441	Max 770	33.0	1990	Mediterranean, N Europe, S America	Standard
MV CostaAllegra	29,500	Max 806	36.6	1992	Mediterranean, N Europe, S America	Superior
MV CostaClassica	53,000	Max 1,304	40.6	1992	Caribbean, Mediterranean, Transatlantic	Superior

COSTA CRUISES (cont.)

Ships	Tonnage	Passengers	Space Ratio	Built/ Refurbished	Cruise Area	Rating
MV CostaRomantica	53,000	Max 1,346	39.3	1993	Caribbean, Mediterranean, Transatlantic	Superior *Brit's Guide Favourite*
MS CostaVictoria	75,000	Max 1,928	38.9	1996	Caribbean, Mediterranean, Transatlantic	Superior *Brit's Guide Favourite*

Cruise line notes: The takeover of this Italian company by Carnival/ Airtours in 1997 led to much speculation about possible changes in the fleet, although Carnival, now past masters of acquiring lines and making them more profitable, insist it will be business as usual. The Italian nature of their operation is very much part of their style and they attract large numbers of European passengers on their Mediterranean sailings. In fact, Costa can largely sell out their July and August cruises out of Genoa from the Italian market alone (with a high percentage of honeymooners).

The difference between the European and Caribbean sailings is quite marked, though, with the American market providing the bulk of the passengers in the 45-plus age profile in the latter. Unusually, the *CostaClassica* operates a series of sailings out of the French island of Guadeloupe, which adds to their European flavour. On the European routes, the atmosphere and ambience are distinctly Italian, i.e. lively, fun and a little noisy, and Brits sailing aboard need to be open-minded and good

Open-air dining is a typically lively, European affair aboard all Costa ships

Europeans. The style is quite informal, and don't expect the queues to be as nice and orderly as on American or British vessels, either! Costa are also increasing their seven-day product, even to the extent of introducing some seven-day fly-cruises to Northern Europe, and so attracting a younger crowd on those sailings than the 10-day and longer itineraries. Cuisine is typically Italian, too (great for pasta-lovers), while service is friendly without being memorable. Costa has moved away from all-Italian waiter service, which many repeat passengers think is a shame as it loses some of the essential Italian ambience.

 **BRIT TIP**

Unless you are a real fan of all things Italian, Costa's summer sailings are not recommended for Brits as you will be among a small minority of non-Italian speaking passengers. Beware, also, of the rather tedious long announcements in all the different languages on most ships.

Ship notes: There is a distinct difference between the older and newer ships of the fleet, with the older veering towards the more traditional ocean-going liner style, with unusual itineraries, while the newer ones have all the latest in the way of modern facilities and a more up-market feel to attract the American market. The newer ships are invariably more spacious, too, offering bigger standard cabins and with quite an inviting, airy feel to all the public rooms. The interior styling is where they score heavily for the European market as they veer drastically away from the American preference for glitz and concentrate instead on an understated chic that is more relaxing and comfortable, especially for British tastes. The *CostaClassica* and *CostaRomantica* are both fine examples of this bold difference in emphasis (and make them more Brit's Guide Favourites), while the *CostaVictoria* delivers an even greater level of quality while sticking with this style. Indeed, the *Victoria* possibly sets new benchmarks for this contemporary European design, with a four-storey forward observation lounge area, complete with waterfall, a state-of-the-art shopping gallery, an indoor pool and jogging track, a tennis court and a proper wrap-around promenade deck. All the ships, new and old, feature generous amounts of open deck space.

 BRIT TIP

Costa's sailings out of Venice are most popular with the British market, especially in May, June, September and October. Brits make up a good 15 per cent of the passenger profile at these times.

Extras: Costa's early-booking discounts make them extremely attractive as they promise to pass on any late reductions to passengers who take the early option. (BUT – check the cut-off date for this discount in the small print. It doesn't apply across the board.) The line also has its own private island off the coast of the Dominican Republic which makes for a relaxing day's visit on Eastern Caribbean routes, while shore excursions generally are quite sporty and active-minded, as well as being hugely varied on the European routes. The ships feature the extra culinary delight of a 24-hour pizzeria, which goes down especially well with youngsters. Excellent year-round kids' clubs in the Caribbean and Mediterranean, with free baby-sitting for 3- to 6-year-olds on the European routes, too. In the Caribbean, Costa offers couples the chance to renew their wedding vows in a special ship-board ceremony. The five newest ships all feature wheelchair-accessible cabins. *CostaRomantica's* back-to-back seven-day itineraries around the East and West Caribbean are a popular choice with British passengers looking for a two-week cruise.

Average price range: £995–£2,720 on seven-day Caribbean routes, £830–£1,860 in the Med. For their UK office, phone 0171 323 3333.

CRYSTAL CRUISES

Ships	Tonnage	Passengers	Space Ratio	Built/ Refurbished	Cruise Area	Rating
Crystal Harmony	49,400	Max 960	51.4	1990/ 1997	World-wide	Deluxe
Crystal Symphony	50,000	Max 960	52.0	1995	World-wide	Deluxe

Cruise line notes: How do you start to describe arguably the most lavish large-ship experience in the world? It isn't easy as there is so much to recommend on these two ships which have set new standards for the Deluxe end of the market. The small Deluxe ships may do things to a slightly higher degree of service and opulence, but this Japanese-owned and American-marketed line has carved out its own niche in terms of providing big-ship variety and facilities with small-ship quality of service, cuisine and elegance. For large, modern cruise ships they even look classy, which is no mean feat these days. A Crystal cruise is characterised by what they like to call the Crystal Experience, an atmosphere of friendly, personal charm that is never too formal but never too familiar. From the moment you step on board to the last morning, you are looked after with a wonderfully eager-to-please yet efficient manner which befits a line that includes butler service throughout its Penthouse Decks, a high percentage of balconied cabins, two additional restaurants, high-powered guest lecturers and a breathtaking range of quality entertainments, from paddle-tennis tournaments to classical concerts and ballet. It should go without saying the cuisine is on a par with many fine restaurants. Crystal also sets great store by its big-production shows, and they can be very elaborate indeed with costumes worthy of any top West End theatre. Staff are all highly-motivated and extremely personable, daytime activities diverse and extremely sociable and shore excursions wide-ranging and always excellently escorted and presented. Indeed, for the up-scale expense of a Crystal cruise, their excursions are remarkably well-priced and offer some of the best value of any in the cruise world. The passenger profile tends to be 40-plus and children are a rarity (although Crystal does provide children's counsellors on sailings where there are going to be a number of kids), while the style is distinctly formal, with more days at sea than most of the American cruise lines.

Paddle-tennis is a great Crystal favourite

Ship notes: As well as state-of-the-art engines and high-tech navigational equipment, the ships feature a huge range of choice in whatever you want to do aboard. Lounges and bars abound, there are two swimming pools, a proper promenade deck and no less than six alternatives outside the main restaurant for meals and snacks (in addition to free 24-hour room service), including an ice cream bar and a wonderful bistro for mid-morning speciality coffees and pastries. The two small speciality restaurants – Prego and Kyoto on the *Harmony*, and Prego and Jade Garden on *Symphony* – are both extremely popular so it is advisable to book early to get your choice of when to dine there. It should go without saying that both ships are wonderfully spacious, and the public rooms are all done out in individual but elegant fashion. The newer *Symphony* is virtually a sister ship of the *Harmony*, but with even more balconies and enhanced cabin space in the lower grades, a bigger casino and central Plaza, and a much-needed bigger Lido Café, which provides buffet breakfast and lunch, as well as a video games room. Club 2100, the ships' second evening lounge, is a stunner on the *Harmony*, while *Symphony's* outstanding venue is the Starlite Club. Even the standard cabins are quite beautifully appointed and fitted out, with queen-sized beds, proper baths, bathrobes, hair-dryers, personal safes, sitting areas, VCR as well as TV and mini-fridges. Attention to detail everywhere is terrific.

Extras: All this luxury obviously comes at a price, and Crystal cruises are not cheap. But, by taking a basic grade cabin, you could be on to some of the best value anywhere at sea. The Gentlemen Host programme is a much-appreciated touch for ladies travelling alone, while dinner can also be served

 **BRIT TIP**

Both ships feature a full-size paddle-tennis court which is among the best sporting facilities at sea and is a great way to meet some of your fellow passengers

in your cabin, course by course as it would in the restaurant. Indeed, eating breakfast on your own balcony in the morning must be one of life's great extravagances. Both ships are fully-prepared for disabled passengers and possess extensive book and video libraries. In fact, the only flaw in the up-market nature of the Crystal operation is their two-sitting dining policy, which is impossible to get round on a 960-passenger ship. However, the alternative dining options easily counteract that one small defect, and, particularly if you choose the second sitting, you are likely to have a dining experience as exclusive as on any of the smaller ships. The only minor surprise is that tipping is not included in the price as it is with the other Deluxe range lines although this is being included in some 1998 cruises and, say, Crystal across the board by 1999. Call 0171 287 9040 for brochures.

Average price range: £3,200–£10,600 on a 13-night Panama Canal cruise.

CUNARD

Ships	Tonnage	Passengers	Space Ratio	Built/ Refurbished	Cruise Area	Rating
MS *Vistafjord*	23,492	Max 732	33.4	1973/1984	World-wide	Premier *Brit's Guide Favourite*
TSMV *QE2*	70,327	Max 1,500	46.8	1969/1996	World-wide, inc Transatlantic	Superior-Deluxe, *Brit's Guide Favourite*
MS *Royal Viking Sun*	37,845	Max 740	51.1	1988/1993	World-wide	Deluxe
MV *Sea Goddess I*	4,250	Max 116	36.7	1984/1997	Caribbean, Europe	Deluxe
MV *Sea Goddess II*	4,250	Max 116	36.7	1985/1997	Far East, Alaska	Deluxe

Cruise line notes: There has been an enormous amount of press speculation over the future of this famous line since its parent company Trafalgar House was taken over by Norwegian conglomerate Kvaerner in 1996. Ship-builders Kvaerner made it fairly clear they were not keen to run a cruise line business, hence regular rumours of buyouts and sell-offs. Happily, Cunard just carried right on going with its reduced five-ship fleet, rebuilding its image in the Deluxe end of the market and showing an increasingly healthier return in the annual balance sheets. The sale of the *Cunard Countess, Cunard Dynasty* and *Sagafjord* (the latter to Saga) in 1996 left a still varied choice of ships and styles which the company has finally put together in one, well-balanced brochure, making for a more identifiable product. The *Royal Viking Sun* and two *Sea Goddess* ships deal in the most luxurious end of the market, and Cunard are keen to raise their profile in Europe. The beautifully-maintained *Vistafjord* remains something of a secret in the British market, but her classic style and European appeal are also being put more obviously in the shop window. All four ships also serve to destroy the common misconception of Cunard as simply the *QE2*, although the last of the great ocean liners has been up-graded a touch, too, with a reduction in passenger capacity from 1,800 to 1,500 and an extra day on her transatlantic voyages that should make for a more comfortable all-round experience (less speed and therefore smoother sailing and a more hospitable arrival time from the previous 5am touch).

Cunard's Sea Goddess *ships offer an exquisite level of quality and service*

Ship notes: Despite the loss of the lower-grade ships, the fleet still boasts quite a variety of choice. The *Royal Viking Sun* is popular with the North American market in particular for her big-ship luxury, which allows for top-quality service and cuisine, along with some huge cabins, a wide range of ship-board facilites (including the only croquet played at sea), Gentlemen Host programme and world-wide itineraries. Her slowly increasing number of British passengers include many who want more than just the traditional elegance of the *QE2*. *Sea Goddess I* and *II* are the nearest things to owning your own private yacht. There are no non-stop activities, Broadway shows, casinos and deck games, but instead you will find top-drawer individual service and pampering, impeccable cuisine and open-seating dining, a highly social atmosphere and all-inclusive extras like drinks and watersports. Caviar, champagne and other fine wines are available at all times (and it is always Beluga and not the slightly inferior Sevruga caviar here). Their itineraries are some of the most intriguing and exclusive at sea and they attract a

Cunard's QE2 *sailing into New York*

discreet, discerning (not to mention wealthy) client from both Europe and America. The classic liner *Vistafjord* is another one-off vessel in the modern cruise world, featuring beautifully tasteful and original décor throughout (notably in the cabins), unusual itineraries (including South America and the Panama Canal) with longer sea-time, and a notably friendly and relaxed ambience provided by her Scandinavian and German crew. The good old *QE2* is destined to continue providing a source of great cruise tradition for many years yet after more than £45 million was spent on refits in 1994 and 1996. Better bathroom facilities, in-cabin TV, complete with satellite and video channels and the reduction in capacity all serve to keep her up to date, yet aloof from the rest of the cruise world. Her Deluxe range of cabins, too, display a magnificent roominess that goes hand in hand with the subdued elegance of the fittings, while the suites all boast butler service as well. As a result of her traditional heritage, the *QE2* is the last ship still operating a type of class system, with four standards of restaurant (one, the Queen's Grill, having its own exclusive lounge) that reflect the grade of cabin you select (with the most expensive grades getting to dine in the most extravagant of the restaurants). This exclusivity harks back to the days of First, Second and Third Class bookings aboard the same ship, and the modern version is much cherished by those who can afford it. It does leave the ship open to different ratings according to cabin type and where you dine, and the lowest 'class' (consisting of the inside cabins and the two most basic outside categories, whose passengers get to dine in the Mauretania Restaurant) is rather the poor relation of the others, with a distinct difference in the quality of food, too. She is still largely the preserve of Cunard's more elderly passengers, with few young couples and even fewer honeymooners on board, even allowing for the ship's programme of itineraries which varies from as few as two days right up to grand World cruises. She also attracts as many as 50 per cent American customers. She remains, however, almost a museum to the great bygone age of the classic liners, with her labyrinthine corridor network and seemingly endless companionways, huge expanses of open decks, timelessly elegant furnishings and subdued décor – a world apart from the new breed of mega-liner today. She is still effortlessly spacious, has superb sailing characteristics and boasts the two single most spectacular suites at sea, the Queen Mary and Queen Elizabeth, which are both split-level and have their own private deck space as well as conservatories, lounges, walk-in closets and marbled bathrooms. When you win the lottery, this is the way to spend your winnings. Ultimately, a *QE2* cruise is as much an experience in British heritage as it is a sea voyage.

 BRIT TIP

For those who find the glitz and glitter of the new breed of mega-liner just too ghastly, the *QE2* is the perfect answer. She is also well-suited to first-timers on her short-range cruises of three to six days.

Extras: Gentlemen Hosts are available on the *QE2*, *Vistafjord* and *Royal Viking Sun*, and the World cruises are still a feature of the *QE2* and *Sun*. The varied itineraries mean you can cruise virtually anywhere in the world under the Cunard banner. The *QE2* also possesses a massive range of health facilities and spa treatments, along with the only Harrods at sea. Singles might find the *Sea Goddess* vessels a bit restrictive as they are geared primarily towards couples, and unlike all the other Cunard ships, there are no wheelchair provisions.

Average price range: From £2,970 on a 14-night *Vistafjord* Med cruise, £15,150 on *Royal Viking Sun's* 61-night South American Discovery, £4,170 aboard *Sea Goddess* for a week in the Med, £1,470 transatlantic on *QE2*, up to £195,450 for the World Cruise in one of those exclusive suites!

DISNEY CRUISE LINE

Ships	Tonnage	Passengers	Space Ratio	Built	Cruise Area	Rating
MS *Disney Magic*	85,000	Max 2,400	35.4	1998	Bahamas	Premier (expected)
MS *Disney Wonder*	85,000	Max 2,400	35.4	1998	Bahamas	Premier (expected)

Cruise line notes: The arrival of the Walt Disney company on the cruise scene is possibly THE shipping event of 1998, with enough advance publicity to warrant a book on its own. Certainly, my knowledge of the company (I also write *A Brit's Guide to Orlando and Walt Disney World*) leads me to suggest their ships will be unrivalled for fun, family-style activities for both children and adults, in a sophisticated, ultra-imaginative environment. There is a distinct aura of magic, what the company likes to call Pixie Dust, about their theme parks, and they aim to translate this lock, stock and barrel on to their first two cruise ships (there are already hints of more ships to come). They aim to bring their renowned levels of quality and service, plus a new level of all original entertainment, to an already well-endowed industry, but stress that they do not intend to be simply a floating theme park. To this end, Disney Cruise Line will cater directly both to the family market and adults without children, setting aside adults-only areas of the ships as well as having the most extensive kids' facilities of any vessel to date. The cruise experience will also be primarily a short one, with voyages of only three or four days from their dedicated new terminal at Port Canaveral to the Bahamas and back. Their cruises can be taken ONLY in conjunction with a Walt Disney World stay, too, meaning packages are on a week's basis (although longer stays can be arranged through individual tour operators – see below) with the cruise element only half of it. Walt Disney World is not generally a cheap place to stay, hence the cruises shape up slightly on the expensive side to my mind, but the quality should be unimpeachable. I fully expect

© Disney

The lobby of Disney Magic, *the new ship from Disney Cruise Line*

Disney to slot into the Premier ship category, therefore, rather than the Superior level of many of their obvious competitors, although this is subject to review.

Ship notes: *Disney Magic* comes out of the Fincantieri shipyard in Italy ready to sail for the first time in March 1998, with *Disney Wonder* due to join her in December. Their twin-funnel appearance and classic styling are geared towards reviving notions of cruising's Golden Age, but the identical sisters will also be full of Disney gadgetry and 'imagineering' (the company's builders, architects and ideas men are all called 'imagineers') which have to be experienced to be fully appreciated. The basic facilities are, however, quite awesome to contemplate: three themed dining rooms (guests dine at each one in turn); a deck devoted purely to kids' activities; a 270-seat cinema; both adults' and kids' pools (the latter with the inevitable water slide); a 1,040-seat formal theatre showcasing Broadway shows and Disney classics; an evening entertainment zone called Beat Street, featuring a live rock 'n' roll bar and disco, a comedy club and a romantically-themed lounge; an interactive Sports Club located in the forward of the two funnels; and a massive fitness spa and beauty salon offering the latest in gym technology and health pampering. Add in some generous-sized cabins, 75 per cent with outside views and 44 per cent with balconies, a grand, three-storey atrium lobby, a veritable shopping mall (5,500 square feet, one of the largest at sea) and the guaranteed Disney service with a smile, and some people may not want to get off.

 BRIT TIP

Disney's cruise programme has obviously yet to be fully evaluated and so does not feature in the Brit Awards this year, but I fully expect them to be strong contenders in the Best Family Ship category next time.

Extras: Both Orlando International Airport and Port Canaveral will have Disney-dedicated operations designed to make transfers, embarkation, etc. seamlessly smooth. The cruises will call at Nassau in the Bahamas and Disney's own private island, Castaway Cay, which will feature more impressive development along a tropical paradise theme, again with family and adults-only areas. Both ships will have self-service launderettes, free pushchair hire, conference facilities and a high crew-to-passenger ratio, with the largest number of children's counsellors of any ship at sea. There is also, of course, the chance to enjoy Walt Disney World itself and the dazzling attractions of neighbouring Orlando. You can book Disney Cruise Line holidays only through their approved tour operator partners, who are Virgin Holidays, Bridge Travel (the only operator with a fully-dedicated Disney cruise brochure), British Airways Holidays, Unijet, Jetsave, Thomas Cook Holidays, First Choice, Kuoni, Destination USA and Transolar.

Average price range: £818–£1,428 on a week's cruise-and-stay package.

DOLPHIN

Ships	Tonnage	Passengers	Space Ratio	Built/ Refurbished	Cruise Area	Rating
SS OceanBreeze	21,486	Max 776	27.6	1955/1992	Caribbean, Bahamas	Standard
SS SeaBreeze	21,900	Max 842	26.0	1958/1991	Caribbean	Standard
TSS IslandBreeze	38,175	Max 1,383	27.6	1962/1978	Caribbean	Standard

Cruise line notes: This Greek-American operation specialises in three- and four-day Bahamas cruises out of Miami, and budget-priced alternating seven-day East and West Caribbean itineraries over the well tried and trusted routes. Now owned and run by Cruise Holdings, a company that specialises in getting the most out of older ships (CH also owns Seawind and Premier Cruise Lines). There is nothing fancy about their operation, although their kids' programmes with cartoon characters from the Hanna-Barbera stable offer some nice touches and are well received by mums and dads as well as the youngsters themselves. The shorter-length cruises can be quite hectic, but there is plenty to do for the more active cruisers, especially with snorkelling and scuba-diving programmes. It offers friendly, relaxed and informal cruising on a trio of refurbished old-style liners. Dolphin brochures should be available through most travel agents, but their main sales point in Britain is Victoria Travel Service's Cruise Collection, tel. 0121 445 1010.

Ship notes: Neither of the two smaller vessels can claim much in the way of sophistication and they are both quite high density when full, with open deck space at a premium. Daily activities and entertainments are rather identikit and repetitive, but service is surprisingly keen and friendly for such a budget operation and the food is hearty and plentiful with reasonable drink prices. As you would expect from older ships, cabins come in all shapes and sizes, some even fitting families of five (at a squeeze) and cupboard space is pretty good. The public rooms are typically glitzy and a little garish but well maintained, while *OceanBreeze* sports a particularly smart, two-level casino. The *IslandBreeze* (formerly the *Festivale* and before that the SA *Vaal* which was my first cruise ship in 1969) has been chartered from Carnival and on to Thomson year-round, alternating in the Med and Caribbean, with a great degree of success after a generous 1997 refit. A classic ocean liner retaining many of her original fittings, she remains a lively customer and offers some of the most spacious cabins in the Standard market.

Extras: *SeaBreeze* is blessed with a proper promenade deck, while all three ships offer Dolphin's popular 'Weddings on Board' service before sailing and themed music cruises along the lines of Country and Western, Jazz and the

'50s. *OceanBreeze* calls in at the company's private island on its three-day voyages. None of the trio is suitable for disabled passengers.

Average price range: £999–£1,949 for a nine-night Caribbean fly-cruise.

FESTIVAL

Ships	Tonnage	Passengers	Space Ratio	Built/ Refurbished	Cruise area	Rating
MS *Bolero*	15,781	Max 900	17.5	1968/1995	Mediterranean, Canaries, Caribbean	Standard
MV *Azur*	15,000	Max 770	19.6	1971/1994	Mediterranean, Canaries, Red Sea	Standard
MV *Flamenco*	17,270	Max 980	17.6	1972/1995	Mediterranean, N Europe, Caribbean	Standard

Cruise line notes: Festival are relatively new on the Mediterranean scene and added their second ship the *Bolero* (formerly NCL's *Starward*) only in 1996 with a third, *Flamenco* (formerly *Southern Cross*), a year later and rumours of a fourth soon. The ambience is Mediterranean once again, but both ships are already attracting a high percentage of British passengers with their keenly-priced operation, offering a good-value product, friendly service and plenty of well-organised activities. Cruise style on board is fairly informal and there are some imaginative itineraries on both ships, including many of the Greek islands and the Corinth Canal. Courteous staff help to mask the general lack of finesse which is especially revealed when these high-density ships are full, but food is surprisingly good and plentiful (there's even a post-midnight buffet snack). Festival use six regional UK airports for their linking flights to Venice and Genoa and offer some enticing add-on packages in Corfu, Crete, Rhodes and Kusadasi. Their brochure gets better year by year, and they DO list their shore excursions, which is a bonus (more cruise lines should follow this example). Most itineraries are quite port-intensive, so there are few at-sea days. The daily programmes are geared mainly towards active couples, although there is a children's playroom on the *Azur* and *Flamenco*.

 BRIT TIP

The often-overlooked Topsiders bar on *Bolero* is a lovely quiet retreat for a cocktail or two before dinner.

Ship notes: Both *Azur* and *Bolero* are quite smart and stylish in appearance and will appeal to young, first-time cruisers as very different from what they might believe the cruise experience to be like. The constant multi-language announcements are a bit tedious, but the ships are well maintained and the décor is quite bright and stylish, if a little plain in the cabins. Cabins on *Bolero* are only adequate for two in many cases and a real squeeze where they take three or four, but two cabins are now adapted for disabled passengers. The *Bolero's* Windows on the Sea restaurant offers some lovely views out from the stern of the ship. *Flamenco* was due for a £3m refurbishment before she sailed under Festival colours, which was a touch overdue when she was under CTC ownership. She still boasts a good range of facilities (although, as in the other two, a decent gym isn't among them) and continues to be popular with the British market.

One of the two pools on Bolero

Extras: The prices, the prices and the prices! Festival were good value in 1997 and have continued to build on that with better child-pricing (the reduced rate for kids sharing with their parents now covers up to 17-year-olds) and a new category called Fortuna which offers a reduced rate for cabins assigned only when you board. There are also big savings on back-to-back cruises. For their UK office, phone 0171 436 0827.

Average price range: £599–£1,495 for a week's Mediterranean cruise.

HEBRIDEAN ISLAND CRUISES

Ships	Tonnage	Passengers	Space Ratio	Built/ Refurbished	Cruise Area	Rating
MV Hebridean Princess	2,112	Max 55	38.4	1964/1989	Scotland, Ireland, Norway	Premier, *Brit's Guide Favourite*

Cruise line notes: This all-British operation is a real gem for lovers of the outdoor life with plenty of comfort. Cruise the Scottish coastal waterways, cross over the Irish Sea to visit Cork and Kerry or take a trip north east to view some of the splendid fjords around Bergen in Norway. That's about as exciting as it gets, but this is the cruise experience for people who have been there, done that and bought copious numbers of T-shirts. Relax, enjoy the wonderful social ambience and be carried away into a world that is several light years removed from the normal hustle and bustle. Specialist guides accompany all cruises and give informal talks and lectures.

Ship notes: Not so much a cruise ship as an elegant, floating country hotel that delivers a charming level of service as you travel through and around some breathtaking scenery. It is the luxury of your own private yacht, the quaint atmosphere of a nineteenth-century inn and the sheer beauty of real quality décor and furnishings. The experience is mainly about the places you cruise, getting well off the beaten track and stopping to visit some splendidly remote town or village, but there are also a few on-board facilities like a mini-gym, deck quoits, clay pigeon shooting and an excellent library, while the use of the ship's bikes, speedboats and fishing gear is included. Every cabin, including several especially for singles, is individually designed in best Laura Ashley style to provide a luxurious level of fixtures (down to gold bathroom fittings in some instances) and the service is equally high class. The Tiree Lounge, complete with a real stone fireplace, has to be one of the most sumptuous public rooms of any ship at sea. The bar also carries (as you'd expect) a magnificent range of whiskies.

 BRIT TIP

Don't forget this is Scotland and the Northern Isles we are talking about. Take plenty of warm clothing (it is an outdoor experience) and waterproofs for the inevitable liquid sunshine that highlights Scottish summers!

Extras: All your entrance fees at places of interest along the way are included, and the ship usually anchors in some sheltered inlet at night so you are unlikely to miss much of the scenery. At prices like these, your drinks ought to be included as well, though, and it can cost as much as £165 to get to and from Oban to pick up the ship on top of your cruise fare. But ultimately it is the sheer uniqueness and exclusivity of the package that is the essence of the appeal, and that is hard to put a price on. It should go without saying that this is not a cruise for children, and there is no provision for the disabled. For a brochure, call 01756 701338.

 BRIT TIP

The Columba Restaurant can accommodate all 55 passengers in one sitting and boasts fresh, local produce served with great style.

Average price range: From £675 for a six-night Highland Escape cruise to £9,975 on the 14-night designated Cruise of the Year.

HOLLAND AMERICA LINE

Ships	Tonnage	Passengers	Space Ratio	Built/ Refurbished	Cruise Area	Rating
MS Nieuw Amsterdam	33,930	Max 1,350	25.1	1983	Caribbean, Alaska	Premier
MS Noordam	33,930	Max 1,350	25.1	1984	Caribbean, Alaska	Premier
MS Westerdam	53,872	Max 1,733	30.3	1986/1990	Caribbean, Alaska	Premier
MS Statendam	55,451	Max 1,627	34.0	1993	Caribbean, Alaska	Premier
MS Maasdam	55,451	Max 1,627	34.0	1993	Caribbean, Europe	Premier
MS Ryndam	55,451	Max 1,627	34.0	1994	Caribbean, Alaska	Premier
MS Veendam	55,451	Max 1,627	34.0	1996	Caribbean, E Coast USA and Canada	Premier
MS Rotterdam VI	62,000	Max 1,320	46.9	1997	Caribbean, Alaska	Premier

Cruise line notes: This originally Dutch line can give P&O and Cunard a run for their money in the longevity stakes since Holland America has been carrying passengers since 1871, and even its 1989 acquisition by the ever-increasing Carnival Corporation failed to alter their chosen commitment to 'A Tradition of Excellence'. Even allowing for their recent ships being some of the most modern in the world, HAL remain as one of the dwindling band of traditional cruise exponents and tend to attract a more knowledgeable, mature passenger, primarily American, but with a growing following in Europe. They are even starting to attract a slightly younger crowd, couples in their 30s on some of their Caribbean and European routes, but one of their undoubted strengths is the Alaskan routes they offer with great precision and style, and these still attract an older clientèle. HAL's attention to detail and polished style more than make up for food that doesn't quite live up to its Premier rating (with the exception of some spectacular buffets), while their activities are increasingly varied and lively and the range of entertainment is good if not startling. Service is a HAL watchword – it tends to be formal but personal, efficient but relaxed, helping to create that refined, elegant atmosphere that was the key to the cruising of yesteryear. Décor tends to be a little garish in places as for some reason the interior designers are keen on lots of oranges and reds, but otherwise they manage contemporary design with a more cultured appearance (although some call it a bit bland). While they have been something of a well-kept secret in Europe, that promises to change over the next couple of years as a result of the Carnival Corporation's new links with Airtours, who have already produced their first British-dedicated HAL brochure.

Alaskan scenery is a Holland America speciality

Ship notes: Just about the only thing you won't find aboard a HAL cruise ship is extensive kids' facilities, but even this detail is changing (see Extras). Otherwise, they have got the lot, including some of the best fitness facilities at sea, great deck sports, two large pools – one covered by a sliding glass roof – multi-storey atriums, fountains and elaborate showlounges. The newest ships are clearly striving to attract a younger clientèle while still appealing to their traditional passengers, and it isn't at all a bad compromise. Entertainment varies from high-energy stage shows to classical concerts, and the public rooms are never less than elegant and occasionally, in the case of the trademark piano bars, real romantic little hideaways. HAL also score heavily with their cabins, which offer a level of spaciousness way beyond most expectations, even among the lower grades. Once again the message is to choose the lowest grade possible for the best value, although the high proportion of cabins with balconies (not on *Westerdam*) is also quite tempting and they are all complemented by some extremely smart fittings and furnishings. Another HAL trademark is the use of millions of dollars-worth of antiques throughout their ships, providing additional focal points. Brilliant passenger flow is aided by the clever use of lots of smaller rooms to break the ship up well, although the split-level dining room, complete with grand staircase and musicians' gallery, goes against this trend and is equally impressive. The new *Rotterdam VI* takes HAL's traditional appeal in the modern idiom to a new level. A real one-off, she eschews the formula style inherent in many new builds and delivers a classic experience, with more use of woods and darker colours for that true liner feel. However, she is still bang up to date in her choice and range of facilities, which include the first dedicated children's playroom on a HAL ship and a two-tier showlounge.

Extras: New in 1998 is Half Moon Cay in the Bahamas, HAL's own private island, with a shopping plaza, food pavilion, white sand beach and an array of water sports on offer. Classic afternoon tea is given a Dutch twist at least once every voyage, while top-of-the-range suites all feature an in-cabin dining alternative. HAL's Dutch officers and Filipino crew make for a warm and friendly service combination. The company's shore excursions in Alaska are some of the best in the market due to their long-standing expertise in this area. Check out the top level observation lounge on each ship – always called the Crow's Nest – for a wonderful place to sip cocktails. Good provision for disabled passengers, especially with the generous-width wheelchair-friendly cabins. HAL is making a big effort to win over 'junior cruisers' with a dramatically enhanced activity programme for children, Club HAL, aboard its Caribbean and even Alaska sailings. A full-time youth co-ordinator is on every ship, with assistants to maintain a ratio of one adult to every 30 children, and their Alaskan programme will even offer special shore excursions for 6- to 12-year-olds and teenagers. For Holland America's UK office, ring 0171 613 3300.

 BRIT TIP

The 'No tips required' policy should be a bonus, but most American passengers still tip their waiters and stewards at the end of the cruise, so beware the all-inclusive tag on this count unless you are happy to be the odd one out. Annoyingly, tipping guidelines are not given out.

Average price range: £1,585–£4,355 on a 12-day Caribbean voyage; £1,790–£4,080 on a nine-day Alaska.

LOUIS CRUISE LINES

Ship	Tonnage	Passengers	Space Ratio	Built/ Refurbished	Cruise Area	Rating
MV *Princesa Victoria*	14,538	750	19.4	1936/ 1993	Eastern Mediterranean	Standard
MTS *Princesa Amorosa*	5,026	354	14.1	1957/ 1990	Eastern Mediterranean	Standard
MV *Princesa Marissa*	10,487	853	12.3	1966/ 1995	Eastern Mediterranean	Standard
MV *Princesa Cypria*	9,984	733	13.6	1968/ 1990	Eastern Mediterranean	Standard

Cruise line notes: This Greek-Cypriot line has proved popular with the British holiday market on Cyprus and has now opened up a fully-fledged London office in a bid to raise their profile outside the island and encourage more direct bookings from the UK. Their stock-in-trade is a two- or three-day tour to Egypt and the Holy Land, where the transport is largely incidental to the itineraries. The ships are all ageing liners, and are pretty crowded when full, functional rather than remarkable, but, at the prices they charge, a lot can be overlooked. Also on the plus side, the food is good and plentiful and you are not likely to spend too long on board with their port-intensive schedules. You can choose from two-day trips to Egypt or Israel, three-day Egypt-Israel combinations, five-day Greek island adventures (mainly for the local Cypriot market) or a seven-day Greek islands cruise, which again represents good value. The passenger profile is likely to be a fair European mix, with a good percentage of Brits, hence the irritation of public announcements in several different languages. Evening entertainment is limited to non-language-specific acts and the staff are eager to please without having any great finesse.

Ship notes: While all four ships are approaching their sell-by date, Louis maintain them well and they are ideally suited to the short runs they do, although the *Princesa Amorosa* is a touch spartan for a full week's cruise. The *Marissa* possesses a few cabins

The Louis line *Princesa Victoria*

without private facilities, which is unusual these days, and there is not a great range of facilities, as is common with the modern style ships. *Cypria* is geared up more for the five-day local market, while the venerable *Victoria* remains a minor classic of old-world style, with generous open deck space and some larger-than-average cabins.

Extras: At these prices it is churlish to quibble about the relative lack of facilities aboard Louis vessels (the two ships chartered to Thomson Holidays, the *Emerald* and *Sapphire* are a different story), especially as their main focus is providing an excellent value trip to the sights of Israel (with all-inclusive tours to Jerusalem) and Egypt (all-inclusive tours to Cairo and the Pyramids of Giza). They also have a flair for the friendly if you are a fan of Greek hospitality. In the UK, phone 0171 383 2882.

Average price range: £94–£209 on a two-day cruise to the Holy Land, £158–£278 on a three-day Egypt-Israel combination.

MEDITERRANEAN SHIPPING CRUISES

Ship	Tonnage	Passengers	Space Ratio	Built/ Refurbished	Cruise Area	Rating
TS *Symphony*	16,495	Max 845	19.5	1951/1996	South Africa	Standard
SS *Monterey*	21,051	Max 638	32.9	1952/1988	Mediterranean, Canaries, South Africa	Standard
MV *Rhapsody*	17,495	Max 959	18.1	1977/1996	Mediterranean, South America, Transatlantic	Standard
MV *Melody*	36,500	Max 1,600	22.8	1982/1997	Mediterranean, Caribbean, Transatlantic	Standard

Cruise line notes: This wholly Italian company, formerly StarLauro until a name change in 1995 to link up with their larger parent company, is proving ever more popular in the British market for its combination of traditional cruise ship style with modern appeal at a budget price. MSC has only recently become a four-ship operation yet already they are in the market for ship number five, which gives some idea of their rapid evolution. The majority of passengers on board (around 65 per cent) are Italian and the age range tends to be not much more than 40–45, making for a boisterous and lively cruise profile, but there are rarely less than 50 Brits aboard and up to 100 on most sailings. This does make for the bugbear of constant lengthy multi-lingual

Enjoy a drink at the pool-side aboard Monterey

announcements and the entertainment has to be of more universal appeal (i.e. jugglers, singers and dancers) than on British- or American-dominated cruises, but the whole style of the cruise is genuinely friendly and warm, with lashings of Italian verve (not least in the food, with great pasta in particular) and service. It's broad-based, cosmopolitan and informal, and your waiter is likely to join in the dinner table conversation along with the guests. It is a style that goes down well with seasoned travellers and repeat cruisers and anyone devoted to Italian holidays generally. Like Costa, mid-July through to the end of August is MSC's peak European period, and the number of Brits aboard drops off.

 **BRIT TIP**

In typical Italian fashion, MSC ships make much more of meal-times, particularly dinner, than their American counterparts. There is no hustle to get first-sitting diners out, and so there is more emphasis here on the service, food and ambience than on the typical evening showtimes.

Ship notes: *Monterey* and *Symphony* are both classic ocean liners that have been given a thorough modern overhaul to provide facilities such as fitness centres, jacuzzis, nightclubs and beauty salons. They sail well (in keeping with all ships of their vintage), and the cabin varieties tend to be less uniform and more individualistic, compact but comfortable (although *Monterey* possesses some extremely spacious suites). They also feature excellent prom decks and boast plenty of open deck space (a feature they are keen to highlight for the British market), and there are some lovely authentic touches with the décor, like wood panelling and brass railings, that hark back to their original lives. *Rhapsody* is more of a purpose-built modern cruiser, and her 1970s build means cabins tend to be a bit more cramped and not so well insulated, but she still has a good amount of deck space for the sun-worshippers and some outstanding public rooms, like the Top Sail Lounge and indoor-outdoor 8 Bells Nightclub. *Monterey*'s split-level dining room, with original engraved glass from its early days, is another eye-catcher. Newcomer *Melody* (formerly the *Star/Ship Atlantic* of Premier) is another of the more recent build of cruise ship that started to provide more spacious cabins and be more generous with deck space, so she should suit MSC admirably. She also has MSC's first children's programme and is a good prospect for families.

Extras: The on-board currency is the lire (although, like all other lines, you just sign for drinks and other purchases as you go along), so you may want to take a calculator along to work out how much money you are really spending! None of the ships have any disabled passenger facilities. *Rhapsody* and *Melody* will offer two attractive transatlantic re-positioning cruises in autumn and spring, with *Melody* going on to a series of 11-night Caribbean sailings out of Fort Lauderdale that offer some more innovative itineraries plus the option of a completely European cruise atmosphere.

Average price range: £570–£1,430 on a seven-night Mediterranean cruise, £1,770–£3,860 on 14-night cruises. In the UK, phone 0171 637 2525.

NORWEGIAN CRUISE LINE

Ships	Tonnage	Passengers	Space Ratio	Built/ Refurbished	Cruise Area	Rating
SS *Norway*	76,049	Max 2,370	32.8	1962/1980	Caribbean, Med, N Europe	Superior, **Brit's Guide Favourite**
Norwegian Star	28,018	Max 765	36.6	1973/1991	Caribbean (out of Houston)	Superior
Leeward	25,000	Max 1,150	21.7	1980/1995	Caribbean,	Superior
Norwegian Sea	42,276	Max 1,798	23.5	1988	Caribbean	Superior **Brit's Guide Favourite**
Norwegian Crown	34,250	Max 1,221	28.0	1988	Bermuda, Canada, S America	Superior
Dreamward	39,217	Max 1,450	28.2	1992	Caribbean, Mediterranean, N Europe	Superior
Norwegian Majesty	32,396	Max 1,501	21.5	1992	Bermuda	Superior
Norwegian Dynasty	19,089	Max 800	23.8	1993	Alaska, Hawaii, Panama Canal	Superior
Windward	39,217	Max 1,450	28.2	1993	Caribbean, Alaska	Superior

Cruise line notes: The pioneers of one-class, Caribbean fly-cruising, NCL have suffered at the hands of their competition through the early 1990s to the extent that the line's future was in doubt under mounting debt at the end of 1995. However, thanks to a company restructuring, they remain one of the key players in the Caribbean business and deliver an extremely well-organised and consistent product. They have also announced their intention of getting back among the front-runners by acquiring the lovely *Royal Majesty* and ex-Cunard ship *Crown Dynasty* (now the *Norwegian Majesty* and *Dynasty* respectively), announcing a new build for 1999 and taking over Costa's abandoned *Olympia* project from the German shipyard where she is still just a hull. The *Windward* and *Dreamward* will undergo a shipyard 'stretch' in 1998 to add extra capacity, and they will be re-named the *Norwegian Wind* and *Dream*. As befits pioneers in their field, they still deliver some imaginative touches, like their alternative Le Bistro dining (at no extra cost), weekly Chocoholics Buffet (watch the Americans pile into THIS one), Dive In snorkelling programme, themed sports cruises (especially for American football lovers), Sports Bars and non-smoking cabins. They attract a younger, livelier crowd without going as far as Carnival's rather raucous image and have an excellent, well-supervised children's programme on all ships. NCL maintain a small element of formality while enjoying several themed, casual evenings per cruise, and their Caribbean staff can be a real delight, especially with the Brits they meet. The cuisine is typical American cruise ship fare, i.e. stylish, eye-catching but a bit bland to the taste, but there is always plenty of it. Entertainment, both day and night, is plentiful, high energy and well-organised, as are the shore excursions, and the big showtimes are both ambitious and eye-catching.

 BRIT TIP

Being situated over the stern, the Terraces restaurants on *Dreamward* and *Windward* experience a bit of vibration that is a little off-putting for first-timers. Opt for the Four Seasons or even the Sun Terrace restaurant, given the choice.

Ship notes: Quite a varied and growing fleet offers a good mix of possibilities, especially for first-timers. The classic liner *Norway*, formerly the magnificent SS *France*, was the largest cruise ship at sea until the *Sun Princess* arrived on the scene, and is still a real treat for proper ship lovers, even if she is showing her age in places. The cabin decks are a positive maze of corridors and it is easy to walk for miles before you get your bearings. Her sheer size (she remains the LONGEST cruise ship still sailing) gives rise to a huge range of public rooms of all shapes and sizes, while cabin space is particularly generous, even among the lower grades. The fixtures and fittings could be better in a few places, notably some of the companionway carpeting and the soft furnishings of the Junior Suites, but there are worthwhile extras with the *Norway* that few other ships can match, like the huge Roman spa centre, the wide, enclosed promenade down International Deck, the classic Club Internationale with its stylish, period décor and the elegant Windward dining room, plus the all-round atmosphere of being on a throwback to the days of true cruise elegance. The *Leeward* is NCL's short-haul, high-density specialist, offering three- and four-day cruises to the Bahamas and Mexico. Cabins can be pretty small (she was originally built as a Scandinavian ferry), but the fixtures and fittings are all quite contemporary and smart and all the typical NCL features are aboard. The nice wooden prom deck offsets the shortage of sunning space when the ship is full, while the upper deck Observatory

Lounge is eye-catching and the Stardust showlounge has quite an intimate feel to it. Sister ships *Dreamward* and *Windward* are the jewels in the NCL fleet, a pair of bright, innovative, medium-size cruisers that have an above-average feel for the Superior market. While some of the décor is a bit bland, the ships both have a warm, friendly ambience that perfectly suits their cruise style. Both inside and outside cabins are reasonably spacious (although a bit short of drawer and cupboard room, and the shower-bathrooms are tiny), the outside decks are very attractive, especially with the tiered stern, and they maintain a pleasant, small-ship feel while providing all the amenities of something bigger.

Dreams are made of this – NCL's Dreamward

Seaward again succeeds in creating this more intimate ambience at the same time as providing big-ship style, although she makes more pretence at being outwardly glamorous. Her standard range cabins could do with being a bit bigger for a seven-day cruise, especially for cupboard space, but the finish is never less than smart. She is quite novel in the American market for possessing a full, wrap-around promenade deck, and there is also an impressive range of public rooms, from the small, intimate Oscar's piano bar to the impressive, large-scale Cabaret showlounge, and there is a surprisingly spacious pool and sun deck. Again, she offers a good product for first-timers, which is where NCL aims much of its marketing.

The newest additions to the NCL fleet all help to boost the line's appeal as well as capacity, with the two former Royal Cruise Line ships *Crown Odyssey* and *Royal Odyssey* (now renamed *Norwegian Crown* and *Star*) adding an extra touch of class. *Star* is also being used as a trail blazer with her re-positioning for a series of year-round cruises out of Houston in Texas to the Western Caribbean, Mexico and Costa Rica. *Crown* offers extra space in her cabins (almost 80 per cent of which are outside) and some truly opulent suites, as well as elegant public rooms that feature good use of marble, brass and wood. *Norwegian Majesty* is quite a chic, refreshing alternative to the bland, identikit ships, with outstanding features like the outdoor Piazza San Marco, serving pizza, ribs and ice cream, surprisingly spacious cabins and good attention to

 BRIT TIP

There is little real distinction in *Majesty's* main grades of cabin (with the exception of the few suites), so the lower grades are by far the best value.

detail. The provision of open deck space could be better, though (American ships, you see). *Norwegian Dynasty* also offers some rather more thoughtful internal design and styling than many of her American counterparts as a result of her Cunard influences, with an impressive atrium foyer that doesn't try to be *too* impressive. The cabins could be better off for cupboard space, however. She should continue to appeal to the British market as an alternative to the much larger ships in this class, too.

 **BRIT TIP**

Watch out for a rare summer season of European sailings in 1998 with the *Norway* for the chance to experience this unique vessel which remains a throwback to cruising's traditional era.

Extras: NCL offers an especially good product for younger singles, with a Guaranteed Singles Rate, and promises to keep everyone busy and involved if they want to be. Families will also enjoy being aboard, with the different Kids' Crew programmes for 3- to 17-year olds. NCL runs golf clinics in Bermuda and Barbados and an excellent range of shore excursions in Alaska. All the ships offer cabins for the disabled, although the *Norway* is not well equipped for wheelchair users otherwise. In addition to their many other innovations, NCL was the first line to develop the 'private island' port of call, with the uninhabited tropical island of Great Stirrup Cay in the Bahamas being acquired to provide passengers sailing out of Miami and Fort Lauderdale with their own paradise beach retreat. Six beaches, two bars, a barbecue buffet, water sports, volleyball and table-tennis are all laid on and add an extra dimension to any cruise. For brochures, call 0800 525483.

Average price range: £465–£945 on three-night cruises, £1,265–£3,345 on a nine-night Caribbean holiday with seven-night cruise.

FRED OLSEN

Ships	Tonnage	Passengers	Space Ratio	Built/ Refurbished	Cruise Area	Rating
MS *Black Prince*	11,209	Max 517	21.6	1966/1987	Mediterranean, Canaries, N Europe, S America, Caribbean	Standard ***Brit's Guide Favourite***
MS *Black Watch*	28,492	Max 920	30.9	1972/1996	Mediterranean, N Europe, Far East, Caribbean	Superior ***Brit's Guide Favourite***

Cruise line notes: In many ways, Fred Olsen's *Black Prince* is the epitome of traditional British cruising, with a strong and loyal following attracted to its no-frills, sensibly-priced, year-round consistent quality and its intelligent programme of well-designed itineraries. They are one of the prime movers in ex-UK cruising and, to a large extent, pioneered the way for the provision of ambitious new cruise facilities at Dover, which offer an attractive new gateway to the cruise world. The line sails far and wide to give its predominantly 50-plus age group great value for money in a consistently smart, clean and relatively sophisticated environment. The addition in late 1996 of the *Black Watch*, effectively more than doubling Olsen's capacity, has given the line a new dimension with a much bigger-scale, modern product and they have done a fine job in adapting her for the British market (she was a typically American product for Royal Cruise Line) after a few teething troubles. With the advantages of sailing out of a British port, Olsen passengers begin their holiday as soon as they reach Dover (although there are now a handful of fly-cruises after the introduction of the *Black Watch*), and the line makes sure everyone is made to feel welcome and part of the family from the outset. It provides quite a formal atmos-

Black Prince *with Ibiza town as the backdrop*

phere on the whole, accentuated by the old-fashioned charm of the décor and the informative port lectures and other talks. Cuisine is good and consistent without being spectacular and service is never less than friendly. On-board entertainment tends towards the homely, with bingo, singalongs, gardening lectures and dance classes complementing the more predictable cabaret evenings, which include old-time music hall acts. The entertainment staff have to be quite versatile to handle a number of different activities and on the whole they do a remarkable job. Like only a handful of her fellow ex-UK operators (P&O and Swan Hellenic being the others), on-board currency is sterling for a change and drinks charges are more modest British pub prices.

 **BRIT TIP**

The brochure makes choosing your grade of cabin rather confusing for newcomers. There are no less than 14 categories on *Black Prince*, but the best value are the E grade of the outside two-berths, H grade of the inner two-berths and the few B grade family cabins which are the only ones on board with double beds.

Ship notes: The *Black Prince* has an almost yacht-like feel to her and the small-ship ambience is complemented by the intimate atmosphere of most of the public rooms, even the two-tiered Neptune showlounge. She also possesses some quite upmarket touches, like a new fitness centre, complete with indoor pool and solarium, non-smoking restaurants and a remarkable outdoor marina centre which swings into action off the stern and port side in calm waters, offering an enclosed pool in the sea for swimming, and the chance to waterski, windsurf and sail from its teak decks. Typically with a ship of this vintage, there is a vast range of cabin types, including a surprisingly high number of singles. They are generally quite spacious (although not when the fold-down beds are in place in the cabins where the second berth is of this type) with pleasant fittings and furnishings, including TV and hairdryers, but cupboard space varies from generous (E and A grades and the Junior Suites) to miniscule (F and H and the majority of Lido Deck cabins) and the bathrooms (shower-rooms in most cases) are tiny and far from high-spec. Pleasingly, though, they all have (admittedly rather small) portholes instead of the windows which are now so popular on modern ships, and these add the proper nautical flavour to your cabin.

There are four cabins classed as Suites, but for the extra price they don't seem worth the addition of a bit more space, a fridge, settee, half-tub bath, picture window and some smart dark wood panelling. Outstanding public rooms are the elegant Aquitaine Lounge and the upper level of the showlounge, the Lido Lounge, which has a pleasant conservatory atmosphere. Outside, the pool deck has a neat wooden terrace arrangement surrounding it, but the sunning space is quite limited and the stairs are quite steep for elderly passengers (although there are lifts to all decks). The new Balblom Restaurant offers indoor/outdoor buffet dining with excellent all-round sea views. The addition of the *Black Watch* to the line is a fascinating development as she previously cruised for the now defunct Royal Cruise Line as the Premier-rated *Star Odyssey* and represents a step up in class rating as well as size for Fred Olsen. She features larger than average cabins (all with hairdryers and TV as standard), some generous suites (choose the Marquee rather than Premier Suites for better value), and an excellent range of public rooms, right down to the alternative brasserie-type restaurant, the Garden Café, which offers evening dining without the formality. Good open deck is complemented by the top-level Observatory lounge, complete with binoculars. Extra quality touches come in the form of the Explorers Library and Dalreoch Card Room, both new and both the product of the traditional feel supplied by British ship designers McNeece. More than anything, however, *Black Watch* gives her passengers a *choice* about almost everything (there are no less than six bars aboard, four lounges, two pools, an attractive gym, a night-club and a cinema/lecture room) and in a style as good as anything else in the Superior range. Her itineraries (from three nights to almost three months and from Dover to Hong Kong) also add to the ship's flexibility. Again, best value is in the lower grade cabins which are equally as spacious as more expensive ones, but have portholes rather than windows.

Extras: The high number of single cabins are a notable feature of the *Black Prince*, although she does not have cabins adapted for the disabled (there are four aboard *Black Watch*). Only the new ship carries children's facilities (there is really not much call for them aboard the *Prince*, which employs children's hosts only for the main summer holiday sailings). Fred Olsen's themed cruises, such as Classical Music, History and Antiques, are always popular and the *Prince* also boasts a unique giant-sized chess deck game. The other attraction of Olsen cruises is their flexibility, from three nights to 35-night adventures from Dover to the Caribbean and back, right up to the grand 82-night Far East Explorer. And I bet you never knew Dover was the gateway to Barbados and beyond! For their UK office, call 01473 292222.

Average price range: £1,340–£3,315 for a 14-night *Black Prince* cruise, £1,565–£4,655 on *Black Watch*.

ORIENT LINES

Ship	Tonnage	Passengers	Space Ratio	Built/ Refurbished	Cruise Area	Rating
MV *Marco Polo*	22,080	Max 860	25.6	1966/1993	Mediterranean, Far East, Indian Ocean, Australasia, Antarctica	Premier *Brit's Guide Favourite*

Cruise line notes: This is a wonderfully original product in the modern-day cruise world, covering as it does some of the most exotic, exciting and innovative destinations in genuine comfort and style and yet with the feel of an actual expedition ship. Orient attract those cruisers (and well-travelled holidaymakers generally) who have just about been there and done it all but still want something different. The rating is fairly arbitrary as there is little to compare Orient with in those terms, but suffice it to say it is a relatively formal and distinguished cruise experience with top quality food and service, a really comprehensive level of lectures and specialist talks, a high comfort level in the public rooms and a low-key level of entertainment and facilities, apart from the destination-orientated programme of lectures. This ship is ideal for those who enjoy relaxing days at sea, to make the most of the ship's attractions (with the exception, however, of their destination-intensive Mediterranean programme), who like a social, relaxed atmosphere in the 50-plus age range (with a healthy Anglo-American mix, plus a strong Australian contingent on the South Pacific cruises) and who take a keen, intelligent interest in the flora, fauna and culture of the more unusual areas it visits. Their Antarctica programme is possibly the best at sea, offering as it does a real close-up experience, but in the maximum possible ship-borne comfort. It is also keenly priced against the more out-and-out expedition ships. Orient are keen to spread their gospel to a younger audience as well (especially on the summer Med itineraries), and their cruises would certainly suit couples who don't demand the non-stop party atmosphere, late-night discos and the latest in cruise gimmicks. A link-up in 1997 with new airline Debonair has helped to keep the cost of their Med cruises down, too.

Pre-dinner drinks at Le Bar on Marco Polo

Ship notes: The *Marco Polo* was originally built under Soviet Union ownership and spent part of her early life as a spy ship before British entrepreneur and travel addict Gerry Herrod bought her up from her cash-hungry owners to turn her into the sophisticated world traveller she now is. Her ice-toughened hull and heli-copter facility allow her to venture deep into the Antarctic regions and she has gradually built up her repertoire of fascinating itineraries, with an increasing number of seven-day voyages to add to longer ones of up to 30 days. She has good sea manners (which is nautical-speak for she sails well in rough seas) and provides an elegant cruise vehicle with a limited range of on-board facilities, including some tastefully-decorated lounges, a good-sized gym and health centre, a small pool and an alternative dining arrangement that is proving extremely popular. The ship also boasts Zodiac landing craft for getting to land on the frozen wastes of Antarctica.

The standard range cabins are a little cramped for more than seven-day cruises, but, typically with a ship of this age, there is a wide choice of categories and the top level ones offer some superb extra amenities such as separate living rooms, queen-sized beds, marbled bathrooms, mini-bars, bathrobes and room safes. As an older ship, her crew have to work harder to maintain her overall appearance, but the fact she is a proper ship, as opposed to one of the new floating hotels, is worth the occasional cleaning inconvenience.

BRIT TIP

It is advisable to book early in the cruise for the alternative dining nights in the Raffles Lounge which can accommodate only 75 at a time. A pre-dinner drink at Le Bar is also recommended.

Extras: Orient's itineraries remain the main attraction, but they also offer an attractive programme of add-ons, hotel stays and land tours tied in with many of the cruises. Single supplements are as low as 125 per cent and there is a cabin-share scheme, while there is also a Gentlemen Host programme for single lady travellers. The line provides a particularly high and sophisticated level of pre-cruise information to tie in with the extensive lecture programme, which includes guests of the calibre of David Bellamy. However, the ship has no special children's facilities and, while there are two cabins adapted for the disabled, the use of tenders and Zodiacs at many ports is rather limiting for wheelchair-bound passengers. Orient is another cruise line taking part in the Royal Geographical Society Tours programme on the Antarctic itineraries which promotes the Society's work and enhances the geographical and environmental elements of the cruises. The genuine friendliness of the largely Filipino staff is another big plus of an Orient cruise.

BRIT TIP

Orient's Antarctic programme has been expanded to every winter instead of every other season, but still proves highly popular and books up extremely quickly. It offers a high degree of variety and flexibility, but, the line warns, the itineraries cannot be set in stone because of the vagaries of the ice conditions. And, because of the near 24-hour daylight, shore visits are just as likely to be 8pm as 8am where conditions allow. The on-board routine is consequently fairly low-key.

Average price range: From £995 on an eight-day Mediterranean cruise up to £10,950 on 26-day Antarctica voyages. For the UK office, call 0171 409 2500.

P&O

Ships	Tonnage	Passengers	Space Ratio	Built/ Refurbished	Cruise Area	Rating
MV *Victoria*	28,891	Max 743	38.8	1966/1997	Mediterranean, Caribbean, Canaries	Standard
MS *Arcadia*	63,500	Max 1,650	38.4	1989/1997	Mediterranean, Canaries, N Europe, Caribbean, World Cruise	Superior
MS *Oriana*	69,153	Max 1,975	35.0	1995	Mediterranean, Canaries, Caribbean, World Cruise	Superior, *Brit's Guide Favourite*

Cruise line notes: Along with Cunard, P&O are one of the most well-known names in the cruise world and maintain their long and distinguished tradition in the business in the best British style. Really, P&O epitomise the British mass market, catering as they do for virtually all social tastes and pockets and all ages, from toddlers to pensioners. They maintain a high element of formality and traditional cruise elegance while being able successfully to satisfy the demands of bingo and karaoke, classical music and theatre. Along with Airtours, Thomson, Fred Olsen and Swan Hellenic, they offer an almost exclusively British product, from the currency, to the officers, to the provision of one proper pub-style bar on each ship (and check out the prices – £1 a pint and no automatic service charge added!). For those wary of committing themselves to an American environment, P&O is the perfect answer, especially in the shape of the flagship *Oriana*, as wonderful an example of modern cruise design in the traditional ethos as there is. There is

Deck sports for all the family are a traditional P&O feature

more emphasis on days at sea and enjoying the cruise experience than trying to do a port a day. P&O also avoid the typical American-style glitz and glamour (although *Oriana* does have her moments) in favour of a more typically reserved nautical mode; however, that doesn't mean they can't be quite innovative, as with their kids' programmes, health and fitness facilities and the provision of a state-of-the-art theatre aboard the new flagship. Service comes with charm and a smile from the Goanese waiters and stewards, even if their English is occasionally a little suspect. Cuisine is a better-than-expected mix of traditional British fare, Goanese curries and a little extra continental flair, and is improving all the time as the *Oriana* brings everything up a level. There is also a good range of moderately-priced wines.

 BRIT TIP

Try not to arrive late for shows and plays in *Oriana's* beautifully-appointed Theatre Royal as the design makes it difficult for latecomers to find a seat, even when it is not full. P&O should really employ proper ushers here.

Ship notes: If 1997 was the farewell year for P&O's grand old lady *Canberra*, 1998 is the year of *Arcadia*, the new ship brought in to replace her. With a question-mark still over the long-term future of the fleet's other old-timer *Victoria* (the company are officially looking for a replacement), P&O could well have one of the most modern fleets in the market before long, with the bold *Oriana* leading the way and *Arcadia* adding to the up-to-date touch. The newest acquisition was formerly the *Star Princess* of sister company Princess Cruise Line, and so was one of the new breed of American superliners, built for large-scale glamour rather than the more reserved hallmark of British tastes. Hence *Arcadia* was headed for a major refit in November 1997 to remove all the overt Americana and substitute some more traditional P&O style, while retaining her range of facilities. These include six bars, two pools (one with a swim-up bar), a pizzeria and ice cream parlour, an impressive, tiered theatre and three-storey atrium lobby. The P&O touches come with the installation of The Oval pub, a proper library and card room, an enlarged Conservatory buffet dining alternative and reduced casino, a teenagers' disco and a night nursery for the little 'uns, and a more sophisticated emphasis on the décor. Cabins are all well fitted and quite spacious (especially the Premier grades and Suites, all with balconies), and P&O have configured 64 for singles and eight for disabled passengers. She is considerably larger than *Canberra*, hence with a much greater array of choice, but traditional aspects like deck sports and the friendly service will be transferred to the new arrival, along with many of *Canberra's* crew. The only remaining question will be if the die-hard *Canberra* loyalists find *Arcadia* such good value for money at the budget end of the market as there is a significant difference in price (up about 10–15 per cent). *Oriana* was launched with much fanfare in 1995 and, despite some early problems over excessive vibration in the stern of the ship (notably the Oriental Restaurant, Pacific Lounge and the aft-most cabins), quickly lived up to her billing as the first ship to be tailor-made for the British cruise market. With her combination of speed to reach her main cruising areas quickly, plus good seaworthiness to sail the Bay of Biscay in comfort, *Oriana* is perfectly suited to ex-UK voyaging and offers a sophisticated level of traditional charm while also catering for

You can always find a quiet corner of the deck for a drink

modern cruise developments such as a higher degree of entertainment, particularly in the evenings, activities to keep the kids amused and in health and fitness facilities. Children under 12 can also benefit from lower fares (75 per cent off rather than 60 per cent) outside the main school holidays.

In keeping with *Canberra's* appeal, *Oriana* possesses a full range of public room options, from the Lord's Tavern pub, through the classically-styled Curzon Room to the gentlemen's club atmosphere of Anderson's. There is a small casino (a bit smoky and not too inviting for non-gamblers) and cinema (where the air-conditioning works rather too well – take a sweater), an excellent library and card room, three children's areas plus an outer deck area and pools devoted especially to the youngsters, as well as a night nursery for 2- to 5-year olds (a master-stroke for the family market), a disco and multi-purpose nightclub, two adults' pools, excellent deck games provisions, golf nets and a general sports net that allows for paddle tennis, football and cricket.

The range of cabins is also quite high compared with the American identikit format as P&O try to offer something for everyone, from some generous-sized suites, larger cabins with balconies, family three- and four-berths, single rooms and eight cabins especially adapted for disabled passengers. All cabins

 BRIT TIP

Be warned. For those of a sporting persuasion there is enough to keep you busy all day long and you can end up quite exhausted, especially cruising in the warmer climates, trying to fit it all in. Again, I speak from experience.

BRIT TIP

Parts of *Oriana* can get quite busy, especially in the holiday periods when larger numbers of families are on board, but there is always a quiet corner to be found for those not wanting to indulge in the non-stop frenzy. Try Tiffany Court for a cup of tea or coffee, Anderson's or the Curzon Room during the day for a peaceful corner to read that book, the aft areas of A, B and C decks for a bit of sunbathing and the aft Terrace Bar in mid-afternoon for a cool drink.

have a fridge, TV, hairdryer and room safe, and are all nice and bright and airy, with good use of artwork and soft furnishings, although cupboard space is a bit limited. Inside cabins are also equally spacious as those with an exterior view. The choice of two restaurants and the bright indoor/outdoor Conservatory for buffet meals is likely to be augmented in the near future by a 24-hour dining option. Other planned developments include providing a bar in the second showlounge, the Pacific Lounge, which is the one area of the ship rather lacking in atmosphere, and increasing the list of daytime activities even further. For a brochure, call 0990 726726.

Extras: Children's provisions are second to none, and all three ships are an attractive proposition for singles with their cabin choice and range of social activities, while *Oriana* and *Arcadia* are well adapted for the disabled, although the use of tenders in some ports can make shore visits difficult. Check the itinerary carefully for the ports to gain maximum access. Themed cruises – notably football, antiques and classical music – are always popular and port taxes are included (hooray!). For repeat passengers, P&O offer special deals through their POSH Club (which really does

Arcadia in the Caribbean

stand for Port Out, Starboard Home from the traditional era of cruising), while they are also quite aggressive in the discounting market. The World cruises are another outstanding P&O feature. There is also the option of fly-cruises as well as ex-UK cruising for those with preferences and a full range of short- and long-duration choices, from three days up to the 90-day World cruise. In fact, the only real reason to avoid a P&O cruise is if you can't stand being surrounded by fellow Brits on your holiday.

Average price range: From £1,545– £5,295 on a typical two-week ex-UK *Oriana* cruise.

PREMIER CRUISE LINES

Ships	Tonnage	Passengers	Space Ratio	Built/ Refurbished	Cruise Area	Rating
Star/Ship Oceanic	38,772	Max 1,800	21.5	1965/1986	Bahamas	Standard

Cruise line notes: This American short-cruise company, known in the US as The Big Red Boat, is marketed in Britain only through the brochures of Jetsave and Transolar, but is worth seeking out in conjunction with an Orlando holiday, especially if you have children. These family-orientated three- and four-day cruises to the Bahamas offer a really budget-priced opportunity to sample fun cruising at the beginner's level to see if it really takes your fancy. The accent is on kids having as much fun as possible, hence it is a lively, if not rowdy experience, with Looney Tunes cartoon characters, four different age group programmes, group baby-sitting, kids' menus and sundae parties. For adults, there is plenty of evening fun and entertainment too (although all of an American flavour), and the cuisine is pretty good for a Standard level product. Premier is now run by Cruise Holdings, who also own Seawind and Dolphin Cruise Lines, in a bold attempt to make these classic liners more marketable and provide an alternative to the megaships.

Not for nothing do they carry the name The Big Red Boat

Ship notes: *Star/Ship Oceanic* features excellent deck space and a full range of facilities, from casinos and showlounges to ice cream parlours and karaoke bars. With the number of children on board, it is not a relaxing cruise, but the short durations and shore visits in Nassau and Port Lucaya in the Bahamas ensure you should never be bored. Cabins are quite spacious for just three- and four-day cruising and the service is friendly and efficient.

Extras: Fully-trained children's staff and cartoon character Tuck-In service (for a little extra) make it a holiday heaven for kids. A new kids' activity centre features a computer learning area. The choice of cruise-and-stay options make it an attractive option, especially at Premier's prices. There is a good choice of on-board duty-free shopping and there is a snorkelling and scuba-diving programme.

Average price range: £719–£1,415 for a two-week holiday featuring a three- or four-night cruise plus Orlando stay.

PRINCESS CRUISES

Ships	Tonnage	Passengers	Space Ratio	Built/ Refurbished	Cruise Area	Rating
MS *Island Princess*	19,907	Max 717	27.7	1972/1992	Mediterranean, Far East, Indian Ocean, Alaska	Superior
MV *Pacific Princess*	20,636	Max 717	28.7	1971/1993	Mediterranean, Africa, N Europe	Superior
TSS *Sky Princess*	46,314	Max 1,350	34.3	1984/1992	Far East, S Pacific, Australasia, Alaska	Superior
MV *Royal Princess*	44,348	Max 1,275	34.7	1984/1994	Caribbean, N Europe, E Coast US S America	Premier ***Brit's Guide Favourite***
MS *Crown Princess*	70,000	Max 1,910	36.6	1990	Caribbean, Alaska, Panama Canal	Premier
MS *Regal Princess*	70,000	Max 1,910	36.6	1991	Caribbean, Alaska, Panama Canal	Premier
MS *Sun Princess*	77,000	Max 2,322	33.1	1995	Caribbean, Alaska	Premier ***Brit's Guide Favourite***
MS *Dawn Princess*	77,000	Max 2,322	33.1	1997	Caribbean, Alaska	Premier ***Brit's Guide Favourite***

Cruise line notes: The American arm of P&O is a much bigger, glitzier and, well, more American proposition and is something of a secret to British mass-market cruising. With 80–90 per cent US passengers, there is little of the traditional style that marks out P&O's ex-UK operation, although the older ships and the new *Sun* and *Dawn Princess*, while retaining a sense of trans-atlantic style and glamour, do go some way to redressing the balance, and

Princess also offers a greater level of formality than many rivals (although still less than P&O). Their ships cruise far and wide, but the core business is the Caribbean, Alaska (where they and Holland America remain the foremost lines) and Europe, and they offer a well-honed, sophisticated and port-intensive programme. They do also boast quite a variety of cruise durations,

The smart Lido Deck on Princess Cruises' Royal Princess

with those of 10 days and above attracting a significantly older passenger profile (50-plus) than the seven-day versions, which draw a lot of families, who are extremely well catered for in both facilities and children's programmes. There is less variety of entertainment, but what there is tends to be more spectacular and showy, with the evening presented around the big production shows (which is fairly typical of the American lines). There is also a difference in the crew nationality, with half the ships having British officers, and the other half having Italians, while the service staff members can be Italian, Portuguese or Filipino. Service generally is friendly and almost unobtrusive, but the dining room staff could be more consistent and the cuisine is currently undergoing something of an overhaul, from thoroughly American (and a bit bland) to something a bit more contemporary and cosmopolitan. It is also entirely a fly-cruise operation (apart from a handful of northern European voyages from the new cruise facilities at Dover).

Ship notes: The big event of 1998 (with the accent on big) will be the launch of 'the world's largest crusing ship'. After Carnival's 101,000-ton *Destiny*, Princess will inaugurate the *Grand Princess* at Southampton on May 14th, and it is not just her 109,000-ton bulk that will catch the eye. At 935ft in length, 118ft wide, more than 155ft high and with 13 passenger decks, this floating city will dwarf just about anything else at sea. Carrying up to 3,300 passengers (Space Ratio 33.1), she also needs a lot of on-board facilities, and the advance publicity is truly mind-boggling. (Pause for deep breath . . .) Start with three main restaurants, five other food outlets (including a 24-hour pizzeria), 14 (count them, 14) bars, one with a sports theme and satellite TV, five swimming pools (including a lap pool with a constant current for keen swimmers) and three lounges in addition to the grand, two-storey Princess Theater. For sports, try the Princess Links, a nine-hole putting green and golf simulator, paddle tennis, jogging track and huge gymnasium and aerobics room. Of course, there is also a library (with CD-

ROM access), card room and writing room, plus a casino with hologrammatic lighting and ceiling effects that change from dawn to dusk every 20 minutes, a beauty salon and a health spa with all the latest treatments. For children? The Fun Zone is a two-storey toddler playroom complete with a whale-shaped pool and waterspout, while Off Limits is the teen club. A separate bar area offers children their own food and drink service. Now add in the Limelight Studio, a blue-screen fantasy world where you can be filmed with your favourite movie star, and the hugely innovative Voyage of Discovery, a virtual reality complex featuring a simulator submarine voyage and other motion-based rides. The *pièce de résistance* is the 'nightclub in the sky', a glass-walled, wing-shaped room the width of the ship suspended 150 feet above the stern, full of dazzling

Princess Cruises' spectacular Contemporary Circus showtime

lighting effects and sound systems. It all promises to be the futuristic new benchmark of the cruise world – but a ship? I wonder. Europe will get her first look at this cruise vehicle of the twenty-first century when she operates her maiden season in the Mediterranean. It will certainly be cruising with a difference!

 BRIT TIP

Beware one transatlantic difference – in keeping with American laws, alcoholic drinks are available only to those 21 and over.

The relative diversity of the rest of the fleet also gives rise to a number of other differences. The virtually identical *Island* and *Pacific* are used for the more exotic itineraries, and so attract an older passenger to their small-ship style and their elegance and extra spaciousness, both in the cabins and public rooms.

The *Sky* is also a touch more traditional, despite her modern appearance, although she suffers from an appalling outbreak of blandness in the interior décor and design that makes many of the public rooms less than inviting. The main dining room is particularly utilitarian, the stairwells uniformly subdued and the soft furnishings just plain dull. However, the Starlight Lounge and Disco is very smart, the trademark Princess pizzeria is quite attractive and the library has a good traditional feel. The *Crown* and *Regal* are Princess Cruise's hotel-type ships, still a little unimaginative and clinical in terms of the interior décor, but a definite step up from the *Sky* and with a well-worked range of facilities. They both qualify in the Premier range for their more than ample selection of facilities and amenities, but none of them features a proper prom deck. The *Royal* is a bit of a one-off and a real gem in the Princess range, a more notably up-market, sleek and sophisticated cruiser, having only outside cabins and a more marked degree of design elegance. Generously spacious cabins feature throughout and many public rooms (although fewer of the latter than on many ships of the same size) come with a wonderfully light, airy feel that makes for relaxing long-distance cruising which should also appeal to the British market. Small touches, like fresh flowers, cutlery placed in linen napkins on the tables in the buffet Lido and overall attention to detail, mark her out as well above average.

 BRIT TIP

The *Royal Princess* has a surprisingly small cinema and, for the more popular films, you should arrive early to ensure a seat. Don't expect to find an array of energetic daytime events, either, as she concentrates on providing a more relaxed atmosphere for her passengers.

The new *Sun* and her 1997 sister ship *Dawn Princess* add an extra element to the Princess appeal and will also be more noteworthy for the British market. As well as being quite stunningly beautiful internally (if still rather of the slab-sided, floating hotel block in overall appearance) they demonstrate an almost unique ability to bridge the transatlantic taste gap.

With a generous range of public rooms on a much smaller scale than hitherto seen on Princess designs, coupled with an almost overwhelming use of eye-catching architecture (check out the four-storey main lobby and pool decks) and some distinctly traditional touches (notably in the Wheelhouse Bar and full promenade deck), the *Sun* and *Dawn* break new ground in mega-liner appeal and sophistication. There is also a full, 24-hour dining option, as well as a pizzeria, to take some of the pressure off the two main dinner sittings and provide more flexibility to enjoy the evening entertainment. Her cabins are unfailingly spacious, many with balconies, and the top-of-the-range suites are truly Deluxe. The only likely drawback with a ship containing more than 2,000 people is for the one-off events, embarkation, debarkation and booking shore excursions, when queues are unavoidable.

Extras: There are some great honeymoon packages, the Princess pizzerias are an outstanding feature, kids will adore the range of facilities on the newer ships and there is a comprehensive scuba-diving programme for everyone, from newcomers to experienced divers. Shore excursions are carefully thought out and well executed, and their information literature is among the best in the business. All the ships feature self-service launderettes. In addition, there are some attractive land-stay add-ons on the more exotic itineraries, and their Alaskan programme is one of the best for offering a Canadian Rockies tour before the cruise. Midnight buffets, notably on the *Royal Princess*, are truly spectacular. For the disabled passenger, the *Sun* and *Dawn Princess* offer 19 specially-adapted cabins, while all the others have at least four. Port taxes are included, and there are attractive discounts for both early bookers and repeat passengers. Newcomers' cruises are another Princess feature.

Average price range: £1,195–£3,145 on Caribbean nine-nighters, up to £3,345–£7,550 on the 23-night Australian Adventure, including 21-night cruise.

RADISSON SEVEN SEAS CRUISES

Ships	Tonnage	Passengers	Space Ratio	Built/ Refurbished	Cruise Area	Rating
MS *Song of Flower*	8,282	180	46.0	1986/1990	World-wide	Deluxe
SSC *Radisson Diamond*	20,295	354	57.3	1992	Caribbean, Panama Canal, Transatlantic, Mediterranean, N Europe	Deluxe
MS *Paul Gauguin*	18,800	320	58.7	1997	French Polynesia	Deluxe (expec-ted)

Cruise line notes: This is a true World Traveller series (485 ports visited in 1996) and attracts a slightly older (45-plus), more discerning and well-travelled passenger who still wants to see the sights in great comfort, enjoy five-star cuisine and service and take a keen interest in the flora, fauna and culture along the way. The itineraries are exciting, exotic and, in many cases, unique, offering the chance to get off the beaten track with well organised shore excursions and intelligent and comprehensive lectures to accompany them. It is not a chance to enjoy glitzy entertainment, non-stop activities and the latest in cruising mod-cons, and the overall atmosphere is one of relaxed formality, sophisticated charm and an almost club-like exclusivity.

Song of Flower visits Stockholm

Fine dining is a Radisson Diamond *hallmark*

Ship notes: All three vessels are complete individuals, with the *Diamond* coming closest to traditional style modern cruising. Her innovative design (which makes for exceptionally smooth sailing) is a real attraction for many, and internally she is quite stunning, too, with a five-storey central lobby atrium, split-level main lounge, and one of the most elegant dining rooms afloat. Cabins are all outside, many with balconies, and are wonderfully spacious and beautifully appointed, and the suites all feature superb bay windows which add to the feeling of spaciousness. Sports facilities are excellent, with a jogging track, golf putting area and driving cage, comprehensive fitness centre and a watersports marina offering waterskiing, wind-surfing, sailing and jet-skiing. There is an alternative dining option, The Grill, which is very popular but seats only 50 at a time, so you need to book early. Passengers are 75 per cent American, with the rest a good European mix. *Song of Flower* is a 'softer' version of the adventure type of cruise ship, visiting out-of-the-way areas but providing a more luxurious level of service and cuisine. Public rooms and cabins are relatively low-key in their décor, but the dining room is a great feature and her regular passengers will tell you she provides some of the most memorable cuisine at sea and a level of service found usually only in the most exclusive land-based resorts. There is a well-stocked library and a small, subtle casino that is, refreshingly, a million miles removed from the usual Las Vegas glitz. There are 10 no-smoking cabins, but bathroom and cupboard space in all of them could be better. A recent addition is a 30-seat alternative dining option, Angelino's, featuring Northern Italian specialities. Book early on for this.

There is a small pool and quite generous deck space for such a small ship, but the fitness centre is a bit of an after-thought. The main lounge is neat without being overly pretty, while the top level Observation Lounge offers excellent views in a quite intimate setting.

 BRIT TIP

The top category A-class suite on *Song of Flower* has plenty of extra space, but, surprisingly, no balcony. The B category offers much better value with its balcony and full-sized bath.

Maintaining the line's tradition for classy, one-off vessels is the new *Paul Gauguin*, a French-built and owned ship operated by Radisson out of Tahiti for 7- and 14-night cruises around French Polynesia. She is another of the small, boutique ships along the lines of Seabourn and Silversea, only less formal. Two restaurants, three lounges, a small pool, fitness centre, spa, beauty salon and casino, and that's about it for the facilities (although the finish promises to be of the highest quality). But, once you add in Radisson's five-star service and Michelin-starred cuisine, plus sumptuous cabins (all with queen-sized or twin beds, marble bathrooms, robes, hairdryers, TV and VCR, fridge and personal safe), half with balconies, it should add up to a Deluxe experience. The itineraries promise unforgettable crusing – with the price tag to match. But, for those who have tired of the cruise mainstream, this should be the perfect antidote.

Extras: Virtually everything is all-inclusive on Radisson Seven Seas ships, from tips and drinks to most of the shore excursions, but, amazingly, port taxes, the old bugbear, are still extra. All meals are single, open seating, which means you dine when YOU want, not at pre-selected times. None of the ships are suitable for children, and only *Radisson Diamond* and *Paul Gauguin* have disabled-adapted cabins. For the UK office, call 0171 287 9060.

Average price range: £2,405–£4,405 on 7-night *Song of Flower* Mediterranean fly-cruise, up to £9,100 on an 18-night cruise to Australia and the Spice Islands.

ROYAL CARIBBEAN INTERNATIONAL

Ships	Tonnage	Passengers	Space Ratio	Built/ Refurbished	Cruise Area	Rating
MS *Sun Viking*	18,556	Max 818	22.6	1972/1988	Far East	Standard
MS *Viking Serenade*	40,132	Max 1,863	21.5	1982/1990	Mexican Riviera	Standard
MS *Song of America*	37,584	Max 1,552	24.2	1982/1991	Mexico, Bermuda	Superior
MS *Sovereign of the Seas*	73,192	Max 2,540	28.9	1988	Bahamas	Superior
MS *Nordic Empress*	48,563	Max 2,020	24.0	1990	Bahamas, Caribbean	Superior
MS *Monarch of the Seas*	73,941	Max 2,744	26.9	1991	Caribbean	Superior
MS *Majesty of the Seas*	73,941	Max 2,744	26.9	1992	Caribbean	Superior

(continued overleaf)

ROYAL CARIBBEAN INTERNATIONAL (cont.)

Ships	Tonnage	Passengers	Space Ratio	Built/ Refurbished	Cruise Area	Rating
MS *Legend of the Seas*	70,950	Max 2,064	34.3	1995	Panama Canal, Alaska, Hawaii, Mexican Rivera	Superior
MS *Splendour of the Seas*	69,130	Max 2,064	33.4	1996	Caribbean, Mediterranean, N Europe	Superior, Brit's Guide Favourite
MS *Rhapsody of the Seas*	75,000	Max 2,441	30.7	1997	Caribbean, Alaska, Hawaii	Superior
MS *Grandeur of the Seas*	74,000	Max 2,446	30.2	1996	Caribbean, Alaska	Superior
MS *Enchantment of the Seas*	74,000	Max 2,446	30.2	1997	Caribbean	Superior

The splendid Solarium Pool on Legend of the Seas

Cruise line notes: The second of the giant American cruise companies, RCI have grown steadily with some of the most impressive hardware and deliver a consistent level of service to suit both first-timers and repeat cruisers with a touch more sophistication than Carnival, their main rivals. The passenger profile tends to vary according to the length of cruise, with the three- and four-day cruises attracting a younger, party-minded crowd, the seven-dayers drawn from right across the board, but especially families, and the longer voyages (12-day sailings to Northern Europe, the Mediterranean, Panama Canal and Alaska and 14-day cruises in the Far East) likely to be more in the 45–60 age range. The Caribbean is their core product, but they have now branched out further afield and are currently pioneering a year-round market in the Far East. The arrival in Europe in spring 1996 of *Splendour of the Seas* raised RCI's European profile quite considerably, and they now attract around 12 per cent of British passengers aboard many of their sailings, with the possibility this number will increase, particularly on the more attractive itineraries such as northern Europe, the Far East and Alaska. They don't claim to offer a luxurious product, but the most recent hardware certainly puts them well into the upper end of the Superior range, beyond many of their obvious competitors. Being American, the style is necessarily glitzy (the *Splendour* has been toned down a little for the European market), lively and straightforward, lacking a lot of cruising's formality (although still retaining several formal nights per cruise) but also some of the personal touch that goes with more small-scale ships. With the exception of *Sun Viking*, all RCI vessels cater for at least 1,000 passengers, with the largest well in excess of 2,000, and that can make for high-density cruising, although the newest series of ships are more spacious and thoughtfully designed to improve passenger flow. Kids are well catered for with their own menus and activity programmes in four age groups and RCI are keen on sports of all kinds, from deck games, to their health facilities, shore-side golf opportunities and watersports. Cabins (except the largest suites) are of the identikit variety, with little real difference between the categories except for which deck they are on. They are always comfortable, but tend to lack cupboard and drawer space and the fixtures and fittings are rather bland. The most recent build (*Legend, Splendour, Grandeur, Rhapsody* and *Enchantment*) all incorporate more balconied cabins and offer rather more all-round space although the cabins still lack hairdryers. Each RCI ship also incorporates a Viking Crown lounge, usually set into the ship's funnel or otherwise at the top of the ship, which provides a trademark visual look to the line as well as an excellent observation lounge. Cuisine is consistently American, and there is always plenty of it, and the newest quintet all possess wonderful split-level restaurants that add to the dining experience. Finally, entertainment: RCI set great store by the quality and quantity of their shows, and there is plenty of razzmatazz served up every night, while they also manage to find some extremely sharp comedians. Incidentally, their name change from Royal Caribbean Cruise Line was to emphasise their more world-wide nature these days. And, with four new ships in the last two years, and another in 1998, RCI expect to be a serious international player.

Ship notes: The heart of their operation is now dominated by the two most modern sets, the *Sovereign, Majesty* and *Monarch*, which introduced a new level of sophistication to the mega-liner concept, and the even newer quintet of the *Legend, Splendour, Grandeur, Rhapsody* and *Enchantment*, which have achieved the near impossible task of making these huge vessels seem quite manageable and almost small-scale (as well as providing distinctly bigger standard cabins than was previously the case with this line). A greater variety of public rooms is the key to the latter five, while all eight benefit from the impressive central multi-storey atrium lobbies, complete with glass-sided lifts, that prove a handy reference point to negotiating the many decks. The 18-hole mini-golf courses on the *Legend* and *Splendour* are fun for the kids, although at $5 a time they are not cheap, and they are perhaps a bit too gimmicky, but the splendid Solarium pool and deck area, with optional sliding glass roof, is certainly a winner. The amount of glass used on these ships, and consequently the amount of natural light that streams in, provides another pleasant feature. It has real practical application in places like Alaska where it can be chilly yet you still want a good outside view, and it is more

RCI ships are big on showy Las Vegas-style casinos

likely to appeal to European tastes. Their sheer size dictates a slight lack of ship character, however.

The *Sovereign*-class ships all possess, for my money, the most pleasant indoor/outdoor buffet dining options of all the mega-liners, the Windjammer Café, which is a beautifully airy, split-level affair complete with plants and waterfalls. It was this sort of innovation, plus the big atrium lobbies, which convinced the mass market of the wisdom of such large-scale operations, and RCI carry it off

probably better than anyone. *Nordic Empress* and *Viking Serenade* are RCI's short-cruise options, and, to that end, are a bit of a chalk and cheese product. *Serenade* is the company's Odd One Out, an ultra-high density converted ferry that plies the Californian coast down to the undistinguished Mexican port of Ensenada; décor is uninspiring, cabin decks are cramped and confused (with many inside cabins, all with tiny bathrooms), deck space is minimal when the ship is full and there are not enough public rooms to spread the passenger load comfortably. Her appeal is limited to the younger, good-time set who will enjoy the non-stop activities rather than any quality of cruise experience. *Empress*, on the other hand, was purpose-built for the short-haul market to the Bahamas and, with a similar passenger load, offers a much greater level of sophistication, from her light, airy design to her proper promenade deck and excellent pool deck, which is a focal point day and night. Cabins are still on the small side, but are far more inviting and comfortable, and the public rooms have more eye appeal and commonsense passenger flow attributes. There is still razzle-dazzle, but it is of a far more acceptable kind.

 BRIT TIP

Nordic Empress, for all she is a high-density ship, is a great first-time cruise experience, especially for the young. For, as the company insists: "We try to cram a seven-day cruise into three or four days!"

Song of America is RCI's traditional cruiser, offering a good mix of the old and the new, especially on her summer runs from New York down to Bermuda. Standard range cabins are a bit on the small side, but the provision for deck space is more generous than some much bigger ships and the range and décor of the public rooms are also appealing. Finally, *Sun Viking* has been employed as RCI's trail-blazer in the Far East to test the waters for mass-market cruising out there. RCI haved proved popular with their programme here, especially with the European market, and it can't be long before *Viking* is sold off and replaced by one of the newer ships.

Extras: The opportunity to do back-to-back 7-day cruises in the eastern and western Caribbean is another popular British choice, with the new *Enchantment* taking over this role in 1998. RCI have their own private islands, off the coast of Haiti and at CocoCay in the Bahamas, to allow for their popular beach parties. Their Breakthrough price structure should help to stabilise the huge mountain of discounts in the Caribbean cruise business, pledging as it does to give the LOWEST prices to the EARLIEST bookers. For singles, they offer a Single Guarantee cabin assignment at reasonable rates and a Share Programme, but only the most recent ships offer cabins for the disabled.

Average price range: From £1,229–£2,969 for a week's Caribbean cruise, and £2,269–£4,599 on Far East two-week voyages.

ROYAL OLYMPIC CRUISES

Ships	Tonnage	Passengers	Space Ratio	Built/ Refurbished	Cruise Area	Rating
MTS Orpheus	5,092	Max 280	18.1	1952/1969	E Mediterranean	Standard
SS *Stella Solaris*	17,832	Max 620	28.7	1953/1973	Mediterranean, Panama Canal, Amazon, Transatlantic	Standard
TTS *Olympic*	31,500	Max 1,386	22.7	1956/1994	E Mediterranean	Standard
MTS Odysseus	12,000	Max 400	30.0	1962/1987	Mediterranean, S America, N Europe	Standard
MS *Stella Oceanis*	6,000	Max 300	20.0	1965/1967	E Mediterranean, Red Sea	Standard
MS *Triton*	14,155	Max 620	22.8	1971/1992	E Mediterranean, Caribbean	Standard

Cruise line notes: The merger of the two biggest Greek cruise lines – Epirotiki and Sun Line – in late 1995 has given the Mediterranean another serious operator in the mass market end of the business. And, while their foothold in Britain may not be big to start with, they promise to make their product an attractive alternative. Basically, Royal Olympic has taken the personal, friendly service of Sun Lines and mixed it with Epirotiki's fun style to provide a fascinating blend of lively Greek ambience and traditional elegance. The two lines will maintain a lot of their former characteristics, but the new combination will stress a comprehensive range of itineraries in the Eastern Mediterranean and the Red Sea offering quite port-intensive tours and trying to get a little off the beaten track thanks to their smaller ship size, visiting some of the smaller Greek islands and places like Albania, Egypt and Jordan. New for 1998 will be a series of 14-day Baltic Sea fly-cruises out of Copenhagen. The on-board style will continue to be unfailingly Greek, and so it should appeal not only to the more adventurous cruisers but also to the two million-plus Brits who holiday in Greece every year. The accent is not on a full range of day-time activities so much as on using the ships to explore the ports of call and sailing at night (a rather American concept), when the company can really turn on the Greek charm and produce a taverna-like atmosphere, complete with Greek dancing. Royal Olympic promise 'professional service, but in a fun way,' with continental cuisine and more spontaneous entertainment. Of course, there will still be the more traditional elements of cruise entertainers, gift shops, hairdressers and photographers, but outside those it will be an entirely Greek experience. The ships are all individuals, too, and attract a more particular type of cruiser according to the area and time of year. The Sun Line ships (*Stella Oceanis* and *Solaris*) attract a high percentage of Americans, while the Epirotiki vessels typically draw their passenger base from all over Europe plus about 35 per cent from the US, but these current distinctions will gradually blur as the merger develops. The age profile tends to be in the 45- to 50-plus range, but July and August see all the ships welcome a younger, more boisterous holiday crowd of all nationalities – but the first language will always be English.

Ship notes: *Stella Solaris* is the ROC flagship, a mature, classic liner which has aged well and continues to be elegantly fitted out to higher levels than most Standard class ships. Her passenger profile alters according to the season, with her winters spent sailing the Caribbean and Amazon on longer routes and therefore drawing an older crowd, while the summers get younger and livelier on seven-day Greek island cruises. Despite the relatively high density when full, *Solaris* is quite a spacious vessel, both in terms of her deck capability (including a proper prom deck) and the amount of cabin space.

 **BRIT TIP**

ROC is not the company for shy, retiring wallflowers. You will be expected to join in the party and there is no escaping those Greek dancing lessons!

Stella Oceanis is much smaller and lacks a lot of the usual creature comforts such as in-cabin TV, a health centre, gymnasium, cinema and a wide range of public rooms (although her Taverna is a real winner), but the reduction in scale allows for an increase in more personalised service, particularly in the well-appointed dining room. Her cabins are pretty small, but all have private bathrooms, and the only real drawback for a ship in the Med is the relative lack of open deck space. Epirotiki's oldest ship in the merger is the tiny *Orpheus*, until early 1996 on long-term charter to Swan Hellenic and therefore quite a chic little adventurer. Her role in ROC is also as something of a pioneer, sailing north from Piraeus (the main port for Athens) to classical Greece and even up to Albania, providing cruise access to parts of the country usually open only to coach tours. She will feature cultural and archaeological experiences and lectures in the best Swan Hellenic style – but more cheaply than her former operators. *Orpheus* is hampered by tiny cabins and limited public space, but once again the accent will be on the ports of call rather than the ship herself. *Olympic* is the largest ship of the fleet and is another old-style cruiser, who does get pretty busy in the summer months when the mainly European crowd can be a boisterous lot. But again she maintains a traditional charm and some of her fixtures and fittings are real classic cruise ship material, with lots of warm wood panelling and brass railings, and her cabins are quite generous for space, with the notable exception of the cramped bathrooms. *Olympic* is the cornerstone of ROC's three- and four-day cruises out of Piraeus which can be incredibly hectic (as many as EIGHT ports in that time) so they are not for the faint-hearted. *Odysseus* joins her on the short-cruise run, offering more traditional cruise ambience, bags of Greek style (notably in the Taverna, which really hums at night) and a surprisingly good range of public rooms, all very tastefully decorated. Cabins are again quite generous and the sun-tan brigade are well catered for on deck. The newer *Triton* completes the fleet and is another quite high-density, bustling cruise ship with the benefits of a good promenade deck, lovely Greek artwork, a rather chic forward observation lounge/nightclub and more generous deck space. Cabins tend towards the small, but are all fitted out in warm, inviting fashion. Like *Olympic*, *Triton* is a lively customer in summer, when there are plenty of children aboard, but more sedate at other times. In the UK, phone 0171 734 0805.

Extras: ROC operate a no-discount policy, promising their brochure prices are the LOWEST they can go, in order to encourage early booking and eliminate the awful possibility of someone finding out their neighbour paid substantially less for the same cruise by booking at the last minute. Early bookers will therefore get the best cabin availability. Port taxes are still extra and none of the ships is really suitable for disabled passengers.

Average price range: £579–£2,249 for a week's Mediterranean cruise.

SAGA CRUISES

Ship	Tonnage	Passengers	Space Ratio	Built/ Refurbished	Cruise Area	Rating
MS Saga Rose	24,474	Max 620	39.4	1965/1997	Mediterranean, N Europe, Canaries, Caribbean, World cruise	Premier (expected)

Cruise line notes: Over-50s tour operator Saga opted to join the cruise world full-time in 1997 as they bought Cunard's redundant *Sagafjord* and turned her into *Saga Rose*. While still chartering with other lines, Saga now offer their own complete package, with some thoughtful European and Caribbean itineraries which build to a grand world cruise that undercuts most of the competition. Saga aim purposely at the formal element and traditional style as befits their passenger profile, and so, while modern

comforts are provided (including a well-appointed gym), the accent is on pursuits for the mature passenger. Her reputation for fine cuisine under Cunard remains unchanged.

Ship notes: After a brief charter with German operator Transocean, *Sagafjord* has 'come home' to life as the *Saga Rose* and the prospect of graceful cruising aboard one of the world's few classic liners. She had been allowed to run to seed a little under her later days with Cunard, hence Saga were sending her in for a much-needed re-fit and facelift in November 1997, and consequently her definitive *Brit's Guide* rating awaits the outcome of this overhaul. But the essence of her magnificent public rooms should ensure she maintains high-quality traditions for some time, even if her bewildering variety of 18 (admittedly all quite spacious) cabins could do with being

The dining room on Saga Rose

simplified. The main dining room is still one of the most timelessly gracious restaurants afloat and her wide, open deck spaces hark back to bygone days of old-fashioned elegance.

Extras: Saga offer a range of single cabins and the chance of an arranged share in a twin berth. There is also an exclusive cocktail party for singles. Tipping is another welcome inclusion, as are port taxes and travel insurance, and there is a free private car service for passengers within 75 miles of home port Dover. Four cabins are due to be adapted for disabled passengers in the refit. The World Cruise can be taken in 12 sectors, from 13 to 85 days, and there are extended tour options at some ports.

Average price range: £1,439–£5,269 on a 13-night Canaries cruise, up to £37,899 on a 97-day World Cruise. For brochures, call 0800 505030.

SEABOURN CRUISE LINE

Ships	Tonnage	Passengers	Space Ratio	Built/ Refurbished	Cruise Area	Rating
MS Seabourn Pride	9,975	Max 204	48.8	1988	World-wide	Deluxe
MS Seabourn Spirit	9,975	Max 204	48.8	1989	World-wide	Deluxe
MS Seabourn Legend	9,975	Max 212	47.0	1992/1995	World-wide	Deluxe

Cruise line notes: The exclusive world of the small, Deluxe ships is perfectly illustrated by the example of the Seabourn line, a three-ship fleet known as the Rolls Royce of the cruise world – and very nearly as expensive! Imagine having your own large, private yacht, with impeccable service, the best cuisine, magnificent but under-stated décor and an ambience of relaxed affluence, then add in the more up-scale qualities of modern-day cruise ship facilities, like health spas, fitness centres, night-clubs, casinos and chic piano bars, and you have the Seabourn ships. The itineraries are the other big distinguishing feature of this utterly luxury-clad cruise experience, circling the globe in their search for sunshine, exotic ports of call, rich cultural experiences and beautiful scenery. The ships' size allows them to explore areas where the big ships can never venture, yet they are not small enough to feel cramped or limiting. Even standard cabins are suites, and all are outside, sumptuously appointed with every conceivable amenity, although only the 16 largest have balconies. Seabourn also got a publicity boost in 1997 when the *Seabourn Legend* was featured in the film *Speed 2: Cruise Control*.

Ship notes: The three are identical sisters, yet the *Seabourn Legend* was only a recent acquisition and is already in her third incarnation having started out as the *Royal Viking Queen* and then moved to Royal Cruise Line's colours as the *Queen Odyssey* before RCL folded and Seabourn moved in. The sleek trio all boast quality wherever you look, from the lower deck main restaurant, with its open dining arrangement and Monte Carlo chic, to the top deck observation lounge, with its floor-to-ceiling windows and passenger radar screen linked to the bridge. The Veranda Café now offers an evening dining arrangement without the formality of the main restaurant as part of Project 2000, which also calls for complimentary spirits and wine to be included as standard (except for premium and vintage brands), a new late-night entertainment programme and a systematic interior redecoration of all three ships by the turn of the century. The cabins all feature queen-sized beds, TV and VCR, walk-in cupboards, fridge, hairdryer, sitting area and the finest in soft furnishings. Dinner can also be served in your suite if the restaurant seems too much of a drag. Other facilities include a marina platform that fits round the stern of the ships, offering the chance to swim in your own sea pool, go water-skiing, wind-surfing or paddle-boating, or use one of the two speed-boats to go off scuba-diving or snorkelling. Evening entertainment is a sophisticated mix of classical music, up-market cabaret and easy-listening live music, while the day will feature guest lecturers, gourmet chefs and authors, and a comprehensive talk programme on the ports of call and local culture, which can vary from Asia to Alaska, the Seychelles to the South Pacific, Nova Scotia to Norway and Athens to the Amazon. In all, the ships visit 117 countries and nearly 300 ports of call.

Extras: The service, the service and the service! If all passengers can agree on one thing, it is that Seabourn offers the ultimate in refined, impeccable, unobtrusive service. On top of that, NO tipping is allowed. As a result, Seabourn has a high percentage of repeat passengers. Single passengers are also especially well catered for, with one of the lowest single supplements of any cruise line. There is no discounting as such (perish the thought), but there are early-booking and repeat passenger savings to be made. The only possible drawback you could mention would be the price – Silversea offer a similar product for less, but on larger ships. *Pride* and *Spirit* are also just starting to show their age externally too. In the UK, call 0171 930 4447.

Average price range: From £3,300 on a seven-day cruise up to £55,000 for the 60-day South American adventure.

SILVERSEA CRUISES

Ships	Tonnage	Passengers	Space Ratio	Built/ Refurbished	Cruise Area	Rating
MS *Silver Cloud*	16,800	Max 296	56.7	1994	World-wide	Deluxe
MS *Silver Wind*	16,800	Max 296	56.7	1995	World-wide	Deluxe

Cruise line notes: If you cross the up-scale facilities of Crystal's operation with the small-scale quality of Seabourn's service, you arrive at Silversea, the fourth major player in the Deluxe end of the market along with Cunard's *Sea Goddess* ships. Silversea are also the newest in the business, having started only in 1994, but they have quickly established a solid reputation for a lavish, all-inclusive experience at a price that undercuts Seabourn, their main rivals, and offers a much higher percentage (75 per cent) of balconied cabins. They can't quite match the latter for the seamlessly smooth service and magnificent cuisine, but they are not far behind and they are already the most popular Deluxe product with the British market, to the extent that Silversea have ordered two new ships of the same design specifications, only bigger – 22,000 tons – for 1999 and 2000. The larger size of their vessels means they have better economies of scale which allows them to incorporate more items into the all-inclusive package, including all your drinks, port taxes, tips and some shore excursions. There is also a more European feel to Silversea, hence a slight increase in formality. There is more emphasis on European desti- nations in their itineraries, from Istanbul to London and all the up-market ports in between, but they also seek out the exotic ports of the Far East and Africa, as well as a range of South American voyages, including the Falklands and magnificent Chilean fjords. Increasingly, Silversea passengers are being converted from the more exclusive land-based resorts and so they include a relatively high percentage of newcomers to cruising (although there is also a 32 per cent repeat factor), but the age profile is solidly middle-aged (40-plus) and primarily couples. Once again, there is little American razzmatazz about the entertainment or décor, although the multi-tiered showlounge offers a touch of big-production style and is capable of putting on some quite elaborate shows and cabaret acts. Elsewhere, things are fairly restrained, with just a classical musician or two, in-cabin films and videos, a small casino, fitness classes and watersports to while away the time.

Ship notes: Unusually for small ships, there is a wrap-around prom deck that allows for walking and jogging and a good-sized pool deck that caters for a large number of sun-worshippers (there is a well-planned spread of sea- days and port days on the longer itineraries, and the ship's facilities will be well-used). The fitness centres are state-of-the-art and the health spa offers a full range of treatments, while the Terrace Café has to be one of the most elegant buffet-style dining option at sea and the main restaurant is quite wonderfully opulent, full of warm woods, rich drapes and subtle lighting, offset by the finest china table settings. The Terrace Café is also proving popular for its occasional themed dinners in either Thai or Italian style. The all-suite cabins are typically spacious and lack nothing in the way of ameni- ties, from the fully-stocked cocktail cabinets to the marbled bathrooms.

Extras: Your only extra expenditure on board will be for the beauty salon, boutique, casino, the occasional shore excursion and premium wines at dinner; otherwise this really is an appealing all-inclusive package. Each cruise also features the Silversea Experience, a unique on-shore event for passengers that may be a beach barbecue in the Virgin Islands, wine-tasting in Bordeaux or dinner in a Victorian castle. Repeat passengers can enjoy savings on future cruises and other benefits through the Venetian Society. Children are not encouraged or well catered for, but there are two wheelchair-adapted cabins on both ships. For brochures, call 0171 739 4029.

Average price range: £2,795–£5,495 on a seven-day Med Cruise, up to £7,995 on the 18-day Chilean Discovery cruise.

STAR CLIPPERS

Ships	Tonnage	Passengers	Space Ratio	Built/ Refurbished	Cruise Area	Rating
SV *Star Flyer*	3,025	Max 170	17.7	1991	Aegean, Far East	Superior
SV *Star Clipper*	3,025	Max 170	17.7	1992	Caribbean, Mediterranean	Superior

Cruise line notes: Star Clippers are the most relaxed, informal and authentic of the classic sailing cruise vessels. They attract an enthusiastic mix of passengers from both America and Europe, average age around 45, who may well not have cruised before but are active travellers or just love the idea of real, old-fashioned sailing. The cruise experience is stripped to the bare minimum here; there are no casinos, beauty parlours or showlounges, and there is only one small shop. The nearest you get to all-out entertainment is a small piano bar, so it is up to the folks on board to use the unstructured pattern to its best advantage. Swimming and wind-surfing are popular, and there are lectures on navigation and sailing as well as organised aerobics and snorkelling classes. The cuisine is hearty rather than *haute cuisine*, but that is not why the majority are aboard. It is to enjoy the experience of real sailing, sitting on the bowsprit safety net and watching the sea whoosh by at close hand under full sail, and delighting in the friendliness of all aboard, from the captain down to the waiters. Star Clippers are marketed in Britain through the

Classic sailing on the Star Clipper

Fred Olsen line and you should find their brochure next to the *Black Prince* and *Black Watch* in most travel agents (or call Fred Olsen on 01473 292222).

Ship notes: These handsome vessels do offer a sound basic level of cruise ship comfort, with clean, well-equipped (if a little cramped) modern cabins, a couple of small pools and a splendid dining room. The emphasis is more on helping to raise the sails than helping to raise your on-board credit, although the varied water-sports programme is extra. The décor is classic maritime Edwardian – notably in the smart library/writing room – but the overall style is pretty casual – no jacket and tie needed here.

 BRIT TIP

Because you are largely at the mercy of the winds, you cannot set the ship's itinerary in stone and must be prepared for last-minute alterations.

Extras: Standing by as the captain gets the ship under sail is a wonderful experience, while the watersports will keep even the most energetic at full stretch. There are some welcome add-ons to the Caribbean and Far East voyages. Deluxe cabins feature a whirlpool bath. However, this is definitely not the cruise for the physically disabled as there are no wheelchair provisions at all. The constant multi-lingual announcements (in English, German and sometimes French as well) can be irritating and their brochure takes some unravelling, too. Both ships are officially recognised scuba-dive centres and have professional courses visiting some magnificent dive areas. In addition to their main itineraries, each ship makes two long positioning cruises a year, the *Clipper* between Cannes and the Caribbean and the *Flyer* between Athens and the Far East.

Average price range: £1,130 for a week's Mediterranean cruise, up to £4,145 on a 15-nighter in the Caribbean.

STAR CRUISE

Ship	Tonnage	Passengers	Space Ratio	Built/ Refurbished	Cruise Area	Rating
MS SuperStar Gemini	19,046	Max 900	21.1	1992/1995	SE Asia	Superior

Cruise line notes: This Singapore-based line is attempting to enter cruising's main-stream by attracting more passengers from outside its obvious Asian stronghold, including Britain, for the first time. There are currently six vessels under the Star Cruise banner, but only the medium-sized cruiser *SuperStar Gemini* (formerly the *Crown Jewel* of Cunard's Caribbean operation) is actually aimed at the European market with its five-day cruises, as the other five ships, two 40,000-tonners, the 28,000-ton former *Golden Princess* and a pair of small, luxury ships, are all one- and two-day attractions only. The line has some big plans, though, with orders for two new vessels, both weighing in at a whopping 75,000 tons, for delivery in 1998 and 1999, working attractive seven-night itineraries. The basic experience is likely to be an Oriental one, from the cuisine to the entertainment to a significant number of your fellow passengers, but that will find plenty of favour in Europe and the US, and the accent will be on smart casual rather than any great formality (DJs are not required), which will appeal to first-time cruisers, and the age profile is often quite young compared to the more traditional European markets. Expect plenty of karaoke and more relaxed meal-times (Asian folk tend to snack little and often), but there are also Western-style cuisine and American and Australian entertainers on board. The mix of passengers is likely to be up to 50 per cent Australian, 35 per cent European (with up to 25 per cent Brits) and some 15 per cent local business, with a handful of Americans. There are plenty of activities for children, too, with full-time, qualified child minders, plus a video arcade. Be aware that this region of the Far East suffers from heavy seasonal weather – high humidity, rainfall and the occasional tropical storm or typhoon – between May and October.

Ship notes: The old *Crown Jewel* was a fine product for the seven-day cruise market and she is well-suited to short-hauls around Malaysia, Sumatra and Thailand. The cabins could be more spacious, but they are all well-furnished and quite airy and there is a generous selection of public rooms and a splendid five-storey central atrium in the best new-ship tradition. There is a full range of ship facilities, from the beauty salon (operated by the British Steiner concession) and fitness centre to the library, casino (members only – gambling is taken very seriously in the Far East), the shopping centre, disco and smart Galaxy of the Stars showlounge. The open deck space is good for sun-worshippers and there is also a jogging track around a proper promenade deck.

Extras: Their Asian expertise provides a good introduction to the area in a totally safe environment. There is also a No Tipping policy and port taxes are included. Star Cruise are being marketed in Britain by 16 different holiday operators, including Airtours and Thomson, who also have some attractive cruise-and-stay packages. Thomson include Star in their main cruise brochure, while Airtours feature them in their long-haul Far Away and Tradewinds programmes.

Average price range: From £969 for a 14-night Thomson package, including 5-night cruise.

SWAN HELLENIC

Ship	Tonnage	Passengers	Space Ratio	Built/ Refurbished	Cruise Area	Rating
MS Minerva	12,500	Max 392	31.8	1996	Mediterranean, N Europe, Red Sea, Indian Ocean Far East	Premier *Brit's Guide Favourite*

Cruise line notes: After operating on a small scale successfully for 21 years by chartering Epirotiki's little ship *Orpheus*, Swan Hellenic, the cultural cruise arm of P&O, have finally taken the plunge with a bigger, purpose-built vessel (chartered from the Monaco-based Vlasov Group who also operate Silversea) and have already expanded their horizons as far afield as the Indian Ocean and Far East in the winter. Their basic philosophy is that 'travel broadens the mind,' hence there is a strong educational content to all Swan Hellenic cruises, and they attract a well-travelled, more mature passenger who is there primarily for the itinerary rather than the style of travel. The new *Minerva* offers a much greater style than previously, however, incorporating as she does some up-to-the-minute features and outstanding design by British architects RPW, who are more famous for their work at the Gleneagles Hotel, Wentworth Golf Club and Claridge's in London. The line's strong suit continues to be her lecture programmes, however, with a 90-seat auditorium augmenting the main lounge for this purpose. Passengers get an insight into the art, history and archaeology of each destination from prominent guest speakers, and they now offer a greater mixture of cruise lengths, from 10 to 26 days.

Ship notes: Former managing director Rupert Morley explained their strategy behind the new vessel thus: 'We set out to produce a ship that does justice to the good taste of our passengers – cultivated and traditional. Cabins are elegant and simple, while public room finishes are predominantly oak with bronze fittings rather than chrome or mirrors. The design of the ship reflects the great British traditions of travel and learning,

The elegantly-appointed Wheeler Bar on Minerva

while a strong marine element will constantly remind passengers they are at sea.' And how! The *Minerva* is a little stunner in the best cruise traditions, and her cabins are all quite generously spacious and beautifully appointed, with the top-of-the-range suites offering a new level of comfort and sophistication for this line. The public rooms are truly gorgeous, with the provision of good spacious sunbathing areas, plus a health and fitness centre, beauty shop, library and self-service launderette. The dining room maintains Swan Hellenic's open-seating policy in fine style and the cuisine is a cut above many of the competitors in the Premier range.

Extras: The line maintains its No Tipping stance and, along with the extended itineraries, there are a series of attractive add-ons in places such as Dubai, Colombo, Singapore and Hong Kong. Many shore excursions and all port taxes are also included, and bar prices are nearer British pub prices than the rather inflated ones aboard American ships. Children are not really catered for, but there are four wheelchair-accessible cabins. The overall package is a wee bit pricey compared to many other lines in this range, but you do get a lot for your money, especially with the new ship, and no one does the educational content quite as well. For brochures, call 0171 800 2200.

Average price range: £1,670–£3,330 on a 10-night Aegean fly-cruise, up to £5,585–£8,190 on a 26-night Far East voyage.

THOMSON CRUISES

Ships	Tonnage	Passengers	Space Ratio	Built/ Refurbished	Cruise Area	Rating
MS Sapphire	12,183	Max 650	18.7	1967/1996	Mediterranean, Red Sea	Standard
SS Island Breeze	38,175	Max 1,383	27.6	1961/1997	Mediterranean, Caribbean	Standard
SS Emerald	24,851	Max 1,153	21.5	1958/1992	Mediterranean, Caribbean	Standard

Cruise line notes: The rapid growth of the UK cruise market through 1994 and 1995 and the startling initial success of Airtours in producing a package holiday cruise product has brought the country's biggest tour operator hot-foot into the business, with three contrasting ships on charter from Louis and Dolphin Cruise Lines. Their target, therefore, is people who have enjoyed a Thomson holiday in the past and might fancy a change to what is, in theory, only an extension of the same company's product, plus previous cruisers who are looking for a good deal on their next trip. Thomson view the biggest block on more people going cruising as the perception of it as being expensive, and so they have made value for money their principal concern. They are out to attract primarily couples of 40-plus, as well as a certain element of the family market – kids' prices lead in at just £99 (for under-17s) and there is a kids' club as well as well-stocked playrooms. The itineraries are all well-tried Mediterranean fare out of Majorca in the summer, with *Emerald* and *Island Breeze* switching to the Dominican Republic in the Caribbean in winter, while *Sapphire* moves to Cyprus and Egypt. For Thomson's latest developments, see Chapter Seven.

Ship notes: Like Airtours, Thomson aim to make cruise brochures easier to understand and so have reduced the number of categories and ask their customers to book only a category rather than a specific cabin (however, the earlier you book, the better cabin you are likely to get within a category as there is an on-board system of priority which works on a first-come best-served basis). They also strip away some of cruising's formality with some imaginative staff, many of whom are drawn from non-cruise sources and therefore have a fresh approach. The East European waiter and stewardess staff are all eager to please, if occasionally difficult to communicate with, and the food is also plentiful and good quality. Embarkation procedure at Palma could be better, though. The ships themselves vary a fair bit, which is the one real drawback with Thomson's evenly-priced operation. *Sapphire* is a small, homely, but high-density vessel, with a limited range of public facilities, although she still boasts good open deck space and features like casino, beauty salon and cinema. Cabins are neat without providing any great level of sophistication, and the passenger flow can be awkward as the majority of public areas are on one deck. *Emerald* displays far more choice and some up-to-date touches with in-cabin TV, a small gym, a dedicated night-club and a lively all-day bar/café called Monte Carlo Court. She still retains plenty of character from her early days (as in the stained glass ceiling and musicians' balcony in the dining room), but the main Show Lounge couldn't be more modern and inviting. Cabins still vary quite a bit, despite the reduction in categories, and the standard outside variety on Concerto Deck look better value than some of the superior ones, but they are all quite spacious and include hairdryers and pleasant soft furnishings. Deck space is good (especially forward on the often-overlooked Sun Deck with its neat little bar). *Island Breeze* is an old favourite of mine having been my first cruise ship under Union-Castle colours before sailing (garishly) for Carnival and now with Thomson/Dolphin for two contrasting seasons. She has been extensively refitted for the European market and now displays some strikingly modern areas while retaining her classic liner ambience. At three times the size of *Sapphire*, she also boasts a much greater range of facilities, with masses of open deck space and more cabin types. It pays here to choose the higher grades as they retain much of their essential character while being extra spacious (the 10 balconied suites, in particular). All cabins, though could do with new cupboards and drawers, and the soft furnishings in the lower grades are looking rather tired. Outstanding public rooms are the elegant Portofino Lounge, the inviting Cordoba Lounge (don't miss afternoon tea here), the well-constructed Piccadilly Theatre, the nautically-themed Capri

Bar and Grill (for buffet breakfast and lunch), the wonderfully old-fashioned Library and The Pub, completely redecorated under Thomson to provide a truly splendid bar at sea. There is also a cinema (as there is no in-cabin TV), a small beauty salon, three shops, a large casino, two pools and a paddling pool, a night-club, a dining room that retains a little of her old, grand style and a smart, modern gymnasium. If you can overlook the majority of cabins being a little spartan, *Island Breeze* remains a great cruise experience and easily one of the best in the Standard level.

Extras: Praise be! A major Standard operator has decided to include all tips, removing one of the biggest bugbears at this level. Thomson's general holiday expertise also makes for quite a slick operation, especially for shore excursions, and their comprehensive flight programme means you can set out from any of 20 regional airports. They also offer a number of attractive cruise-and-stay packages in Majorca, Cyprus, Egypt and the Dominican Republic. The children's programme features clubs for the 4–7s and 8–12s for two to three hours a day, providing a parent is on the ship, while kids also have their own early-evening menu. Two cruises can be taken back-to-back to give a full two weeks' worth of Mediterranean fun. And, at these prices (especially on *Island Breeze*), you'll be hard pushed to get better value anywhere in the cruise world. The transatlantic positioning cruises are also well worth noting for value, too. For a free Thomson Cruise video, call 0990 275587.

Average price range: £499 for a week's fly-cruise.

WINDSTAR CRUISES						
Ships	Tonnage	Passengers	Space Ratio	Built/ Refurbished	Cruise Area	Rating
MYS *Wind Star*	5,703	Max 148	38.5	1986	Caribbean, Mediterranean, Canaries	Premier
MYS *Wind Song*	5,703	Max 148	38.5	1987	Costa Rica, Panama	Premier
MYS *Wind Spirit*	5,703	Max 148	38.5	1988	Caribbean, Mediterranean	Premier
MYS *Wind Surf*	14,750	Max 395	37.3	1989	Caribbean, Mediterranean	Premier

Cruise line notes: Despite being owned by the giant American Carnival Corporation, Windstar maintain their own style and continue to grow with the acquisition of the much larger Club Med vessel, now renamed *Wind Surf*. They attract a high percentage of Americans keen to sample the sailing experience (although this one is a bit of a cheat as the sails are computer-controlled) in an elegant atmosphere that manages to retain a relatively informal manner. Passengers tend to be quite active couples in their 30s and 40s, and slightly older groups who are attracted by the line's more exclusive itineraries, like their new Pacific coast cruises from Costa Rica. On board, the main attraction is as much the open, friendly ambience as any great sophistication in the facilities, although the Windstar ships do possess the highest general comfort levels of the ships in this market. 'Casual elegance' is the theme of the dress code (i.e. jacket and tie not required) while there is no great organised schedule of events. Life is relaxed, unstructured and definitely for the hearty, outdoor type who enjoys his watersports more than his showlounges. The dining is open-seating and the cuisine and service are distinctly sophisticated, especially when compared to the fare on standard American cruises. All three vessels maintain an open bridge policy to allow passengers to see how it is done at any time.

Ship notes: Uniquely, there is just one class of cabin (with the exception of a couple of suites), and all are outside, airy and well-appointed, with a queen-sized bed (that converts to a twin), teak-deck bathroom (but with shower only), TV, VCR and CD player, mini-bar, fridge and 24-hour room service. The use of wood generally throughout the ships is an admirable feature, and the few public rooms (restaurant, shop, library, casino, lounge and piano bar, plus fitness room, sauna and the Verandah open-air dining option, while bigger *Wind Surf* also boasts three extra bars) are quite elegant in a traditional fashion. The ships also feature a water sports platform astern that allows for wind-surfing, sailing, water-skiing, snorkelling and scuba-diving.

Extras: The wonderful feeling of freedom with sail travel is never better felt than aboard a Windstar vessel with her more up-market elegance. You can arrive in some of the smaller, more exotic ports of call and really feel you are a privileged individual to be there. The friendly nature of everyone on board only accentuates this feeling and it is the ideal 'Get away from it all' type of holiday. For honeymooners it also represents one of the most romantic hide-aways possible, provided you are not looking for lots of up-scale evening entertainment (on honeymoon? Come on!). There are no children's facilities, but older children should revel in the great range of watersports on offer. However, the

The Windstar vessels are real classics

ships are not well designed for disabled passengers. Port taxes are extra. For a brochure, call International Marine Agencies on 0171 628 7711.

Average price range: From £1,932–£3,925 on a 14-day Med sailing.

BEST OF THE REST

To complete this section on the cruise lines of the world, there are a handful of others worthy of mention, albeit in more abbreviated form, for more unusual cruises or where their impact on the British market is negligible at the moment, but has scope to increase.

Arcalia Shipping Company: **Area** – Northern Europe, Mediterranean, Canaries; **Ships** – MS *Funchal*, MTS *Princess Danae*; **Rating** – Standard. This Portugese line enjoys a higher profile in the UK thanks to the British marketing expertise of Cruise & Maritime Services, who also promote German operator Transocean (two ships) and Greek company Dolphin Hellas (one, the *Aegean I*). The 16,500-ton flagship *Princess Danae* operates a series of summer charters, mainly from Harwich, to the Baltic, Norwegian fjords and North Cape. Her 1955 vintage (refurbished in 1994) makes for a generously spacious ship, if a little short of quality around the cabins. Festive Holidays (not to be confused with Festival) charter the classic *Funchal* (9,846 tons) for a series of ex-UK cruises each summer, travelling as far afield as Norway and Spain and including the British Isles and Ireland, with regional departures from Cardiff, Dundee, Harwich and Liverpool. The ship is 1961 vintage (refurbished in 1986) but has been well maintained and offers a good cruise experience at modest rates. She is quite a high density vessel, but has a cosy, friendly style all her own, with attentive service from the Portugese staff.

Clipper Cruise Line: **Area** – 7- to 22-day routes around Eastern USA, the Caribbean, Panama Canal and Alaska; **Ships** – MV *Nantucket Clipper*, MV *Yorktown Clipper*; **Rating** – Superior. This pair of tiny (1,471 and 2,354 tons respectively) shallow-draught river-orientated cruisers offer a sophisticated, unfussy version of close-in cruising, geared more toward nature studies than mainstream cruise enjoyment. They have the ability to nose into little-seen parts of the Americas in a relaxed, country-club atmosphere. Facilites are limited, but the accent is more on social and intellectual pursuits. Clipper are marketed in Britain through Noble Caledonia (see p186).

Curnow Shipping: **Area** – 35- to 39-day routes from Cardiff to St Helena, Tristan Da Cunha, Ascension Island and South Africa; **Ships** – RMS *St Helena*; **Rating** – Superior. Not so much a cruise as a sailing experience aboard a modern 6,767-ton cargo vessel operating regular round trips to the South Atlantic with up to 128 passengers. Creature comforts include a pool, a shop, sun lounge and dining room, an excellent library, deck sports and low-key evening entertainments, as well as simple, but perfectly comfortable cabins (although not all with private facilities). But the voyage is not so much about cruise luxury as the chance to enjoy sailing some of the remotest waters on earth, visiting rocky outposts like St Helena, where the ship spends at least one night, affording a unique opportunity (it is accessible only by sea) to explore this fascinating seventeenth century British colony, the quaint capital Jamestown and its extremes of countryside, from wind-eroded desert to mountainous cliffs. For more information, call Curnow on 01326 563434.

Direct Cruises: **Area** – Med, N Europe; **Ships** – TS *Edinburgh Castle*; **Rating** – Standard (expected). New in 1998 will be this bold ex-UK (sailing from Liverpool and Greenock in Scotland) operation from northern-based Direct Holidays, who have chartered the 32,753-ton *Edinburgh Castle* (formerly the *EugenioCosta* of Italian line Costa) to form their own cruise programme, selling direct to the public and therefore with lower prices than their competitors. They have targeted fans of Fred Olsen and the now-discontinued *Canberra* of P&O plus past CTC passengers who enjoy the all-British experience of sailing round-trip from a UK port, with more days at sea and with a good variety of itineraries (from the Mediterranean to Norway and even Greenland). The ship is of 1966 vintage, but extensively refurbished in 1997, and offers classic cruise style with an excellent array of public rooms (including a pub and cinema) and generous open deck space. All tips and travel insurance are included and, if they can deliver the quality of product they promise at these prices (from £799 for a two-week Canaries cruise), it represents superb value. For a brochure, call Manchester, 0161 237 5600, or Glasgow, 0141 221 0077. Their brochure is also wonderfully clear and readable, although, like Thomson and Airtours, they do not allow passengers to select a particular cabin as you book a grade only. Unlike Thomson and Airtours, there is no flying involved.

Hapag-Lloyd Tours: **Area** – world-wide adventures; **Ships** – MS *Europa*, MS *Bremen*, MS *Hanseatic*, MS *Columbus*; **Rating** – Superior-Deluxe. The merger of German companies Hapag-Lloyd (which celebrated its 150th anniversary in 1997) and Hanseatic Tours has created a new, four-ship fleet operating in some of the most far-flung corners of the world in five-star, expedition style. The clientèle is largely German, but all the ships are officially bilingual, with a highly personal, indulgent level of service. *Hanseatic* (9,000 tons) and *Bremen* (6,752 tons) are the two adventurers of the group, with ice-hardened hulls to visit the likes of Antarctica and the North-west Passage, as well as Northern Europe, Alaska, the Russian Far East, South America and the Falklands, but still in maximum comfort. *Hanseatic*, in particular, is a wonderfully chic little adventurer, more like a high-class country club than a ship, with spacious cabins, elegant public rooms and an open bridge policy for passengers to visit at any time. Rubber Zodiac boats allow for real close-up nature encounters, and both ships are designed to be as environmentally friendly as possible. *Europa* (37,012 tons) is the line's Deluxe product, a modern ship featuring some classic touches (although no balconied cabins), outstanding cuisine and tempting itineraries, including an annual World Cruise. She is also one of the most spacious ships in the world, with a wonderfully inviting feel to the public areas and conspicuously tasteful lighting. Passengers must feel comfortable in a German-dominated environment, however. *Columbus* (12,000 tons) is the line's brand new ship, a Superior, mass-market product launched in 1997 for extensive cruises of the American Great Lakes, but unlikely to be marketed in Britain in 1998. For more information on Hapag-Lloyd, call their main UK agents Paul Mundy Cruising on 0171 734 4404.

Noble Caledonia: **Area** – world-wide adventures; **Ships** – MV *Caledonian Star* (and various charters); **Rating** – Superior. Not so much a cruise company as 'a collection of random travel ideas', from a seven-day walk in north Cyprus to a 65-day Antarctic circumnavigation. If you are looking for something different, this is the company to turn to, with their cruise operation typically wide-ranging and imaginative. *Caledonian Star* is a thoroughly British product, offering a cruise experience several light years removed from the conventional, around such little-visited areas as the Seychelles, Bali, Australia's Great Barrier Reef, Fiji and down to New Zealand, then back to Northern Europe. The accent is on a warm, convivial atmosphere (maximum 110 passengers on the 3,095-ton ship) and an intelligent programme of lectures, films and shore expeditions with the ship's Zodiac boats. There is no obvious ostentation, but there is plenty of genuine charm in a smart-casual style and with a private yacht level of comfort. In addition to *Caledonian Star,* the company also charters with other expedition-type vessels, including the ice-breaker *Kapitan Khlebnikov*, the *Irrawaddy Princess* river cruiser in Burma, the *World Discoverer* to Antarctica, Alaska and the South Pacific, the *Bali Sea Dancer* around Indonesia, the cruise-ferry operations of Norwegian Coastal Voyages and the *Ambassador* and *Polaris* for trips to the extraordinary Galapagos Islands. Wonderfully heady stuff. Noble Caledonia's expedition cruises are also featured with Royal Geographical Society Tours, a joint venture to enhance the geographical and environmental aspect of each voyage and boost the Society's world-wide programmes. Their brochures won't be found in your local travel agent, but you can call their head office in Mayfair, London, on 0171 409 0376.

Page & Moy: **Area** – Northern Europe, Mediterranean; **Ships** – MS *Ocean Majesty*; **Rating** – Standard. As well as being the largest cruise travel agent in Britain, Page & Moy are becoming increasingly active in the ship charter business, with block bookings with several lines and, in 1998, 18 full-ship sailings of the Greek-owned *Ocean Majesty* (10,417 tons), a well equipped, if high-density, vessel boasting smart public rooms and unfailingly friendly service. The smallish cabins and relatively limited open deck space should not be a major drawback with the ship's destination-intensive itineraries (from 8 to 13 days) to the Baltic, Norwegian fjords, North Cape (all ex-UK from Harwich) and fly-cruises to the Mediterranean. The full-ship charters allow Page & Moy to provide a fully-British service, from the cuisine to on-board currency and evening entertainment, with guest celebrities on many cruises. There is also a special £4 coach offer to Harwich or Gatwick, Stansted and Manchester airports from anywhere in the country. For booking details or a brochure, call 0116 250 7722.

Renaissance Cruises: **Area** – world-wide 7- and 14-day cruises; **Ships** – *Renaissance V–VIII*; **Rating** – Premier. This American line is something of a well-kept secret (almost non-existent PR) in Britain, but currently aims at the

Sea Goddess, Seabourn cruise world, yet without quite the same level of opulence (and expense) and offers a series of unstructured, casually elegant cruises around the more select areas of the Mediterranean, Baltic, Caribbean, Indian Ocean and Indonesia. Their four elegant little ships (all of 4,280 tons, carrying just 114 passengers) are well equipped for their well-to-do passengers who tend to be in their 40s and 50s. Their style and profile are likely to change in 1999, though, when they take delivery of two new 30,200-ton ships with a much greater range of facilities but the same level of quality service and food.

They do not feature with many agents, but if they take your fancy, try one of the specialist consultants like The Cruise Line on 01273 835252.

Seawind Cruise Line: **Area** – 7- and 14- day Southern Caribbean cruises; **Ship** – TSS *Seawind Crown*; **Rating** – Standard. Now being marketed in Britain through Unijet, the Seawind operation is a toned-down, more refined Caribbean product on a classic 24,000-ton liner sailing year-round out of Barbados. The itineraries are a little different and the service totally European in style, dispensing with a lot of typical American razzmatazz in this region. Passengers are slightly older, although they are attracting more young first-timers and honeymoon couples with their keenly-priced packages. The ship is comfortable and old-world, with a more formal ambience and less attention to non-stop entertainment. Expect announcements in a variety of languages as she attracts passengers from Latin America as well as much of Europe. Call Unijet for their Caribbean brochure on 0990 336 336.

Crystal Harmony visits Caribbean St Thomas

Transocean Tours: **Area** – world-wide cruises; **Ships** – MS *Astor*, MV *Calypso*; **Rating** – Standard-Superior. This German line offers two contrasting products that work large areas of the world and so can boast some wonderful itineraries, including a 120-day World Cruise, also available in six sectors, on the 20,150-ton *Astor*. She also cruises Northern Europe, Eastern USA and the Caribbean in a fair degree of comfort, with well-equipped, spacious cabins and a generous range of tastefully decorated public rooms. The more mass-market *Calypso* (11,160 tons) operates solely for the German market from April to December, but still offers a series of Caribbean and South American voyages of 14–18 days for the wider market. She lacks the spaciousness and finesse of her partner, but still delivers an excellent value product. For details of Transocean's British options, call Cruise & Maritime Services on 01322 303399.

Awards
1998

And so we come to the cruise world's equivalent of the Oscars, the first Brit's Guide/What Cruise Awards. This innovative scheme aims to provide an extra insight into the real value of the cruise world as well as lauding the operators who we believe are the 'Best Of' in their categories.

First, let me introduce the panel of experts who have helped to make this all possible and who confer an air of definitive credibility in this field. They represent a full cross-section of the industry and are renowned for their insight into the vast range of products. They are: **Gary Buchanan**, a highly-respected travel writer and author of several cruise books, notably on the *QE2*. Gary is also a Fellow of the Royal Geographical Society and Vice-Chairman of the British Guild of Travel Writers; **Ken Page**, a popular former director of the Passenger Shipping Association who is still respected throughout the industry; **David Short**, Sales & Marketing Director of the big cruise agents Page & Moy, who travels widely to keep his product knowledge up to date; **Paul Mundy**, director of one of the most distinguished cruise businesses, Paul Mundy Cruising, and a founder member of the Guild of Professional Cruise Agents; from America, **Patricia Piacente**, President-Owner of the cruise-orientated Talk About Travel business in Northbrook, Illinois, whose Australian background gives her an excellent all-round appreciation of the industry; **Tony Ripper**, Director of the Cruise Advisory Service, who holds arguably the most complete and up-to-date database on all the ships in the British market; **Chris Coates**, one of the expert voices advising *What Cruise* magazine and a founder of the innovative Cruise & Maritime Services with his partner Richard Bastow; **Ian Buckeridge**, the razor-sharp, opinionated Director of Operations & Marketing for The Cruise Line Ltd., voted Europe's foremost cruise information and booking service by the European Travel Network; **Carolyn White**, Brit's Guide researcher and well-travelled cruise consumer who brings an acute eye for detail to the proceedings; and Canadian **Stephen Thorne**, Brit's Guide research man for North America and an industry insider, having worked aboard many of the main cruise lines, including Princess, Holland America and P&O. Stephen lives in Vancouver and currently works out of Fort Lauderdale as a Port Lecturer. Oh, and **me** (well, someone has to keep an eye on the intellectuals). In all seriousness, I am indebted to the support and advice of the above.

And so to the Awards. The four main categories of *Standard, Superior, Premier* and *Deluxe* each have their own Awards, with *Deluxe* being divided into two sections (small, or below 20,000 tons, and large) to highlight the specialist differences involved; then there are nominations for *Best Family Ship*, where the facilities must be aimed at both children AND adults; *Best Specialist*, to highlight operators who get off the beaten track or offer exceptional opportunities for adventure cruises; *Best Cruise Innovation*, to nominate those operators who strive to do something different in an increasingly regimented business; *Best Brochure*, which rewards those (few) lines who realise their literature can be hard going; and a *Special Service Award* for vessels of pre-1970 vintage which have continued to provide great service through 1997.

The full deliberations of the panel are as follows, with the Nominations given first in each case followed by the winner, which was arrived at by a majority vote, and a note on the winner by one of the panel.

CATEGORY	NOMINATIONS	WINNER
Best Standard Ship	*Carousel* (Airtours), *Celebration* (Carnival), *Bolero* (Festival), *Monterey* (MSC), *Black Prince* (Fred Olsen), *Victoria* (P&O), *Stella Solaris* (Royal Olympic), *IslandBreeze* (Thomson)	**MV *Victoria* (P&O)** 'P&O's edge as a British operator is most noticeable in the Standard category', says Ken Page
Best Superior Ship	*CarnivalDestiny* (Carnival), *CostaVictoria* (Costa), *Seaward* (NCL), *Black Watch* (Fred Olsen), *Oriana* (P&O), *Splendour of the Seas* (Royal Caribbean), *Star Clipper* (Star Clippers), *SuperStar Gemini* (Star Cruise)	**MS *Oriana* (P&O)** 'The best modern, all-British product', says Simon Veness
Best Premier Ship	*Century, Galaxy* (both Celebrity), *Vistafjord, QE2* (both Cunard), *Westerdam, Veendam* (both Holland America), *Marco Polo* (Orient), *Sun Princess* (Princess), *Wind Spirit* (Windstar)	**MS *Century* (Celebrity)** 'Their product is hard to fault', insists David Short
Best Deluxe Ship (small)	*Sea Goddess* (Cunard), *Song of Flower* (Radisson Seven Seas), *Seabourn Legend* (Seabourn), *Silver Wind* (Silversea), *Hanseatic* (Hapag-Lloyd)	**MS *Silver Wind* (Silversea)** 'Elegance personified', says Gary Buchanan
Best Deluxe Ship (large)	*Crystal Harmony, Crystal Symphony* (both Crystal), *Royal Viking Sun* (Cunard), *Europa* (Hapag-Lloyd), *Radisson Diamond* (Radisson Seven Seas)	**MV *Crystal Symphony* (Crystal)** 'A contemporary, quality hotel at sea', says Tony Ripper
Best Family Ship	*CarnivalDestiny* (Carnival), *Century* (Celebrity), *Seaward* (NCL), *Oriana* (P&O), *Sun Princess* (Princess), *Grandeur of the Seas* (Royal Caribbean)	**MS *Oriana* (P&O)** 'P&O have always provided well for families with children', says Paul Mundy
Best Cruise Innovation	*Airtours* (for their wholesale fleet investment), *NCL* (for the use of Houston as a home port), *Holland America* (for building a classic liner in their *Rotterdam VI*), *Royal Caribbean* (for introducing their advanced bookings system), *Royal Geographical Society* (for introducing RGS Tours), *Thomson* (for their dramatically increased cruise investment)	**Holland America for *Rotterdam VI*.** 'Hooray for a line not building a "kit" cruise ship for a change', cheers Ian Buckeridge
Best Brochure	Celebrity, Cunard, Bridge Travel's Disney Cruise Line, Festival, Hebridean Island Cruises, NCL, P&O, Seabourn	**Cunard** 'All five ships in one brochure is a big improvement', says Carolyn White
Best Specialist	*Explorer* (Abercrombie & Kent), *St Helena* (Curnow Shipping), *Hebridean Princess* (Hebridean Island), *Minerva* (Swan Hellenic), *Hanseatic* (Hapag-Lloyd) *Caledonian Star* (Noble Caledonia), *Marco Polo* (Orient)	**MV *Hebridean Princess* (Hebridean Island Cruises)** 'An absolute joy of a little ship', says Paul Mundy
Special Service Award	*QE2* (Cunard), *Canberra* (P&O), *Orpheus* (Royal Olympic), *IslandBreeze* (Thomson/Dolphin)	**QE2 (Cunard)** 'Still the grand old lady of the seas', says Stephen Thorne

*

CHAPTER SIX

Where Can I Cruise?

(or, The World is Truly your Lobster)

In many cases it is a question of saving the best until last when you come to consider your options for exactly *where* in the world to enjoy the cruise experience. It should by now be fairly evident you have a breathtaking range of choice in the style of cruising you select, and the same is equally the case when it comes to deciding the area that most takes your fancy. The long and the short of it is simply you can sample just about anywhere in the world where it is possible for a cruise ship to sail. As already noted, you can choose itineraries that are port-intensive or ones which offer more days at sea; where the accent is on the destinations themselves or where it is more about the style in which you travel; and you can sample extremes of temperature, from the frozen ice continents to the tropical rain forests.

Close encounters of the penguin kind in Antarctica

There is, of course, an extra element in all this which is the cruise season for any particular area. The Mediterranean and Alaska – two of the most popular and rapidly-expanding cruise destinations – are both primarily a spring and summer prospect, while even the Caribbean, for all that it offers year-round sunshine, has some unpredictable weather, notably in the official hurricane season from July to November, which is particularly bad news for cruising (not that it means you are likely to be in danger, just that you can find ports of call cancelled at short notice and the seas a little rougher than their usual tranquil state). The two big hurricanes in the autumn of 1995 effectively took the Caribbean's two most visited destinations, the US Virgin Island of St Thomas and the Dutch St Maarten, out of commission for several months and forced the cruise lines to reschedule hurriedly many of their Caribbean itineraries. It made big news at the time, of course, because it was so extreme and such a rarity, but it does serve to indicate nothing is totally reliable when you have the weather as one of your main operating factors. For this reason, remember that itineraries can change at short notice. When it comes to the cruise seasons, you will find the American lines also divide their operations into three distinct periods according to the demand. *High Season* marks the main holiday periods in the States when the majority of people are all looking to get away, and hence prices are higher, discounts are rare and ships are closest to capacity. The *Shoulder* or *Value Season* marks the periods just either side of the peak demands where larger numbers are still in search of their holiday, but can be more flexible with their vacation time. Finally, the *Low* or *Economy Season* indicates the periods of lowest demand, e.g. early and late in the Alaska run (May and September), when prices are lowest and the ships are likely to be at their quietest. Quite often, only a few weeks can separate the *High* and *Low* seasons for a given area, and it stands to reason that if you can be flexible with your own holiday time you can make the biggest savings on your cruise price.

GATEWAY TO THE WORLD

Seasonality apart, of course, it remains true that your choice is utterly world-wide. If you fancy exploring the North-west Passage, there is a ship (Radisson Sevens Seas' *Hanseatic*, for example) that will take you there; if your family is adventurous enough to want to sail around Cape Horn at the tip of South America, you have that choice open to you as well (try Silversea, Seabourn or Princess); perhaps the less-explored corners of the Mediterranean appeal to you, in which case there is now a growing band of ships eager to satisfy that demand, too (Star Clippers and Royal Olympic both boast some innovative itineraries); or, if you just want to enjoy the general cruise experience, relax and unwind in the sunshine, the Caribbean remains the perfect setting and any one of two dozen cruise lines can tempt you in that vicinity. Whale watching in Alaska? Penguins in Antarctica? Native tribes along the Amazon? Archaeology of the Middle East? Shopping in Hong Kong? Investigating ancient cultures in the Pacific islands? The list goes on and on, and it gets bigger every year as the cruise companies continue to cater for the 'Something new' brigade.

But, before I get too carried away with the exotica of modern cruising, let's try to get a realistic idea of where the major cruise areas are, and where you will find the greatest numbers of British passengers.

The most obvious feature of the differences between where the British market chooses to cruise and where the rest of the world (i.e. the American section, or the other 75 per cent of the market) goes, is in the Mediterranean/ Caribbean percentages. While the Caribbean makes up more than half of the US market, it represents only a quarter of the British choice; and, while Americans in the Med number only 9.75 per cent of their total, it is a whopping 41.2 per cent share of the British market. Alaska is also way up in American popularity, but that is largely because it is so much easier for them to get there. It is one of the biggest growth areas, in comparative terms, for the British passenger, too.

WHERE THE WORLD CRUISES

DESTINATION	THE AMERICAN MARKET	THE BRITISH MARKET
The Caribbean	50.5%	25.8%
East Coast USA (inc Bermuda)	4.13%	0.9%
West Coast USA (inc Alaska)	20.05%	6%
The Mediterranean	9.75%	41.2%
Northern Europe	4.4%	8.4%
The Atlantic (inc Canaries)	1.85%	7%
Indian Ocean	0.24%	0.8%
Far East	2.13%	1.9%
Australasia & South Pacific	1.61%	0.7%
World Cruises & Line Voyages	2.61%	3%
Others (inc Antarctica)	2.73%	4.3%

So, if for British purposes the Mediterranean is Number One, let's start our study of the main cruise areas of the world there.

THE MEDITERRANEAN AND THE MIDDLE EAST
(Including The Black Sea, Cyprus, North Africa and The Canaries)

WHO GOES THERE

Airtours, Costa, Crystal, Cunard, Direct Cruises, Festival, Holland America, Louis, Mediterranean Shipping, NCL, Fred Olsen, Orient, P&O, Princess, Radisson Seven Seas, Renaissance, Royal Caribbean, Royal Olympic, Saga, Seabourn, Silversea, Star Clippers, Swan Hellenic, Thomson, Windstar.

Cruise season: Western Mediterranean, April–October; Eastern Mediterranean (Cyprus, Middle East and Red Sea), year-round

For practical purposes in the modern cruise world, Mediterranean itineraries cover the whole spectrum from Gibraltar to the Middle East (and the Red Sea in some cases nowadays), also including the Black Sea for a handful of Eastern European ports which are now an intriguing part of many agendas. Considering the Med has been Britain's favourite foreign holiday playground since the early 1970s, it is not too surprising this is also our

The Greek isles offer picture postcard sailing

Number One cruise destination. A greater familiarity with European culture, the relatively short distances and the fact it is a slightly cheaper option compared to long-haul fly-cruise all combine to make the area more attractive to the UK market.

It is also, however, arguably the most dynamic and sought-after cruise region in the world, hence more ships are being positioned for a summer season in the Med all the time, offering a greater variety of destination (and price) as the lines seek out more attractive itineraries to offer their repeat passengers. The big American companies Royal Caribbean and Princess are at the forefront of this development, but a number of the smaller players are equally keen to explore the possibilities and in some ways offer a more attractive product, notably the likes of Orient, Star Clippers and Radisson Seven Seas. Not to be outdone in their own backyard, so to speak, giant Italian line Costa (which also deals in the American market) is exploring new routes and bringing its newest ships into the area, while the two main Greek lines, Epirotiki and Sun Line, actually merged in order to create a better marketing opportunity for themselves. P&O and Fred Olsen, both long-established in this field, have continued to expand their repertoire, while newcomers like Airtours, Thomson and Festival have all taken

 **BRIT TIP**

The Mediterranean (and Northern Europe, for that matter) by cruise ship represents probably the most cost-effective way to visit Europe's major cities. It would be hideously expensive to try to visit, say, Florence, Rome, Athens and Istanbul on a flight- and hotel-basis in one go, whereas a cruise can do all that for you without having to unpack more than once.

advantage of the cruise boom generally, as well as the Med in particular, to establish themselves quite firmly in the area. Direct Cruises are the latest to seek a piece of the action here.

As a result of all this hectic development (and much of it has taken place only in the last few years), the Mediterr-

anean cruise passenger now gets a much better deal both in terms of price, as the competition hots up, and the hardware involved, as newer ships compete for your attention. Your choice of where to go is also being broadened almost monthly. As the political situations in the former Yugoslavia, the Black Sea countries and the Middle East gradually stabilise, so the cruise lines will seek to re-establish ports in places like Sarajevo, Albania, Lebanon, Syria, Georgia and the Red Sea. The cruise season has also developed apace, with the frontiers being pushed back all the time from the more obvious spring, summer and early autumn stages to encompass March and November and even the winter months in the cases of the Eastern Med and Red Sea.

Taking the area country by country, these are your choices in broad terms.

Portugal

Yes, I know its not *actually* in the Mediterranean (even my geography is not that bad), but it is commonly a starting point for Mediterranean ex-UK cruises, with the capital of **Lisbon** the main port of call. It offers a spectacular entrance as you sail under the April 25th Bridge, and the city

The Rock is Gibraltar's big attraction

itself is well worth one of the standard half-day tours which most ships will offer as there is a lot to try to see in a few hours.

Don't miss: The historic city's authentic old Alfama Quarter.

Gibraltar

This British colony on the tip of Southern Spain is a popular port of call for just about every cruise line and offers passengers longing for a good pint of

 BRIT TIP

Watch out for the barbary apes on The Rock – they will happily make off with any unsecured item you leave undefended – sunglasses, handbags, hats and even cameras. You have been warned!

beer or a plate of fish and chips the chance to visit a home away from home. You can see all there is to see in the city itself, go shopping in Marks & Spencer, have lunch in a proper pub and take a cable car ride up to the top of The Rock under your own steam in less than a full day, so an excursion is somewhat unnecessary.

Don't miss: St Michael's Cave in the middle of The Rock, with its labyrinthine tunnels and massive cavern which stages regular concerts.

Spain

The old city of **Vigo**, on the Atlantic Coast, is a less common port of call these

The Majorcan port of Palma is home port for Airtours

days (visited on only a handful of ex-UK cruises), but is still an eye-catching place, with some spectacular views over the huge harbour from the castle-turned-hotel at Bayona. With **Barcelona** now operating as a home port for part of the year for Royal Caribbean and Princess, and **Majorca** being the centre of operations for both Airtours and Thomson, it is noticeable that the cruisers' Mediterranean focus is starting to switch away from Italy to Spain, especially for British purposes. Barcelona itself offers more authentic big city charm, a spectacular view from Montjuic, the mountaintop venue for the 1992 Olympics, and an excellent opportunity to walk the local streets (being extra mindful not to carry your valuables carelessly as petty crime is something of a problem). Barcelona is also a fascinating port of call for its architecture, inspired by the unconventional Gaudi and others, shopping, culture (the fiercely proud Catalans), rambling Gothic quarter and parks.

Don't miss: The Picasso Museum for art-lovers.

Cadiz is the port city for **Seville** although several of the smaller ships can sail right up to Seville itself. The city of Seville boasts the largest Gothic cathedral in the world and some magnificent parks and gardens which it is best to explore under your own initiative. The Costa del Sol port of **Malaga** suffers from the summer deluge of European holidaymakers and is best visited for the chance to take a day-trip to the wonderful Medieval city of **Granada**.

Don't miss: The fourteenth-century Alhambra Palace in Granada.

Ibiza offers a more authentic Spanish experience (if you can avoid the high-season sun-worshippers), plus some excellent beaches, while its sister holiday island of **Majorca** should need little introduction to British visitors.

At the centre of the package holiday boom since the late 1960s, the island has some fabulous Roman ruins and charming villages, plus the inevitable beaches and a surprisingly unspoiled historic old quarter in the port of **Palma** itself. Again, shopping is a real pleasure and the city's landmark cathedral is quite an awesome sight.

France

The French Riviera should be an obvious attraction to anyone familiar with film-star style, designer fashions and the playgrounds of the rich and famous. It's expensive, outrageous, a bit tacky in places but otherwise still terribly chic, and those facets are all represented in the main ports of call. **Cannes** maintains its ancient heritage quite well in the face of the annual excesses of its international Film Festival and is a wonderfully relaxed port in which to shop, eat or just wander the well-kept streets. **Nice** (with its adjacent port town of **Villefranche** for all but the smallest ships) offers some pleasant streets to wander (notably the Promenade des Anglais where our Victorian ancestors discovered the winter package holiday!) and excellent museums. **St Tropez** is the epitome of French beach culture and open-air cafe society, but the jewel in the crown here for sheer up-market sophistication (and outrageous prices) is **Monte Carlo**, which can also be visited from Nice. The famous Casino, the Hotel de Paris and the Oceanographic Museum are all complemented by some fabulous views over the Principality from its perfectly-maintained gardens. And, providing you can negotiate a few hills, Monte Carlo is perfectly suited to doing your own thing for most of the day.

Don't miss: The elegant restaurants and shops of the Boulevard de la Croisette in Cannes.

The French isle of **Corsica** is a different kettle of fish altogether, a rugged, mountainous outpost famous as the birthplace of Napoleon and equally idiosyncratic. The main port of **Ajaccio** offers a pleasant, pastel-coloured town with a huge collection of Napoleonic museums, while the fortress town of **Calvi** in the north is quite breathtakingly situated (but suitable only for those who enjoy a challenging walk).

Italy

The most frequent daily port of call for many lines is **Civitavecchia** to allow for excursions to Rome. Much-needed extra cruise facilities are scheduled for 1998, as well as a new rail-link to Rome which will provide a welcome alternative to the two-hour coach journey. Once the work is complete, Civitavecchia will be a delightful visit. The port city of **Livorno** offers trips to **Florence** to enjoy the magnificent treasures and architecture of Michelangelo, da Vinci, Donatello and Raphael. Then there is **Naples**, for a chance to view the remains of Pompeii and nearby Mount Vesuvius, the picturesque, coast-hugging town of **Sorrento** (and its island of **Capri**) and the chic northern port of **Portofino** with its elegant harbour-side restaurants.

Don't miss: The Ponte Vecchio Bridge in Florence and the coastal scenery around Sorrento and Naples.

BRIT TIP

If you opt to go wandering on your own in most of the Italian cities – and especially Sicily – don't carry any valuables with you, since handbag-snatching and other forms of petty crimes are on the increase.

Genoa is the centre of the cruise world in Italy – and the biggest turnaround port in the Med – and is also the birthplace of Christopher Columbus, hence numerous museums and other attractions dedicated to him. If you can negotiate the traffic-choked centre, Genoa offers attractions such as the biggest aquarium in Europe and some great shopping, plus a fascinating medieval quarter and the magnificent Cathedral of San Lorenzo. New port developments are also a feature here, and the local tourist office is one of the most up-to-date in the Med. **Venice** is the other main point of embarkation for many cruises and the attractions of this quite magnificent floating city should be obvious. It is a great place to visit at any time of year (you can rarely avoid the crowds) and makes for a wonderful starting and finishing point to any cruise. Finally, the islands of **Sardinia** and **Sicily** offer two more contrasting Italian experiences, with the former an increasingly up-market, quite chic development, but still with a host of authentic little villages that are best explored on a ship excursion, while Sicily ranges from its crime-hit principal city of **Palermo** to the stunningly beautiful town of **Taormina** (with its port entrance of **Catania**), which is increasingly popular as a port of call. Lovely views, attractive shopping and restaurants and the background of Mount Etna all add up to one of the Mediterranean's most visibly enjoyable ports.

Don't miss: The Greek amphitheatre perched up on the hillside above Taormina.

Pacific Princess sails into beautiful Venice

Malta

Rich in history and diverse cultures, Malta and its little harbour town of **Valletta** is a particular personal favourite. A warm, friendly island at the 'crossroads' of the Mediterranean, the people have not forgotten their historic British ties, including the island's Second World War heroism, and so a visit here offers that extra dimension. The island itself is not outstandingly pretty and is even a little unkempt in places, but the coastline is impressively rugged and it boasts some unique sights, like the silent city of **Medina**, where no motor vehicles are allowed, some prehistoric caves and the full historical experience of the Knights of the Order of St John from the Crusades. The history of this remarkable island is fascinating, and, if you can spare half an hour, start by taking in The Malta Experience audio-visual presentation in Merchants Street in Valletta to get a full perspective of the island's significance.

Don't miss: St John's Cathedral in Valletta and its truly stunning internal architecture and painting.

Croatia

Croatia is another country making a tourist comeback and some cruise lines have reinstated **Dubrovnik** as a port of call, a welcome return for this Renaissance masterpiece of a city. Now a UNESCO world heritage site, Dubrovnik revels in its thirteenth-century traditions and is one of the Mediterranean's best-kept secrets, rivalling the likes of Venice for natural beauty.

Greece

Cruising is just the perfect way to see a lot of what this fascinating country has to offer in the best possible style. Given that Greek accommodation can sometimes leave a lot to be desired in terms of modern creature comforts, and island hopping by the local ferries, while fun for the young, carefree crowd, can be a frustrating and time-consuming experience, the cruise lines have quickly cottoned on to the attraction of offering full and varied itineraries in this area. Due to Greek cabotage laws (which may not survive EU regulations much longer), only Greek-registered vessels are allowed to offer circular cruises from a Greek home port (almost invariably Piraeus, the port for Athens), hence Royal Olympic (the merger of Epirotiki and Sun Line) have currently cornered the market on all the best cruise experiences in this area. However, their competitors do offer a good range of Greek ports in addition to other Med destinations, and no one else is as port-intensive as Royal Olympic (which can be a drawback if you like to spend some time at sea). For a really memorable Greek cruise, the smaller ships can visit a lot of the lesser-known islands where the big vessels cannot get in.

 BRIT TIP

A lot of Greek islands are only tender ports, i.e. the ships don't dock but transfer passengers ashore by tender. This can be a concern for more elderly passengers and those whose mobility is limited. Check your cruise brochure carefully if this could be a problem for you.

Piraeus is quite often the start or finish point for many Greek cruises and, as such, can be a bit of a disappointment, to put it mildly, as it consists of some fairly mundane urban sprawl all the way into **Athens** and its congested streets. Not for nothing is this known as the TV aerial capital of the world, and it is a major feat to take any picture of the sights of Athens without it being disfigured in some way by this unfortunate background. However, if you can survive the crowds and congestion, the Acropolis is still one of the great wonders and there are numerous smaller sites which just crop up at regular intervals around the city. The many museums are a real highlight for anyone with a historical bent, while no visit is complete without seeing the traditional guards in their ceremonial uniforms, complete with pom-pom shoes and 'skirts', outside the Presidential Palace in Constitution Square.

 BRIT TIP

Unless you enjoy an atmosphere of almost pure carbon-monoxide, Athens is not the city to wander around on foot. Apart from the fact it is a good 45-minute drive from Piraeus at most times, it is best enjoyed these days by air-conditioned coach on an official ship tour.

Once you head out from Piraeus, there are a myriad of islands vying for your attention, the main ones of which are the green (and rather British) **Corfu**, mountainous **Rhodes, Crete** (the largest of the Greek islands and therefore boasting several different ports), spectacular **Santorini**, popular **Mykonos** and the tiny uninhabited islet of **Delos**, which has some superb archaeological sites crammed into its two square miles. Corfu offers a graceful old town that is not too crowded with tourists in the height of summer while Rhodes has an equally fascinating old walled city as well as the brilliantly white village of **Lindos** with its picturesque Acropolis (the citadel of the old city). The main port of **Heraklion** on Crete is less than inspiring (apart from its outstanding archaeological museum), but the island itself has two of antiquity's most famous sites, the 5,000-year-old Minoan city of **Knossos** (partly 'restored' in dubious taste by the British archaeologist Sir Arthur Evans) and the more authentic palace of **Phaistos**.

 **BRIT TIP**

For visits to Thera, you have the choice of a short (near vertical) cable car ride, or a donkey ride up the steep, hairpin-bend-littered path. Trying to walk up the path can be hazardous (for being run over by Formula One donkeys or being ankle-deep in donkey 'doings'), and if you choose to come back down by cable car, leave plenty of time as some serious queues build up in the afternoon.

Don't miss: Knossos is just a short taxi ride from Heraklion and one of the great archaeological wonders for all its rather haphazard latterday restoration.

Mykonos offers the more relaxed, simple charms of its beautiful main town and thatched windmills, but Santorini is simply unmissable – a craggy survivor from a huge volcanic eruption around 1500BC, its small towns and villages are all perched high atop the circular cliffs which surround the central 'lake' and small core island that is all that survives of the main volcano cone. The main town of **Thera** is usually full of tourists hunting around the many jewellery shops, but the views from the top are quite stunning and rightly adorn just about every Greek scenic calendar you see.

The other main Greek ports are the mainland Peloponnese ones of **Nafplion** (otherwise spelt Navplion, Nauplia or Nauplion), which is the gateway to the principal archaeological sites of **Epidaurus**, **Corinth** and **Mycenae** and has a fine Venetian fort overlooking its harbour, and **Gythion**, the ancient port town of Sparta. Less-visited ports include **Volos**, with its precariously-perched monasteries, **Preveza**, for the up-market

Radisson Diamond explores many corners of the Med

resort of Parga and the Byzantine churches of Arta, **Patmos**, with the spectacular monastery of St John the Divine, **Cephalonia**, the largest and most unspoilt of the Ionian islands (which include Corfu), **Katakolon** and **Patras**, both offering visits to nearby Olympia (birthplace of the modern Olympics), **Skiathos**, with its pretty town and spectacular beaches, and **Pylos**, for the chance to tour the historic town of Methone and the palace of legendary King Nestor at Englianos.

Don't miss: The incredible ancient theatre at Epidauros (otherwise spelt Epidavros) with 55 limestone rows and room for 14,000 spectators, where, from the topmost row, you can literally hear a coin drop on the stage.

Finally, almost without exception, the Greek islands and other ports of call all offer some outstanding beach opportunities to relax and unwind, as well as some of the most hospitable tavernas in the world.

Turkey

This is an area the cruise companies are only just beginning to take into account, apart from the three main ports of Istanbul, Izmir and Kusadasi. It saw a huge tourist boom in 1995 and to a large extent it is an undiscovered gem of a country. It houses some of the most complete and well-exhibited archaeological remains from the ancient world and is a history buff's paradise. If your cruise doesn't include **Istanbul** at some point, demand a refund! This is one of the most fascinating cities the Med has to offer, situated as it was in antiquity at the crossroads of Western and Eastern civilisations. Even today it exhibits a tremendous array of co-existing cultures, not to mention some fabulous architecture, wonderful museums and a genuinely exotic atmosphere. A few ships now opt for an overnight stop in this city, which lies in both Europe and Asia because it straddles the strait of Bosporus. This just begins to give you enough time to scratch the surface, but if you can arrange a pre- or post-cruise stay, all the better.

Don't miss: The awesome Grand Bazaar for unique shopping and the pedestrianised precinct of Meydani, which boasts the three great wonders of The Blue Mosque, the Cathedral of St Sofia (a truly breathtaking church-turned-mosque-turned-museum) and the Topkapi Palace.

 BRIT TIP

Visiting any mosque, you will be required to cover your legs if you are wearing shorts, in deference to the Muslim religion. Large wraps are usually provided for that purpose, and a small donation is required in exchange, so try to have some Turkish currency with you.

Izmir (or Smyrna in the ancient world) is a busy, modern city with a turbulent history and is mainly used by visiting cruise ships as a gateway to the wondrous archaeological site of **Ephesus**. However, **Kusadasi** is a closer and more suitable port of call from which to take a tour of this absolutely unmissable ruined city, so much of which has been restored to appeal to even the most non-history-minded tourist. It requires at least two hours for a serious tour (which can be taken on your own or with a proper guide), so double check you will have enough time and remember that even though, in the height of summer, it can be uncomfortably hot, it is always a thoroughly memorable experience. Kusadasi has also cleaned up its act considerably in the last year or so to become a pretty little port in its own right.

 **BRIT TIP**

If any of your ship-organised excursions include a stop to check out Turkish carpet-making, beware. There is usually a crafty sales pitch thrown in, so try to give it a miss unless you are genuinely interested in buying (and can afford to splash out £500 or more).

Of the up-and-coming ports (where you usually have to tender ashore), **Bodrum** is a young, lively, happening resort in best Med style, exceedingly busy in the summer months but also boasting a fine Crusader fortress (and some tempting and relatively inexpensive seafood restaurants overlooking the harbour), **Dikili** is the new gateway to the impressively-situated ancient site of **Pergamum**, **Canakkale** offers its bustling waterfront cafés looking out over the narrow Dardanelles Straits, and nearby excursion to the (rather dull) site of ancient **Troy** (the wooden horse has long since gone) and **Antalya**, another major resort city and stopping point, affords visits to more Greek and Roman relics at **Aspendos** and **Perge**.

Don't miss: The Roman theatre of Aspendos, the finest surviving example of its kind.

Of course, all of these Mediterranean and Aegean resorts also boast excellent beaches to get away from it all for a while and perhaps sample the local alcoholic speciality, raki, the Turkish equivalent of ouzo or pernod.

The Black Sea

Another relatively recent addition to many brochures, the Black Sea offers more off-beat destinations and the chance to sample the different cultures of Bulgaria, Romania and the Ukraine. Here, at ports of call like **Nesebur** and **Varna** (Bulgaria), **Constanta** (Romania) and **Yalta** and **Odessa** (Ukraine) you can almost step backwards in time to a different century where the modern world has only just started to intrude. The relative level of poverty can be quite a surprise after Greece and Turkey and, in the Ukraine in particular, the locals seem almost desperate for foreign currency (and there is a seedy side, if you investigate too far – you don't want to get caught short in need of the loo in the Ukraine, the public facilities are indescribable!). All the different ports offer similar levels of cultural experience, but, to be on the safe side, it is better to stay with an organised excursion to get the maximum out of your visit. In the Ukraine in particular you will need a separate visa, which you are required to obtain more than a month in advance, if you want to go off on your own, but don't expect

The beauty of Venice, as seen from Crystal Harmony

too many people to speak English. The city of Odessa has its fascinations with the Potemkin Steps, the neoclassical Opera House and the catacombs, but somehow both it and the fading seaside resort of Yalta (famous as the site of the Second World War peace conference between Churchill, Stalin and Roosevelt) are ultimately rather uninspiring destinations, fun to say you've been there but not on the list for an imminent return.

Cyprus

Limassol has been the principal port of call for the Greek part of this island for many years and received a boost when both Airtours and Thomson opted to use it as a base for some of their cruise operations, offering some attractive cruise-and-stay options. Although Greek is the language, it is a country in its own right and offers a particularly rewarding island tour lasting the best part of a day and visiting the ancient site of **Paphos**, the imposing castle at **Kolossi** and the beautiful **Troodos Mountains** as well as the resort town itself. On the other hand, you could just grab a taxi and head for one of the great beaches.

Middle East

Until the promised development of the ports in Syria, Jordan and Lebanon actually happens, the region tends to revolve around Egypt and Israel. The Syrian town of **Tartous**, although not found on many itineraries, is a minor Eastern Med jewel, boasting as it does access to the fabulous site of the **Krak des Chevaliers** Crusader fortress, or a trip to the capital **Damascus**, almost a scaled-down version of Istanbul. Swan Hellenic currently operate the only really extensive choice to these countries, with the extra options of **Beirut** in the Lebanon (for tours to the 5,000-year-old city of Byblos and the fascinating mountain village of Beit Eddine), **Latakia** in Syria (visiting the massive and ancient Crusader fortress of Saladin or Aleppo, which claims to be the oldest continuously-inhabited city in the world) and **Aqaba** in Jordan (from where there are tours to the ancient city of Petra). Israel's ports of **Haifa** (picturesque and charming) and **Ashdod** (modern and functional) both offer tours to **Jerusalem**, which is the principal reason for visiting this region. It would be hard to see all the main sights under your own steam unless you have been here before, and the majority of ship-organised excursions will be all-day affairs, which even then can be pretty hectic. Alternative tours take in the religious stronghold of **Massada** or the **Dead Sea** (the lowest place on earth!), plus the ancient towns of **Nazareth** and **Bethlehem**. The city of Jerusalem itself, with its mix of Muslim, Christian and Jewish religions, is truly one of the great wonders of the Holy Land and, providing the political situation doesn't become too intense, it is an eye-opening experience.

Don't miss: The Wailing Wall, the Church of the Holy Sepulchre and the Via Dolorosa, the walk to the site of the Crucifixion.

Egypt can be something of a tourist hot-spot and it is difficult to know what to recommend as the official guidelines tend to change from month to month. Suffice it to say, the two main ports of call, **Alexandria** and **Port Said**, are both primarily gateways to (but some two hours' drive from) the city of **Cairo**, which offers an excellent museum and a chance to see the great Pyramids and the Sphinx, and you are best advised to take an official excursion to avoid any possible problems. An alternative tour from Alexandria takes in the Second World War site of **El Alamein**, with many relics of that crucial battle. A trip through the **Suez Canal** to the Red Sea port of **Safaga** offers the opportunity to visit the ancient city of **Luxor**, which is in many ways more fulfilling and less demanding than hot, noisy Cairo, where the appearance of the massive pyramids on the outskirts of the sprawling city can be something of an anti-climax. Aqaba in Jordan, and **Sharm-el-Sheikh**, for visits to Mount Sinai, in Egypt, are also beginning to attract more cruise ship visits as the Red Sea features in more winter programmes.

North Africa

This vast expanse of sun-drenched coastline can boast few genuine ports of interest, especially as the levels of poverty and petty crime are not conducive to comfortable tourist visits. I have been unimpressed with Morocco more than once and heard too many horror stories from European tourists in Algeria and Tunisia to be able to recommend either with any conviction. They can be intimidating countries for women in particular to visit, especially on their own. The most frequent visits are to the Tunisian capital **Tunis** and its port of **Sidi Bou Said**, which are notable for the chance to visit the ruins of the once-mighty city of **Carthage**, from

The city of Jerusalem

where Hannibal set out in his attempt to conquer Rome. The Moroccan port of **Tangier** is another regular stop, offering a taste of modern French-Arab culture and the inevitable shopping experience of the casbah. The inland city of **Tetouan** makes for a fascinating day-trip and rather more authentic Arab atmosphere (which can also translate as a bit run-down and not bearing up to too much close-up scrutiny). **Agadir** on the Atlantic coast has become something of a favourite in recent years with cruises from and around the Canary Islands, but again it is hard to see why. Laughably dubbed 'the Miami of Morocco', it is a modern, almost purpose-built resort designed to attract the European sun-worshipper in large numbers at the beachfront hotels, but, apart from a pleasant enough expanse of beach, there is little to hold your attention. An all-day excursion to **Marrakech** is the other option from here, but that entails a good six-hour round trip by coach and that is a lot of effort for the principal attraction of the huge souk or marketplace (okay, snake-charmers and fire-eaters can be fun, but you will find you are constantly hassled by local 'guides' and it can be an unnerving experience). If you are really determined to try Marrakech, better to find a ship that puts into the port of **Casablanca**, from where the journey is less demanding, and the city itself has a real charm of its own (albeit nothing like the Humphrey Bogart film). The ancient royal capital of **Rabat** is another alternative from Casablanca. But, again, as advised above, for safety's sake it is best to stick with ship-arranged tours.

The Canary Islands

Here is another mini-cruise experience that will appeal especially to British cruisers, particularly if the Portuguese island of Madeira can be included as well. The seven islands that make up the Canaries consist of **Gran Canaria**, with its port of **Las Palmas** (a bustling, lively town on a history-rich island, boasting some impressive architecture and landscapes, including the mini-Sahara of Maspolomas); **Tenerife** served by **Santa Cruz** (a functional town with a rather congested port when full, but gateway to an island of rich contrasts, from mountainous rain forest to wonderful beaches), the touristy **Fuerteventura;** the volcanic and treeless **Lanzarote** and its port **Arrecife**

Oriana sails through the Norwegian fjords

(opening up an island which boasts Fire Mountain, a still-active area of distinctly hot hills which offers a fascinating half-day tour); **La Palma** and its port **Santa Cruz de la Palma** (a tiny island that can boast the greatest altitude in the world relative to its perimeter and one of the largest volcanic craters to boot); unspoilt (and sparsely populated) **La Gomera** with its port of **San Sebastian**, and the smallest and most westerly island **El Hierro**, with the port of **Valverde** and some more wild, volcanic mountains. Surprisingly, the most British-feeling experience of the lot can be **Madeira**, which is some 250 miles to the north, and can be wonderfully pretty in spring with its mountain flowers in full bloom. The port and capital, **Funchal**, is a maze of winding, cobbled streets and red-roofed houses with a lively market where the majority will speak English. You can also stop off for proper afternoon tea at Reid's Hotel.

Don't miss: The traditional wicker sled rides down some of the steep streets, and the chance to wander the fine gardens and call in at the Madeira cellars to sample the fine local wines, of course.

NORTHERN EUROPE

WHO GOES THERE

Arcalia, Costa, Crystal, Cunard, Direct Cruises, Festival, Hapag-Lloyd, Hebridean Island Cruises, Holland America, NCL, Fred Olsen, P&O, Princess, Radisson Seven Seas, Renaissance, Royal Caribbean, Royal Olympic, Saga, Seabourn, Silversea, Swan Hellenic

Cruise season: May–October

As with the Mediterranean, the ports of Northern Europe are also very much on the cruise companies' 'hit-list' of places to expand and develop to make their itineraries increasingly attractive and a touch different. There are two distinct regions to this area's make-up, with the option of 7- to 15-day cruises around the Baltic Sea, taking in some of the major cities of Russia, Latvia, Germany, Denmark, Estonia, Finland, Sweden and Norway, or cruises of 9–14 days along the fjords of Norway as far as the bleak, inhospitable North Cape, Europe's most northerly point and well into the Arctic Circle. In both cases they are very much summer season destinations, and the attractions of the Norwegian fjords, the Midnight Sun and the forbidding northerly outcrops of our continent have much in common with those of Alaska. Once again, the cruise ship package offers the opportunity to take in the region's rich cultural diversity in the most comfortable yet still stimulating fashion. Distances between ports are relatively small, making for some more port-intensive itineraries which continue to attract quite an American following (especially those who have already 'done' Alaska and want to be able to boast the 'something different' factor to their friends). The fabulous scenery, the plentiful wildlife and the fascinating histories of the main cities are all hugely rewarding, hence the area is slowly losing its reputation for attracting only the older, 50-plus crowd. The arrival of Royal Caribbean and their new mega-ship *Splendour of the Seas* for 12-day cruises from Harwich into the Baltic and up to the North Cape has added a glamorous edge to the hardware involved, and, with Costa and Royal Olympic now offering fly-cruises around the area from Copenhagen and Festival from Kiel, the competition is hotting up.

What of Britain?

When it comes to the principal British ports, it hardly seems necessary to mention that they are only the point of embarkation for us, whereas the Americans (of whom there are still a fair number flying in for cruises with Cunard, Royal Caribbean, NCL, Holland America, Costa, Princess, Radisson Seven Seas, Seabourn and Silversea) usually see them as destinations in their own right. However, as there is now a fair bit of competition between the four main departure points for ex-UK cruises, it is quite informative to see how they are gearing up to attract the increasing amount of cruise trade these days.

Southampton remains Britain's busiest port simply in terms of passenger numbers (well in excess of 200,000) as it deals with the bulk business of Cunard and P&O, as well as occasional visits from Princess and NCL. It boasts two fine recently-refurbished passenger terminals with a total capacity (rarely reached) of 10,000 in the space of a weekend. The Mayflower Terminal (Dock Gate 10) serves the P&O ships which all sail from here almost weekly, while the QE2 Terminal (Dock Gate 4) serves, surprisingly enough, the regular visits of the QE2, plus the more infrequent visitors. Both terminals offer good seating space (as there can be a wait of an hour or more to board at peak times), plus bars, a newsagent and a currency exchange. The largest ships can call here and it is most conveniently situated for cruises out into the Atlantic and Mediterranean. Ease of access has been boosted by the completion of the M3 link to the M27 which runs through the city, and the drive from London to Southampton's dockside should not take more than an hour. Rail links are also excellent. Extensive car parking is adjacent to both terminals and there is also a car collection and delivery service, as well as the usual car hire company arrangements.

It may come as something of a surprise to people who know **Dover** only as a cross-channel ferry gateway to the hypermarkets of France, but it is the newest player in the UK cruise port stakes and has quickly established itself as the only major rival to Southampton from a standing start of no cruise ship visits as recently as 1993. A £10 million investment in turning the derelict old Dover marine railway station into a bright, modern cruise terminal was the biggest single development in 1996, and the huge upgrade in the port's facilities has quickly attracted a big increase in cruise business, with Fred Olsen switching their operations here from Southampton, and the likes of Costa, Festival, Princess, Holland America, Crystal, NCL and Radisson Seven Seas all joining the expansion. The clever restoration of the main railway station, incorporating the listed original building itself, has allowed for ample covered parking right next to the smart new passenger facilities, which include modern check-in desks, state-of-the-art security systems for quicker baggage processing, a comfortable 450-seat lounge and a pleasant cafe. Dover is also well served by its road links from London, especially the completed M20 route that skirts Ashford and Folkestone, as well as the M2 and A2 north Kent route. The additional element of sailing out of a port that offers the White Cliffs as the backdrop is also quite appealing to British as well as American passengers.

The port of **London** still offers two quite convenient locations at Tilbury and Tower Bridge, with the latter especially popular with the smaller, more up-market vessels like Seabourn, Cunard's *Sea Goddess* ships, Silverseas and Radisson Seven Seas' *Song of Flower*. The cruise terminal at Tilbury (officially run by London International Cruise Terminal) has rather fallen behind its main competition (Dover and now Harwich) in terms of up-to-date appeal, although it still boasts good road links from the M25 to the A13 and A109 and right into the port, and it is slowly losing business both up and down river. The Tower Bridge berth (Central London Cruise Moorings), alongside HMS *Belfast*, is not exactly a classic facility, but somehow it is typically British and sailing from there does provide the grand opportunity of seeing the beautiful Tower Bridge raised to let the ships out. It is never likely to be able to take ships of any great size however, which is why a planned new terminal at Greenwich is an interesting prospect.

The new cruise facility at the Essex port of **Harwich** is another quite fascinating development as it is geared almost completely towards Royal Caribbean's new mega-ship *Splendour of the Seas*, a 70,000-ton, 1,800-passenger vessel intended to raise the profile of the line significantly in Europe. The brand new terminal facility (completed in 1996) offers passenger, coach and car terminals and brand-new baggage-handling systems. Road links are again quite good (via the M25, A12 and A120), although it is the furthest of all four from the airports of

Royal Princess *in Dover Harbour*

Gatwick and Heathrow. The railway service runs right into the port area as well. Arcalia and Voyages of Discovery are other lines to use Harwich.

Once you board your cruise ship and begin sailing north, there is an exceedingly rich variety of ports that begin to open up for you.

Holland

As the Northern European market has grown, so has the appeal of its smaller ports as they all seek a piece of the action, especially as umbrella organisation Cruise Europe has worked hard to increase the profile of some of its lesser lights. **Amsterdam** has seen its ship visits more than double from a paltry 38 in 1985 as lines like Holland America, Royal Caribbean and Costa discover the city's attractions. For us near neighbours, there is no real secret – just a city with a rich history (dating back to 1275), lively streets, squares and parks, a laid-back culture and a wonderfully convivial atmosphere. Amsterdam will open a new, state-of-the-art passenger terminal in 1998 as further evidence of its long-term appeal to cruise devotees.

Germany

This country is usually the first stopping point for the Baltic Sea cruise, with the majority of ships now taking advantage of the 60-mile **Kiel Canal** (just 148 feet wide and mostly 46 feet deep) to avoid having to sail around Denmark. **Bremerhaven** provides access to the city of **Bremen** 37 miles inland, which is well worth a visit on any ship-organised excursion for its stunning medieval and Gothic architecture. Smaller ships are also able to take in a cruise down the River Elbe to lively **Hamburg**, Germany's second-largest city, and its full range of sights and activities, including canal launch rides, museum visits, the colossal fish market and the famous red light district of St Pauli (Hamburg's answer to Soho only somehow more decadent). The ports of **Travemunde**, near Lubeck (the home of marzipan) and **Warnemunde**, in the former East Germany, are both primarily departure points for visiting **Berlin**, either by coach or train. They are much closer than Hamburg, with journey times of little more than an hour.

Don't miss: Any full-day excursion to Berlin. It is steeped in twentieth-century European history yet also possesses some very modern touches like its shops and the Berlin Zoo. The Wall, of course, no longer exists to any real extent, but famous locations like Checkpoint Charlie can still be seen (albeit now as a museum).

Estonia

The strong medieval appearance and history of **Tallinn**, the capital of this former Soviet Baltic state, which maintains its own traditions proudly in the face of centuries of foreign domination, is well worth pencilling in to your must-see list in this part of the world. The so-called 'City of Colours' is an immaculately preserved fourteenth-century treasure trove of gilded churches, palaces and winding streets, and also boasts the nearby lovely **Kadriorg Park** and Palace, with its State Art Museum.

Don't miss: The Town Hall Square, the focal point of Old Tallinn, and the chance to sip the local strong, black coffee while marvelling at the glorious architecture.

Latvia

Swan Hellenic, Princess and Silversea were the only lines offering the Latvian capital of **Riga** in 1997 which is a shame as it is another of the Hanseatic League (a trading alliance of the thirteenth century) cities (together with Tallinn, Lubeck, Hamburg and Bremen) which means more medieval ancestry and architecture and a rich sense of history and Northern European culture. The **Dome Cathedral**, dating back to 1211, and **Riga Castle**, which houses three museums, are all worth taking in on a general walk around the city; this can be accomplished quite easily under your own steam and in relative safety (although most cruise lines still advise you to leave all your valuables back on the ship).

Don't miss: The Old Quarter, where 17th century buildings are preserved.

 BRIT TIP

There is increasingly a crime risk with visits to most Russian cities these days and St Petersburg is no exception. Wandering around on your own (you would need to have applied for an individual visa in the first place) is not advised, and you are best advised to stick to ship-organised excursions. You will also be hassled in the main tourist areas by street traders who are desperate to get their hands on foreign currency.

Russia

In a similar vein to Tallinn, and also still largely unscarred by modern development, is the main Russian Baltic port city of **St Petersburg**, which is a practically compulsory stop on Baltic Sea cruises nowadays. It offers a wealth of historical and architectural delights, with the world-famous **Hermitage Museum** and the **Palace of Peterhof**. The **Summer Palace** at **Petrodvorets** is another worthwhile excursion, while, as many calls now stop overnight, it is also possible to take in an evening ballet or concert performance – and come out to find it is still light thanks to Russia's summer White Nights.

In addition to the wonderful blend of Russian and Western European architecture (created at the demands of Peter the Great in 1703 as his 'Window on Europe'), the **Nevsky Prospektin** boulevard offers some great shopping.

Finland

The capital of **Helsinki** is another in the Baltic's impressive list of elegant cultural centres, boasting wonderful fish and flower markets which are all well within a good walk of the cruise ship docks. Its overall accent is more modern than historical (and at the same time superbly well-kept), but the **Senate Square** is impressively old-fashioned, with its Cathedral of St Nicholas, Government Palace and Rock Church of Temppeliakuio.

A double helping of style – the Deluxe *Crystal Harmony in Oslo*

Sweden

The typical cruise ship itinerary of Baltic capitals will also probably take in **Stockholm** and some more clean, cultured Scandinavian charm. The old town of **Den Gamle Stan** is a maze of narrow streets and neat little shops, usually chock-full of amusing street performers, and is ideal for a casual wander for a couple of hours. Ship excursions also take in the **Royal Palace**, **Old House of Parliament**, the restored historic seventeenth-century warship **Vasa**, and its attendant museum, and occasionally the beautiful **Drottningholm Palace and Theatre**.

Don't miss: The early-morning cruise through the thousands of islands that choke the entrance to Stockholm's harbour.

Denmark

If it's Denmark it must be **Copenhagen**, and frequently another overnight stop to enjoy the full range of features of this lively city. **Tivoli Gardens** is a prime attraction with its old world amusement park, as are **Rosenborg Castle** (home of the Danish crown jewels), the palaces of **Christiansborg** and **Amalienborg**, and the harbour area where Hans Christian Andersen wrote some of his fairy tales. Shop in the **Stroget** district, the longest traffic-free street in Europe, and tour the Carlsberg Brewery. The best port in the Baltic? Probably.

   Don't miss: Tivoli Gardens at night if your ship stays late enough (many now do).

Norway

Oslo is often the final port of call on the Baltic route and will complete a fascinating tour of the Scandinavian countries in fine style. Once described to me by a Norwegian friend as 'the largest village in the world', Oslo retains the small-scale atmosphere with a clean-city culture that offers friendliness and charm in abundance (if at an outrageous price sometimes if you stop for a beer or even just a coffee). Art lovers will want to check out the many art galleries (and art shops), history buffs the twelfth-century medieval fortress and marine enthusiasts the fine collection of maritime museums, including the **Viking Ship Museum** and Thor Heyerdahl's **Kon Tiki Museum**. The nearby **Norwegian Folk Museum**. Add in the unique **Vigelund Sculpture Park**, the world's largest collection of outdoor sculptures, by Gustav Vigelund, and you have more than enough for any ship visit (or two).

   Don't miss: Oslo.

 BRIT TIP

While the summer weather in Northern Europe is usually predictably pleasant and warm, it makes good sense to take a sweater or two, plus a waterproof jacket for the fjords.

   Norway is also popular for its utterly spectacular fjord coastline up into the Arctic Ocean, which can easily be a cruise in its own right. Starting at **Bergen**, with its huge fish and flower market, quaint streets and colourful wooden houses, the fjord cruise works its way steadily north taking in the increasingly picturesque sights of the mighty **Sognefjord** (Norway's largest), with its attendant picture-postcard villages of **Flaam** and **Gudvangen**, the impossibly steep **Geirangerfjord** (rated Norway's most scenic) flanked by the Seven Sisters and Bridal Veil waterfalls, **Storfjord**, offering a bus ride up the Eid River to the Mabodal Canyon and the roaring Voringfoss Waterfall, past Norway's third city of **Trondheim** (where you can see Nidaros Cathedral, the largest medieval building in Norway and the wooden church at the Trondelag Museum), and up into the Land of the Midnight Sun. Here you will find the ports of **Narvik** (from where you can catch a train into neighbouring Lapland and visit reindeer country), **Harstad** and **Tromsø** and the truly magnificent **Hollandsfjord** and **Ofotfjord** before reaching the **North Cape**, and the tiny fishing village of **Honningsvåg**, from where a bus ride takes you 21 miles through the bleak Arctic tundra to the top of the 1,000-foot cliff that marks the northernmost end of mainland Europe.

Don't miss: The Flaam railway ride to Gudvangen, or the sight of the sun not setting at night in the Arctic circle.

Ireland

From the roof of Europe it is possible to sail back across the British Isles to take in arguably the newest, most surprising and eager-to-please cruise destination. The likes of Seabourn, Cunard, Silversea, Royal Caribbean, NCL, Hapag-Lloyd and Arcalia have now put Ireland firmly on the cruise map, and its appeal is growing annually. **Dublin** is, unsurprisingly, the top destination for its scenic beauty and history, a great literary and cultural tradition and downright hard-to-beat hospitality.

Don't miss: The Jury's Hotel Irish cabaret or just the chance to sup a *real* pint of Guinness.

Cork is another historic city, with passengers able to disembark from the cruise terminal straight into the Cobh Heritage Centre. It again offers the chance to wander some ancient – as well as quite modern – streets, while Blarney Castle is only five miles away. **Waterford** is Ireland's fastest-growing port, with a new £30 million development paving the way for increased cruise traffic. The quaint streets and elegant shops, two great cathedrals and the adjacent Kennedy Park are all good reasons to visit.

Don't miss: The Waterford Crystal factory and the chance to buy some of their wonderful glassware at bargain prices.

Londonderry, in Northern Ireland, is possibly the biggest surprise, with the spectacular journey along the rugged Donegal coastline into River Foyle just the precursor to a city which boasts Europe's only completely walled centre, dating back to 1618. The inner city is a wealth of shops, galleries, restaurants and museums, not to mention the occasional pub (and, again, their hospitable nature is hard to overlook), with the Tower Museum in particular winning numerous awards for its audio-visual displays.

THE CARIBBEAN

WHO GOES THERE

Airtours, Carnival, Celebrity, Commodore, Costa, Crystal, Cunard, Disney, Dolphin, Festival, Holland America, Mediterranean Shipping, NCL, Fred Olsen, P&O, Premier, Princess, Radisson Seven Seas, Renaissance, Royal Caribbean, Seabourn, Silversea, Star Clippers, Windstar

Cruise season: Year-round

The world's biggest cruise playground has been a going concern for more than 30 years and is by far the most tried and trusted product on the cruise holiday shelves. Sunshine is virtually guaranteed, the islands are the stuff of Bounty bar adverts, people are generally amiable and relaxed (in some cases so laid back as to be practically horizontal) and the cruise ships themselves are usually the most modern and user-friendly to make sure of attracting the American market, which accounts for MILLIONS of passengers every year. As with other areas of the world, the search is on for new ports, particularly home ports, and new itineraries, especially on the short haul three- and four-day sailings. As a consequence, some ports like San Juan in Puerto Rico are becoming quite congested with cruise passenger traffic, and some of the

The Caribbean boasts dazzling beaches

bigger islands on the main routes can be equally busy when several 70,000-ton-plus ships are in port. Airtours have tried to avoid this particular problem by basing their winter Caribbean operation on Barbados and the Dominican Republic, with Thomson also opting for the latter. Royal Caribbean bids to compete with Disney by putting *Nordic Empress* into Port Canaveral for the first time, while also repositioning their smart, short-haul cruiser to San Juan in summer. Deluxe line Seabourn are on the point of quitting the Caribbean altogether because of the level of discounting involved in the area while also being aware that the increasing commercialisation is not what their customers want. Happily, there are still plenty of alternatives to the big island congestion, and your choice for ports of call has never been greater.

The cultural, scenic and geographic diversity is also huge, from the mountainous Spanish-American Puerto Rico to the flat, arid Dutch isles of Aruba and Curaçao, from the traditionally British Barbados to the Rastafarian Jamaica, and from the Bahamas off the coast of Florida right down to the Venezuelan coast of South America. In fact, the Caribbean is a huge cultural melting pot, soaking up as it has done for the last 300 and more years the influences of Spain, Holland, France and Denmark as well as Britain, often in quite violent fashion. The climate, of course, boasts a consistently warm, tropical nature, varying in temperature from 80 to 100°F (so remember to take those high-factor sun creams), and gives rise to plenty of rich vegetation as well as being the perfect environment for a host of activities, from water- sports to bird-watching. When it comes to food and drink, there is also an abundance of choice, from pina colada (the national drink of Puerto Rico), daiquiris (first mixed on St Thomas, claim the locals) and the ever-present rum (mixed with fresh-ground nutmeg on Grenada), to paella (Puerto Rico again), rijstaffel (an Indonesian dish popular on the Dutch islands), curries (Trinidad) and Creole cooking (with a festival every August on Guadeloupe). Fresh fruit is also universal, while the whole experience comes topped off with the inevitable diversity of music – salsa, merengue, the beguine, reggae, calypso and steel bands. The lure of the region is manifold.

For the purposes of this book (and most cruise itineraries), the Caribbean is also taken to include the Yucatan peninsular of Mexico and the Panama Canal. The region therefore stretches in an arc some 2,500 miles from the western tip of Cuba, just 90 miles off the Key West tip of Florida, down to the last islands of Trinidad and Tobago and the coast of Venezuela. It consists of the Greater Antilles (the largest islands of Cuba, Haiti, the Dominican Republic, Jamaica, Puerto Rico and the Caymans) and the Lesser Antilles (the string of smaller islands in a rough semi-circle from the Virgin Islands to Tobago). Barbados is the eastern-most point in the area and is therefore more exposed to the Atlantic weather (hence being one of the Windward Islands), while the Leeward Islands all enjoy the tranquil position of the Caribbean Sea.

Cruise capital of the world

The starting point for Caribbean cruises is likely to be either Miami or Fort Lauderdale, just to the north, which together are expected to account for several million passengers in 1998. Tampa, on Florida's Mexican Gulf coast, is actually the state's biggest port, but cruising accounts for only some 16 per cent of its business, while Port Canaveral, on the Atlantic coast, a short drive from Orlando, is primarily a short-haul port, although it will expand considerably with the advent of Walt Disney's cruise operation in 1998, for which a major new terminal is being built. San Juan, as already mentioned, is a thriving (and growing) cruise terminal, while several lines also use New Orleans and Galveston in Texas, although neither is directly applicable to the British market as there are no direct air links.

Houston, in Texas, is the newest port development, with NCL basing their *Norwegian Star* there year-round for cruises to the Yucatan peninsula, plus

Miami's famous Art Deco district

cruise-and-stay options in Las Vegas, New Orleans, San Francisco or on a cattle ranch. Some smart thinking has gone into this.

Miami remains 'the cruise capital of the world' simply because of the volume it handles – some three million passengers a year and 14 large ships year-round from no less than 12 well-equipped (if rather plain, functional) terminals. A £150 million expansion project – Maritime Park – to add four huge new terminals (providing a 40 per cent increase in capacity), plus entertainments, shops and restaurants, is scheduled for completion in 1999. The port is only a short taxi ride from the international airport and is also well situated to be able to enjoy the attractions of the rest of the Miami area (see below).

Check out Westin Resort for an up-market flavour

Port Everglades have enjoyed a massive growth in cruise business in the 1990s, almost doubling the volume of business to become the world's second-busiest cruise port, and welcoming some of the newest, most up-market tonnage on the Caribbean runs (Princess, Celebrity and Holland America are all regulars here). Ten modern cruise terminals, including a near-£3 million investment in Terminal Two for the arrival of the new *Sun Princess* in 1995 and superb links with the international airport of **Fort Lauderdale** (avoiding the usual congestion and hassle at Miami) make for a slick cruise operation. Again, the port is wonderfully convenient for enjoying the relatively undiscovered charms of Fort Lauderdale itself.

In keeping with its Cruise Capital tag, Miami and its surrounding beaches are a great add-on to any Caribbean cruise, offering some outstanding attractions, great shopping and nightlife and some fabulous sports opportunities. The **Art Deco district** of South Beach is Miami's main claim to fame, a series of streets surviving from the classic 1930s architecture style and a real happening area, too. **Ocean Drive** is classic background scenery from many episodes of Miami Vice, a street of hotels, restaurants and bars that attracts all the bright young things morning, afternoon and evening (especially the evening, when it really hums with party spirit until the early hours of the morning). A 15-mile string of white-sand **beaches** – Miami's second most famous feature – sprawl northwards from here and offer plenty of opportunities for a relaxing time pre or post-cruise. The **Seaquarium** at Key Biscayne is another top-rated attraction, an exciting family day out with a fascinating array of sights, from shark-feeding to dolphin and sea-lion shows. For **shopping**, Miami boasts a superb line-up of smart malls, purpose-built tourist traps and some really up-market developments, like the **Bal Harbour** shops with designer names such as Gucci, Cartier and Chanel. When it comes to **sport**, Miami can thrill you with NBA **basketball** (Miami Heat), **American Football** (Miami Dolphins), **ice-hockey** (Florida Panthers) and the great game of **baseball** (Florida Marlins), as well as being home to some spectacular **golf** courses. Downtown Miami offers the chance to ride the

Metromover overhead tramway, to go shopping in Burdines (the oldest and largest department store in Florida) and have lunch at **Bayside**, a lovely harbour-front collection of shops, restaurants and bars, including Miami's Hard Rock Cafe. You can also take a boat tour from Bayside around the miles of waterways that circle the city. Two other areas that should be on your must-see list are **Coconut Grove**, a lively shopping and nightlife development that has quite a

Go shopping on Las Olas Boulevard

chic, European feel to it, and the up-market suburb of **Coral Gables**, where you will find the beautiful Venetian Pool and the outstanding Biltmore Hotel – perfect for afternoon tea.

Don't miss: Coconut Grove at night, South Beach at any time, and the fun water-taxi rides during the day.

For the best place to stay in town, it has to be Miami Beach, where two of the most sophisticated and up-market hotels are the **Fontainebleau Hilton** (pictured in the opening credits of Miami Vice), tel. 305 538 2000, or the **Westin Resort**, tel. 305 532 3600, both of which come fully equipped with a superb range of facilities.

 BRIT TIP

Crime IS a concern in Miami, but common sense is your best defence. Don't go wandering off the beaten track at night and be aware that some fairly run-down areas of this multi-cultural city exist almost side by side with the glamorous ones

If Miami is just too hectic and, well, American, for the land-based element of your holiday (and many lines now offer a week's stay on top of a week's cruising out of Port Everglades), then **Fort Lauderdale** should suit you right down to the ground. The advent of Freddie Laker's direct air service has re-awakened the British holiday industry to the delights of this wonderful resort town, which has altogether a more relaxed air than its neighbour to the south. There are still great **beaches** to be lounged on and great **nightlife** for the younger holiday-maker, but Fort Lauderdale also boasts some sophisticated elements like the **Museum of Art**, **Museum of Discovery & Science** (the latter is particularly suited to children with enquiring minds), **Center for the Performing Arts** and **IMAX cinem**a. Shopping is again first class, from the massive discount mall of **Sawgrass Mills**, to the **Galleria** complex. In addition, **Las Olas Boulevard** offers some smart, boutique-type shops with a dazzling array of individual arts and crafts, plus some of the most enticing restaurants in South Florida. As in Miami, you can take a wonderful water-borne tour of the area, and the **water-taxis** operate conveniently to most parts of the city. For the chance to sample some real native Florida countryside, the **Everglades** are not far inland and there are plenty of opportunities to investigate under your own steam or simply take

an organised excursion that will pick you up from, and return you to, your hotel. Fort Lauderdale boasts a fine collection of Superior Small Lodgings (telephone the Visitors Bureau on 954 765 4466 for details), while two of the more up-market properties are **Marriott's Harbor Beach Resort** (tel. 954 525 4000) and the **Marriott Marina** (tel. 954 463 4000), both with first-class facilities and convenient for the port.

Deep-sea fishing is a popular excursion

Don't miss: Las Olas Boulevard at night, an Everglades airboat ride and, if you are in town in December, the glittering spectacle of the annual Winterfest Boat Parade around the waterways.

Any Caribbean cruise that sails out of Miami or Fort Lauderdale will be likely to include a call at the **Bahamas** as either its starting or finishing point. This ultra-Americanised group of 700 islands (of which little more than 20 are inhabited) is a major beach holiday resort and, as such, can be incredibly busy during the main holiday periods of Christmas, Easter and summer. Visiting cruise ships are allowed to keep their casinos and gift shops open as an extra incentive to offset higher port taxes, and that gives a hint as to some of the principal attractions – duty-free shopping and gambling (which both draw the Americans like bees round a honey pot). The main resort areas tend to be high-rise and very modern, with some distinctly ordinary tourist shopping, not exactly what the Caribbean is renowned for (i.e. laid-back culture and white beaches), but the main town and harbour of **Nassau** does maintain some of its original charm and could not be more convenient to explore on foot from the docks. The islands don't boast a whole range of attractions outside the beach resorts and the towns of Nassau and **Freeport** (the alternative, or sometimes second, Bahamas port of call), so unless you fancy one of the raucous rum party catamaran cruises, a beach party or a fairly unnecessary town tour, save your organised excursions for elsewhere. The marine menagerie of **Coral World** on New Providence (Nassau's island – Freeport is on Grand Bahama) is worth a visit, as is the luxuriant **Garden of the Groves** and **Bahamas Museum** in Freeport.

The **Greater Antilles** will usually be next on the agenda from the Bahamas. **Cuba** is by far the biggest island, but as it remains politically at loggerheads with the US, no American-based cruise ship will visit it. The Cuban tourist business is growing fast, despite its travel restrictions, and this could be a good chance to get a glimpse of the island generally, and the fascinating, multi-cultured city of **Havana**, before the inevitable commercialisation occurs. The political situation in **Haiti** tends to keep the cruise lines away from here, too, although Royal Caribbean do at least have a private beach set-up at **Labadee**, a tiny island off the north coast of Haiti. The

Dominican Republic, which forms the other half of the island mass of Hispaniola with Haiti, is one of those on the list of places to be 'discovered' by the majority of cruise lines as its tourist infrastracture is still limited mainly to beach-orientated pursuits. However, there is the charming old city of **Santo Domingo** to explore (the island's capital, and the oldest city in the New World) with its sixteenth-century cathedral and other relics of the Christopher Columbus era, while the resort

Catch the Caribbean spirit with Windstar

of **Casa de Campo**, with its adjacent port of **La Romanna**, is world-renowned for its full range of sports facilities.

Don't miss: Shopping for amber anywhere on the island.

The large tropical rain-forested island of **Puerto Rico** boasts just the main port of **San Juan**, which is now as much a starting point as a port of call along the way. Its heavy commercialisation makes it fairly unremarkable and a bit like any other major Spanish resort you care to mention (with heavy

BRIT TIP

Not for nothing is El Yunque in Puerto Rico called a RAIN forest so be prepared for some major precipitation – it can experience more than 60 INCHES of rain a month in the wet season from August to November! And, when walking around the San Juan, keep your valuables secure as petty crime is an increasing problem.

American overtones), but the saving grace of the **Old Town**, which can easily be explored on foot, and the chance to take an excursion out of the city to the rain-forest of **El Yunque** still make San Juan worth a visit.

Don't miss: The seventeenth-century fortress of San Cristobal in the Old Town on your self-guided tour.

Jamaica has been at the centre of the Caribbean cruise business right from

Idyllic beaches are a feature of the Caribbean

the word go and it remains popular, although the island has its share of crime problems as its increasing poverty-stricken areas do not sit easily with the wealth brought in by the tourist industry. The capital of **Kingston**, an infrequent port of call, is not the place to go wandering on your own, and organised excursions generally are much the safer option. **Ocho Rios** is increasingly the main port of call to take in the spectacular **Dunn's River Falls**, the classic Jamaican postcard, where you can climb up (or down) the 600-foot falls providing you remembered to pack your swimsuit and some trainers that you don't mind getting wet. Yacht cruising, rafting and visits to the **Prospect Plantation** are the other recommended excursions, while the alternative port of **Montego Bay** offers some superb beach resorts (try Doctor's Cave Beach) and local crafts in the town, where you can expect to be pestered by the many vendors (who also wander the beaches – so keep your valuables safe or, better still, leave them on the ship). Finally, if you leave Jamaica without being offered ganja or 'waccy baccy' then you haven't really seen the island.

The nearby **Cayman Islands** are almost the mirror image of feisty Jamaica – courteous, almost reserved and quite sophisticated. Not for nothing is **Grand Cayman** known as the Switzerland of the Caribbean. It is well-organised and currency-conscious, but delivers great value for money, some wonderfully picturesque views around the main town of **George Town** and its beaches (notably **Seven Mile Beach**) and, more importantly, some of the best underwater viewing in the Caribbean. Whether you take the **Atlantis Submarine** trip or are adventurous enough to go snorkelling or scuba diving, this is the unmissable attraction of Grand Cayman. The Cayman Wall reefs are the most famous feature, along with **Stingray City** – an area of North Sound barely 12 feet deep where you can snorkel among the menacing (but totally harmless) rays and really have something to tell your friends afterwards. An unforgettable experience, but not for the faint-hearted. Grand Cayman also boasts the world's only commercial **Green Turtle Farm**, which helps to play a part in the conservation of this species, but doesn't hold back from offering a whole array of turtle dishes. No turtle products can be imported into Britain, by the way.

Any voyage to the Western Caribbean (especially popular with the four-day winter and spring cruises) is also likely to take in the part of **Mexico** which sticks out into the Caribbean, the Yucatan Peninsula. Here the three main resort ports are all highly Americanised and can be incredibly busy, but they do offer another different cultural experience. The island of **Cozumel** is the most frequent port of call for some brilliant snorkelling and shopping (the latter of which has all but submerged the original Mexican settlement), and it is often combined with a stop at mainland **Playa del Carmen**, from where it is possible to take a tour to the Mayan Ruins of **Tulum** or **Chichen Itza**, which features some impressive towering temples. **Cancun** is a modern, purpose-built beach resort and has little in common with the rest of the region, but it is also slightly closer to Chichen Itza to avoid the six-hour round trip from Playa del Carmen.

 BRIT TIP

Irrespective of whether the island has any great scenic diversity or not, each one will offer the standard ship-organised Island Tour, varying from a half to a full day out. The latter is NEVER necessary, while some of the smaller islands (notably the Dutch Antilles, St Lucia and Tobago) just do not have enough to justify a proper tour.

The **Virgin Islands** are more or less at the centre of the Caribbean for cruise purposes (and also mark the beginning of the **Lesser Antilles**), and the **US Virgin Islands** (St Thomas, St John and St Croix) are an almost obligatory port of call for American ships. Up to 12 vessels at a time throng the harbour and disgorge their passengers into the streets of **Charlotte Amalie** and the biggest duty-free shopping frenzy in the Caribbean. Visit **Mountain Top** for an overview of **St Thomas** and sip a banana daiquiri at the world-famous Banana Daiquiri Bar while you look down on **Magens Bay**, frequently listed among the Top Ten most beautiful beaches in the world. St Thomas and **St Croix** (the Americans pronounce it St Croy) are unfailingly American, right down to the fast food restaurants and hotel resorts, but that does not necessarily make it a Bad Thing – the people, and taxi drivers in particular, are always polite and helpful and crime is not a problem here as it is on some islands. A visit to **St John** is also worthwhile as much of it is designated National Park, including some 5,600 acres under water. This means great, unspoilt beaches (including another Top Tenner, **Trunk Bay**) and a general lack of commercialisation. If the US Virgins still sound a bit too much for European tastes, then Tortola and Virgin Gorda – the **British Virgin Islands** – will have more appeal. The lack of tourist development is quite striking in comparison to St Thomas, and the atmosphere is altogether more rustic and laid back. **Virgin Gorda** offers **The Baths**, another stunning area for underwater exploration, while Tortola is just drop-dead tropical island pretty. The main port, **Road Town**, will keep you amused for an hour or two's gentle wander – longer if you happen to stop off at **Pusser's Company Store**

The beautiful island of St Lucia

and make the mistake of over-sampling their near-lethal rum concoctions! It has real Brit appeal, even this far from home, and Pusser's is also a great place to stop for a bite to eat and to buy some unique souvenirs.

Don't miss: Snorkelling at The Baths and a drink at Pusser's.

Running down the rest of the Lesser Antilles islands is like a trip through all the wonders of paradise, and this is the essential Caribbean that people usually think of whenever you mention the area. **St Kitt's**, **Montserrat**, **Antigua**, **Barbuda**, **Martinique**, **St Lucia** – the names are just as evocative as the places themselves. Here is where it is most tempting to choose an itinerary that gets you to as many of them as possible. That is fine if you have a two-week cruise and can enjoy seven or eight ports in that time, but a typical seven-day cruise that tries to fit in seven or more ports of call can be overdoing it just a bit, even in this eye-catching playground. The differences in style and appearance are not that great along this stretch, and it can all become a bit of a blur if you try to do too much, hence the frequently-heard remark that one Caribbean island looks much like another after a while. Well, they would if you have six or seven successive island tours under your belt with little time taken at each one to enjoy the distinguishing features.

Starting at the top, **St Martin/St Maarten** is split into French and Dutch portions, hence the twin name. For a tiny island (just 37 square miles) it has packed in a lot of tourist development, and the French/Dutch split makes for contrasting experiences, with the Dutch capital and port of **Phillipsburg** offering more rampant commercialisation *à la* St Thomas, while **Marigot** in the French area is distinctly more laid-back and authentic. **St Barthelemy** is a little-visited French outpost that offers the chic town of **Gustavia** and a wonderful walk up to **Les Castelets** for an overview of this uncrowded, unhurried island. **St Kitt's**, and its smaller volcanic twin neighbour of **Nevis**, is one of the former British colonies in the Caribbean that still has overtones of the colonial days as well as some of the most genuine Caribbean charm in the whole region. Fabulous beaches, friendly people, good shopping and lovely walks around the capital and port of **Basseterre** make this a real gem.

Don't miss: A trip to the 37-acre, seventeenth-century fortress at **Brimstone Hill**.

Antigua, another former British colony, is all about great beaches (the locals claim there are 365, one for every day of the year), great watersports (including a world-famous yachting festival every April) and great cricket – it's a stronghold of the West Indies' renowned cricketing prowess. **Montserrat** is another little-visited gem, but has effectively been closed to tourists after the huge volcanic eruption that affected the whole island. The devastation was widespread and, sadly, in August 1997 there was no sign of a return to normal life. **Guadeloupe** returns to French-Caribbean style and is split into two halves, with the city of **Point-à-Pitre** dominating one half and the other boasting the unmissable lush rain-forest of the **Parc Naturel**. The island also features some of the best Creole cooking in the world in numerous little restaurants dotted around, some of which are usually people's homes! Stop at the main tourist information office at the **Place de la Victoire** for up-to-the-minute details on where to eat. Costa's *CostaClassica* also uses Guadeloupe as a winter home-port.

Dominica (not to be confused with the Dominican Republic in the Greater Antilles) is verdant, natural and still home to a large population of Carib Indians who were all but wiped out by the European colonists of the sixteenth and seventeenth centuries. A ship-organised tour is a good idea here as the roads are poor and there are many picturesque corners to see, like **Trafalgar Falls** and its bubbling mud lake, and the glittering waterfall at **Morne Trois Pitons**. **Martinique** is more chic French-Caribbean culture, with its neat town of **Fort-de-France** and some elegant shopping.

Don't miss: The site of Mont Pelee, the largest volcanic eruption in the Caribbean, which killed more than 30,000 islanders in a mind-boggling explosion in 1902.

St Lucia boasts the world's only drive-in volcano (!) and sulphur springs at **Soufriere**, which is also a fascinating little town where some of the smaller cruise ships occasionally call. Otherwise, the big liners put in at **Castries**, with its smart new port facilities and inviting duty-free shops. Here you can take a catamaran trip to beautiful **Marigot Bay**, where the musical *Dr Doolittle* was filmed. **St Vincent** is the largest island of the scattered little **Grenadines**, which include the exclusive **Mustique**, playground of the rich and famous. **Kingstown** is the vibrant capital, while the **Mesopotamia Valley** offers a long, rich tropical flora experience.

Don't miss: St Vincent Botanical Gardens, the oldest in the western hemisphere (dating back to the eighteenth century), for a fantastic collection of the weird and wonderful in the world of vegetation.

Little **Bequia** is an occasional port of call in the Grenadines, with its charming town of **Port Elizabeth**, and is also the gateway for boat tours to some of the many splendid beach islands that dot the vicinity. Princess Lines (and, hence, British parent company P&O) have their own exclusive beach resort development on the private island of **Mayreau** which makes for another pleasant diversion.

Out to the east, largely on its own, sits **Barbados**, which epitomises much of what is good about the Caribbean. Its desperately English-tinged culture, right down to Trafalgar Square and Nelson's Column in the capital **Bridgetown** (and they actually pre-date the versions in London), is still very appealing, and there are some great shops and restaurants (you have to try the local delicacy – flying fish, either grilled or in a sandwich) to be explored. A half-day tour isn't a bad idea here, either, as there is quite a lot of ground to cover on your own, including the **Andromeda Gardens** and **Animal Flower Cave** in the north, the **Tropical Flower Forest** and **Barbados Wildlife Preserve** in the middle and some magnificent old **Plantation Houses** in the south and east. Tours of the local distilleries are definitely over-rated unless you are really into rum. The downside of Barbados is the worrying level of petty crime and the seemingly non-stop hassle of street (and beach) urchins, trying to offer you taxis or souvenirs you really wouldn't want if they were giving them away. A firm but polite 'No thanks!' is the best policy as the vast majority are perfectly harmless, just very poor. For shopping, the **Da Costas Mall** provides a good cross-section of what the island has to offer.

 BRIT TIP

The two coastlines of Barbados are vastly different. The east is rugged, Atlantic Ocean territory, not recommended for swimming but great for surfers, while the western shores are sandy and tranquil.

Grenada, or 'The Spice Island of the Caribbean', sits to the south of the Grenadines and boasts another of the region's most spectacular beaches, **Grande Anse Beach**. Souvenir hunting is enjoyable and, for once, relatively hassle-free, and you will have to sample the local nutmeg-spiced rum cocktails at some point, which add a picturesque haze to everything!

Don't miss: The morning arrival in the port and capital of **St George's**, one of the prettiest harbours in the Caribbean, and a wander around the town's historic warehouses and homes.

Trinidad, and its smaller attendant isle of **Tobago**, offer a different experience yet again, with quite a rich, bustling ambience that stems from its wealth as an oil producer. The main town of **Port-of-Spain** is the most highly-developed in the Caribbean and boasts an eclectic mix of architecture, bustling markets, and the wide open spaces of **Queen's Park Savannah**, ringed by 'The Magnificent Seven' mansions. Its tourism has been carefully developed along ecologically-friendly lines and offers such attractions as the

Caroni Bird Sanctuary and **Maracas Bay**, with its 'Skyline Highway' scenic road from Port-of-Spain.

Don't miss: Asa Wright Nature Centre, an old plantation house-turned-hotel set in a forest preserve boasting some stunning birdlife.

Tobago is smaller, prettier and so sedate it is practically at a standstill compared to the rest of the world. That makes it the perfect place to 'chill out' and enjoy the great beaches, notably **Pigeon Point**.

Completing the full Caribbean sweep are the Dutch Antilles islands of **Aruba**, **Bonaire** and **Curaçao**, a trio of wind-swept, almost desert-like out-crops just north of the Venezuelan coast. The colourful port of **Oranjestad** in Aruba is handy to explore from the harbour, but the rest of the island itself is pretty arid and spartan, unless you are attracted by cacti and masses of windblown, oddly-shaped divi-divi trees. The beaches are still wonderful, though, especially **Eagle** and **Palm** on the west coast. Bonaire is accessible only to the smallest cruise ships, but is often sought out by scuba-divers as offering some of the best dives in the world around the coral reefs in crystal clear waters. Curaçao is the largest and easily most impressive of the three, with the fabulous harbour of **Willemstad** boasting some picture-perfect houses along the waterfront and a floating market that sails over daily from South America. Ships tie up right opposite the town centre, which is then reached by a short walk across the Queen Emma pontoon bridge that opens and closes to admit harbour traffic, a fascinating sight (have your camera ready for arrival and departure). Great shopping can be found in town, while the **Chobolobo Mansion** on the outskirts offers the chance to sample the many varieties of the sweet liqueur that takes its name from the island itself. More great snorkelling and diving is the feature of the **Underwater Marine Park**, while **Christoffel National Park**, a 4,500-acre garden and wildlife park, is the best scenic offering of all three islands, with a wonderful all-round view from the top of Mt Christoffel.

Don't miss: Curaçao Seaquarium for a well-displayed range of marine environments, some larger creatures like sea-lions, glass-bottomed boat rides and a small beach.

The Caribbean coast of South America also offers cruise ships some attractive ports of call and another dimension to a voyage around these parts, hence **Venezuela** and **Colombia** can expect to become featured on more itineraries in the next few years. As the tourist numbers increase, so does petty crime in the cities of **Caracas** and **Cartagena**, and here you are best advised to take a ship excursion and not to wander off on your own (especially as not all taxi drivers will speak English). Shorts, especially for women, are also frowned upon. **La Guaira** is the port for Caracas and is a busy commercial docks as well as a cruise ship harbour, so don't expect a pretty, scenic outlook. The tours into Caracas will feature the old colonial city centre, **Plaza Bolivar**, with its city hall, cathedral and statue of Simon Bolivar, and the **Boulton Museum**, housed in a restored plantation mansion with a very fine collection of period paintings, documents and other artifacts.

Outside the old historic centre, the city is an exceedingly busy, modern conurbation, with a lot of high-rise development and not much thought to the overall visual impact, i.e. a bit of a mess. Alternatively, a few ships offer an (expensive) trip by plane to the spectacular **Angel Falls**, the world's highest, and **Canaima Lagoon**. The prosperous Colombian city of Cartagena is the jewel in that country's Caribbean coastline, boasting a fascinating old city, full

of narrow streets, cute shops and small forts and museums, a lively, modern centre, a seventeenth-century monastery that provides a terrific overview of the city and some magnificent beaches and coastline in either direction. Tourism is gradually becoming a more recognised facet of Colombia's make-up, and the next year or two could be a good time to visit if it really takes off as a major destination for both Europe and America.

The Panama Canal is one of cruising's great sights

Finally, edging along the outline of South America, the last key destination in this part of the world is one of the most outstanding anywhere in the cruise ship itinerary, the **Panama Canal**. As I have already mentioned, the canal is primarily a linear cruise choice, from Fort Lauderdale, Miami or Puerto Rico through to Acapulco or Los Angeles, or vice versa, but there are a few circular options that feature a canal mini-cruise that does not go all the way through, but stops at the mid-point **Gatun Lake** and then returns to the home port. Either way you will experience one of the modern wonders of the world, a 50-mile, all-day crossing that goes 'up' over central America through a series of locks barely wide enough to admit the largest ships and 'down' again into the Pacific Ocean using a series of 'mules' (small trains) to pull the vessels into each lock. The whole process is accompanied by a running commentary over the ship's loudspeakers by a locally-supplied guide, who will astound you with the facts and figures of this awesome operation. There are no ports of call as such associated with the Canal, but a few ships now visit the coral **San Blas Islands**, just to the east of the Caribbean entrance. The San Blas are home to the Cuna Indians, who enjoy having their pictures taken in their elaborate national dress (for a price, of course! Each snap will cost you about $2). It is therefore primarily a cultural experience, although there is also the chance to pick up some unique souvenirs, including the brilliantly coloured molas blouses worn by the Cuna women.

THE US WEST COAST
(Including the Mexican Riviera and Alaska)

WHO GOES THERE

Carnival, Celebrity, Crystal, Cunard, Holland America, NCL, Princess, Radisson Seven Seas, Royal Caribbean, Seabourn.

Season: Mexican Riviera – year-round. Alaska – May–September.

There are two distinct regions to the cruise world on America's West Coast, and they differ in almost every aspect of attraction, from climate and scenery to duration, passenger profile and even the hardware involved. The **Mexican Riviera** run from Lost Angeles is the fast-food version of cruising: cheap, cheerful and primarily for the young crowd. The ports of call, from the Baja Peninsula (otherwise known as Baja California, but don't be fooled, this is all South of the Border) down to the big Mexican resort of Acapulco, are purely an exercise in shopping, beaches and watersports. Fun they may be, but cultural they ain't. In fact, the three- and four-day Riviera cruises are geared almost totally towards the Californian market, and the

Crystal Symphony *in Glacier Bay*

average age can be below 30 at times. Also, while the season generally is a year-long one, the busiest months are November to March, with April to October becoming the distinctly cheaper off-season.

 **BRIT TIP**

When in Mexico think Spanish, i.e. DON'T drink the water. In fact, unless you can be sure your drink comes out of a bottle, give it a miss altogether. Plenty of ice in a drink is also a Bad Thing – it is only frozen water after all.

Ensenada is the first stop travelling south from Los Angeles, an undistinguished town with a scruffy port. Walk in for an hour, do the shops then head back to the ship, unless you are feeling brave, in which case check out Papas & Beer, a wild, raucous bar popular with the young American crowd. You won't believe how they serve shooters (their potent liqueur mixtures), but try ordering one for your friend and stand well back – you have been warned! (See end of chapter for the gory details, if you must.*) The purpose-built resort of **Cabo San Lucas** and its town of **San Jose del Cabo** offer a higher level of sophistication and some crystal-clear waters in which to take a submarine dive or the less adventurous glass-bottomed boat trip. The shopping is more presentable (especially in the markets of the town proper – the main tourist area of **Zona Dorada** is entirely predictable) while deep-sea fishing is a big draw here, too. **Mazatlan** is the biggest city on the true Mexican west coast, with good craft areas for shopping, more fishing opportunities and some good surfing beaches, while you should also watch out for the cliff divers from the main beach wall (although those in Acapulco are traditionally more spectacular). **Puerto Vallarta** is more high-rise beach development in the best Costa traditions, while **Manzanillo** is quieter, more laid-back and includes the glittering resort of Las Hadas, where the film *10* was shot, and the dual resort of **Ixtapa** and **Zihuatanejo** combines a wonderful expanse of beach (check out Playa La Ropa) and genuine village

charm which comes as a welcome relief after the relentless commercialisation elsewhere.

Finally, **Acapulco** is the big resort centre which stirs the most mixed reaction. My brother (younger, trendier and a real night-club person) loves it, while my thoughts tend to the Costa overdose scenario. Whatever, it is a wonderful port to sail into, it offers some more fabulous beaches and unquestionably lively nightlife, the cliff-divers at **La Quebrada** (a short taxi-ride to the west) are a must-see if you have come all this way, and the shopping opportunities are enough to keep even the most ardent shopaholics happy. The eighteenth-century fort of **El Fuerte de San Diego** is a welcome diversion away from the more obvious tourist attractions.

However, if you voyage north from Los Angeles, the cruise experience goes through a complete transformation. Through ports like San Francisco, Seattle and Vancouver and up into **Alaska**, this is one of the most dynamic (not to mention increasingly crowded) cruise areas of the world. It is easily the Number Two choice

Alaskan scenery is breathtaking

for the American market and, with the possibility of adding on a pre-cruise tour of the Canadian Rockies or a few days' stay in the wonderful city of Vancouver (both of which are big Brit attractions), it has quickly become a popular choice with us as well. As with the Norwegian fjords (and possibly even more so in the case of America's 50th State), the main draw is the scenery – bucketloads of it – big, raw, dramatic and, to all intents and purposes, untamed. To get up close (and I mean within a few hundred yards) of one of Alaska's many glaciers, which can be more than 20 miles long, four miles wide and 200 feet high where they slide into the fjords, and watch one of these brilliantly blue-white walls of ice losing huge chunks into the waters (the process called 'calving') is an utterly awesome experience. Add in the lure of wonderful wildlife, from seals, sea otters, the occasional bear and the ever-present golden eagles to killer and humpback whales, and some fascinating ports, and you have a 24-carat-gold cruise experience.

The only real drawbacks with the Alaska run, apart from the big crowds it now pulls, are that the weather can be a touch unreliable early in the season (typically wet and misty along the Inside Passage) and the summer months bring on an attack of mosquitoes in many places. The other off-putting factor, that it is seen primarily for the 50-plus crowd, is steadily being eroded as the region is 'discovered' by the family market, as witnessed by the likes of the ultra-traditional Holland America line laying on children's counsellors and even special kids' shore excursions on many of their Alaska sailings. It truly is a magnificent mainstream cruise product and the one real worry is that the market will quickly become overloaded as the cruise lines try to get more and bigger ships working the area, with a subsequent negative effect on the delicate local eco-systems. Tourism is all very well, but there is no point in destroying the main reason for visiting in the first place, and this is an issue with which the region's various governing bodies are fully involved. The principal attraction of Glacier Bay is a current case in point, as the number of permits that allow ships to sail its breathtaking waters are limited, and the debate in 1996 was over whether to increase the number of permits.

The majority of ships on the Alaskan run use Vancouver as their base port for a series of circular cruises along the Inside Passage as far as Glacier Bay, or occasionally the port of Seward. Just a few (notably Princess, Crystal and Seabourn) offer the opportunity to cruise in linear fashion from either San Francisco or Seattle right up to the main city of Anchorage and then back again on the next cruise.

San Francisco is a marvellous port in which to start (or finish) any cruise, and it offers a wealth of attractions in its own right, especially for visitors from our side of the Atlantic. It has long been one of my favourite US cities, and, with the dock area being surrounded by the wonderful tourist-orientated area of the **Embarcadero**, it offers one of the most scenic and enjoyable ports of call in the world. It is an easy city to negotiate on foot or by the excellent public transport system of trains, buses and the obligatory cable cars, and there is a lot to see, even given a week to try to do it all. Good shopping, museums, sights (including, of course, the Golden Gate bridge), restaurants (especially in Chinatown) and parks all add up to a wealth of opportunities – and that is before you even set foot on your cruise ship. North of California you find the state of Washington and its capital and major port **Seattle**. Many transatlantic flights already operate into here, and then transfer cruise passengers to Vancouver by bus after an overnight stay. A few days in Seattle isn't a bad idea, either, as there is again plenty to do and see here before you tackle the cruise options. Historic Pioneer Square, the 74-acre urban park of Seattle Center, the 605-foot Space Needle (complete with revolving restaurant and observation deck at the top), Seattle Aquarium and the busy waterfront are the things to see, while you can also visit the Boeing Assembly Plant (the biggest aircraft building business in the world), the Maritime and Gold Rush Museums, and tour the surrounding countryside (including the volcanic **Mt St Helens** about two hours' drive from the city) and its charming villages. Its modern, recently up-graded cruise terminal facilities can accommodate some of the biggest ships, while there are also three- and four-day cruises out of Seattle that visit the Canadian Vancouver Island and its wonderfully British centre of Victoria.

Vancouver still remains the Number One port of embarkation for Alaska, and is another city where it is well worth spending some time at either end of your cruise. It is a lively, cosmopolitan city without being at all brash, and Canada's British links mean UK visitors tend to feel rather more at home here than they do in many cities in the United States. An attractive downtown area (including the smart cruise facilities of Canada Place and the charming restored old city area of **Gastown**), magnificent **Stanley Park**, some great beaches, sightseeing (including Grouse Mountain by cable car, Capilano River Regional Park and the Royal Hudson steam train to the little town of Squamish), museums (don't miss Science World for kids and adults) and nightlife all add up to one of the world's great city experiences. Indeed, if you have both San Francisco and Vancouver on your itinerary, you will need an extra month to see it all.

Ketchikan is the first port of call on the Alaska run proper, and, if you don't need your waterproofs here it is a lucky day indeed. Average annual rainfall is close to 200 inches a year – four times that of Britain. But, for all the fact it can be wet and chilly, it gives you your first taste of the frontier country that is Alaska. It is also the totem pole capital of the world, with the opportunity to learn all about the culture of the Tlingit and Tsimshian native inhabitants of the area. Towns like Ketchikan (and virtually all the others on the Alaskan routes) have quickly adapted to the cruise business and have become adept at providing tourists with shopping and souvenir opportunities seemingly at every turn, and here the attraction is the former red light district of **Creek Street**, built on wooden stilts, with the original buildings converted into trendy boutique shops, while **Dolly's House** remains as a 'museum' to the street's past life. Most ships also offer an (expensive) aerial view of the neighbouring **Misty Fjords National Park** by plane or helicopter, which is another awesome sight if you can afford it.

Don't miss: Totem Bight State Historical Park, an 11-mile taxi ride to the north, with its elaborately-carved ceremonial house and focus on the Tlingit totem pole culture.

Juneau, Alaska's capital, offers a magnificent mountainside setting before you even set foot ashore. Here you can pan for gold (over-rated, many find), dine out at a genuine Alaskan salmon bake (and the state is rightly famous for its salmon), raft down the **Mendenhall River** or take a canoe trip on one of the mountain lakes. The town itself offers bags of genuine frontier atmosphere (don't miss the **Red Dog Saloon** and the local Alaskan Amber beer), but the big attraction (and I mean big) is the world's only 'drive-up'

The Sun Princess *is an impressive visitor to Alaska*

glacier, the magnificent **Mendenhall Glacier** 13 miles out of town. The setting, with its attendant Visitor Center, is one of Alaska's great sights. Once again, if your pocket can stretch to it, the most memorable excursion is a helicopter flight that actually lands you on the glacier. Back on your cruise ship, the nearby **Tracy Arm Fjord** rivals the world-famous Glacier Bay for the most awesome glacier views – this is not the time for your camera to run out of film.

Sitka harks back to Alaska's days as a Russian colony, and even boasts a genuine onion-domed **Russian Orthodox church** (rebuilt after a fire in 1966 as a beautifully-restored replica which maintains its authentic atmosphere very well), while the 105-acre **Sitka National Park** is another excellent attraction, with a full historical overview of both native American and period Russian cultures, all in a beautiful forested parkland setting. The twin towns of **Haines** and **Skagway** are pure mining country, gateway to the Klondike Gold Rushes of 1898, with cleverly re-created shop-fronts giving Skagway in particular a genuine period feel and atmosphere.

Don't miss: The White Pass and Yukon Railway trip up into the breath-takingly scenic mountains.

Wrangell is more off the beaten track of the main Inside Passage run, but was again home to more gold rush stampeders. Visit **Chief Shakes Tribal House**, surrounded by beautiful totem poles, and walk the beach at low tide to see the mysterious petroglyphs (carved ancient stones). **Glacier Bay National Park and Preserve** has no port of call but offers the chance to cruise these fabulous waters, into which pour no less than 16 lofty glaciers. Whales are also commonly sighted here, and a humpback whale breaching (leaping into the air) is one of the most unforgettable sights anywhere in the world.

Passing out of the Inside Passage brings you to the final port of **Seward**, quite often a terminus for the linear cruises, and a bit of a disappointment after all the frontier, period charm of the earlier ports, but still notable for magnificent scenery all around, like the **Kenai Fjords National Park** and **Chugach National Forest**. From here you may transfer to Anchorage for the flight back (or the flight in, if you're only just setting out). **Anchorage** itself, for the lucky few who cruise this far, provides some spectacular views over the 400-square-mile **Columbia Glacier**, the **Kenai Mountains** and inland to volcanic **Mt McKinley**. It is a big, bustling, modern city in the best American traditions where luxury hotels and great shopping are only minutes from true wilderness and historic gold trails. If you have a day or two to spare here, consider a trip to the **Denali National Park**, a semi-tamed wilderness of caribou, grizzly bears, wolves, moose, Dall sheep and other wildlife, with the chance to see sled-dog demonstrations or just hike around the nature trails with a wonderful feeling of utter freedom.

US EAST COAST (including Bermuda)

WHO GOES THERE

Celebrity, Cunard, Holland America, NCL, Princess, Royal Caribbean, Seabourn, Silversea

Season: May–October.

Not so much a cruise area but a number of attractive destinations loosely grouped together geographically from as far afield as the Atlantic island of Bermuda (not to be confused with the Bahamas or the Caribbean as it frequently is), some 600 miles out from New York, the coast of New England to the north (especially for the spectacular colours in the autumn), and Canada's Atlantic Maritime area, Nova Scotia, Newfoundland and the historic St Lawrence Seaway. Only a handful of lines operate here, which is a shame as it offers a fresh, uncluttered alternative to Alaska (but without the glaciers). It is very much a seasonal offering, with New York and Boston the key home ports for most ships.

Bermuda is a collection of some 150 islands, of which only 20 or so are inhabited and the main island of **Great Bermuda** is always the principal focus and port of call – three ports in fact, as ships tend to sail out here and then spend at least a day or two around the island shuttling between the various harbours. This self-governing British colony enjoys warm summers and boasts some wonderful beaches (around 100 of them) with the attendant attractions of crystal-clear waters for scuba-diving and snorkelling. The number of ship visits is carefully controlled to prevent the small main island (just 21 square miles and with a

Bermuda boasts eight golf courses, which can be linked with a cruise

population of some 55,000) from becoming crowded (as can be the case with the Bahamas and US Virgin Islands), hence the route is always popular and discounts are rare. Celebrity Cruises enjoy the privilege of being allowed two ships to visit every week, and so they are regarded as the Bermuda specialists. However, local laws require all ships to suspend their full evening entertainments programmes, with only live music allowed so as not to compete with the island's night-time attractions. Being still typically British (down to playing cricket and having proper pubs), they take a dim view of wearing swimsuits anywhere but the beach and going without a shirt in town or wearing shorts into a restaurant are definite no-noes. For all those little idiosyncrasies, the main island has great charm and poise, with a more structured, refined atmosphere than any you would find in the Caribbean, hence it always goes down well with British visitors. The three main ports are also quite contrasting: the **Royal Dockyard** (King's Wharf) berth is at the westernmost tip and offers authentic shopping and the Bermuda Maritime Museum, which reflects the island's rich naval history; **Hamilton**, the capital, is a shopper's Mecca, especially Front Street which overlooks the harbour; and **St George's** is at the picturesque historic end of the island the original capital, offering colonial architecture, churches and several museums. The island also boasts an excellent bus service for getting around cheaply (or bicycle hire for the more energetic) and some spectacular coastline in addition to the beaches, with caves, grottoes and sea arches. For such a tiny land mass, Bermuda has no less than eight golf courses for devotees of that sport.

Don't miss: The Crystal Caves at Harrington Sound, a bizarre collection of stalagmites and stalactites reaching out into underground sea pools.

Boston is at the centre of most of the cruise itineraries for New England and Canada, and, as such, offers another contrasting big city experience, with a wonderful range of attractions, from walking tours of the old city (which dates back to the eighteenth century), state-of-the-art museums, opera and ballet, excellent sports, great beaches at Cape Cod, whale-watching mini-cruises and, yes, you can even visit the famous *Cheers!* bar (just don't expect it to look anything like the TV show internally).

Don't miss: The Freedom Trail, a two-and-a-half-mile walking tour of 16 of the city's most historic landmarks, including the USS *Constitution* and the Paul Revere House.

From Boston, you voyage north to the fishing villages and ports of the state of Maine. **Boothbay Harbour**, **Rockland** and **Bar Harbour** typify the quaint, almost kitsch coastal style, with plenty of relatively unspoiled, friendly shops and restaurants (lobster is a Maine speciality), plus the opportunity to take a tour inland to see the splendour of **New England** (the collective area of the north-east states of Maine, New Hampshire, Vermont, Connecticut, Rhode Island and Massachusetts), the great rural hinterland which boasts the spectacular autumn colours in parks like **Acadia National Park**. Moving up into Canadian Nova Scotia brings the must-see port of **Halifax**, with the second-largest natural harbour in the world and a rich nautical history that gives rise to a number of fine museums, including the **Marine Museum of the Atlantic** with its Titanic Exhibit. Check out the historic district along the waterfront and enjoy a genuinely sincere level of local hospitality and friendliness.

Don't miss: The Historic Properties, a converted nineteenth-century business district now home to an inviting range of shops, restaurants and night-clubs.

The coal-mining port of **Sydney** is another quaint old centre with the bonus of the amazing **Fortress Louisbourg**, a re-created eighteenth-century French fortress peopled with real characters and featuring period atmosphere right down to the food served in the café. Mainland **Labrador** and the huge island of **Newfoundland** are keen to establish themselves as two of cruising's new destinations, with plenty of big, wild landscape to explore, starting from the capital city of **St John's**, with 500 years of history from the explorers to the pirates. **L'Anse Amour** offers the Labrador Straits Museum and 9,000 years of human settlement history, while the coastal waters also see an abundance of whales – and icebergs. And, if you thought the Alaskan scenery was rough and ready, check out Labrador's North Coast for some of the most rugged, daunting coastline in the world as the jagged Torngat and Kaumajet Mountains seem to soar straight out of the sea. Amazingly, there are small communities of fishermen and Inuit native inhabitants, and a flying tour along this stretch can rightly claim to be a unique experience.

Don't miss: Signal Hill National Historic Site in fascinating St John's, the old whaling capital of Red Bay and the incredible Northern Lights in winter.

Completing the leisurely sail up this stretch of coast brings you into the St Lawrence Seaway, entrance to the great St Lawrence River and the five Great Lakes of the interior. **Prince Edward Island**, and its port of **Charlottetown**, offers more quiet scenic charm and fishing villages, the surprisingly good beaches of Prince Edward Island National Park and the shipbuilding museum. Coming into the St Lawrence brings you to the majestic French-Canadian city of **Quebec**, with its proudly-preserved seventeenth-century heritage, that includes a wealth of historical detail, from battle sites to monuments and winding cobbled streets. The walled city of **Vieux Quebec** is the place to wander, while **Dufferin Terrace** offers a fabulous overview of the St Lawrence.

 BRIT TIP

Remembering a few words of your school French lessons is a good idea here as Quebec sticks fiercely to its French traditions and English is not always spoken.

Montreal, a more cosmopolitan, built-up city, is the usual cruise terminus on the St Lawrence, and visitors always marvel at how clean everywhere seems to be, and 'Why can't they keep it like this in our city, town, etc.' Take the Metro into the city centre (London's Underground is Third World by comparison) and enjoy some fine museums (including the unmissable Canadian History Museum), restaurants (notably along Prince Arthur Mall) and shopping. Get your walking shoes on and marvel at how well-designed all cities could be if only common sense was allowed to have a say every now and then.

THE FAR EAST

WHO GOES THERE

Crystal, Cunard, Holland America, Orient, Princess, Radisson Seven Seas, Renaissance, Royal Caribbean, Seabourn, Silversea, Star Clippers, Star Cruise, Swan Hellenic

Season: Year-round (Royal Caribbean, Star Cruise), October–March otherwise.

In many ways the Far East (taking this rather generalised area to stretch from Thailand, Malaysia and the island of Sumatra in the south through Singapore, Indonesia, the Philippines, Vietnam, Hong Kong, China, Korea and Japan) has yet to establish itself in mainstream cruising, despite the fact it has been featured in brochures for many years now. The long distances involved in flying people out to base ports in Singapore, Hong Kong and Japan, the relatively high maintenance costs for cruise ships in the region (not to mention some exorbitant port taxes for less than impressive cruise-ship facilities in some cases) and the fact it is definitely not a cheap cruise option, all mean the Far East has been distinctly under-exploited. Despite the apparently high number of ship visits, only Royal Caribbean and the Singapore-operated Star Cruise are year-round lines, but they both offer the

prospect of substantial growth from opposite ends of the spectrum, RCI as one of cruising's existing major players and Star Cruise as an ambitious newcomer on the world scene, anxious to attract large numbers of European passengers cruising in this area for the first time.

Royal Caribbean offer 16- and 17-day fly-cruises out of Singapore to Bali, Indonesia, Malaysia and Thailand; Thailand, Vietnam and Hong Kong; China, South Korea

The Far East boasts some amazing scenery, like the Chocolate Hills of Bohol in the Philippines

and Japan; or just China and Hong Kong (at least, I think that's what their hopelessly vague brochure says!). Star Cruise (now marketed through various operators including Thomson) stick to shorter cruises from Singapore to Malaysia, Thailand and Sumatra. The other cruise lines are all short-season visitors at best, while the likes of Crystal, Cunard, Holland America, Seabourn and Silversea make only annual visits on their way round the various sectors of the world.

 BRIT TIP

Singapore's Good Retailer Scheme protects against damaged or pirated goods. Look for the red Merlion stickers on doors or windows for guaranteed courteous, honest service. Larger stores tend to be fixed-price establishments, but elsewhere you are expected to haggle! Ask for the retailer's 'best price' then make an offer on that, and away you go.

Once again, it is the huge cultural and scenic diversity which makes the Far East such a tempting destination, not to mention the sheer exotic experience of places like Bangkok, Bali and Shanghai. Mysterious, oriental cities, crowded markets, fabulous temples and spectacular tropical flora and fauna all add up to a real wealth of tourist opportunities, and doing it all from the relative security of a ship means a lot of the possible worries of health and safety are immediately removed. And any cruise line that gives you the chance to visit Beijing and the Great Wall of China should be avidly sought out by the more discerning traveller.

Singapore is likely to become the Miami of the Far East if current developments are anything to go by (and if Hong Kong's business future remains unclear under Chinese rule), and this highly-organised city state on the tip of the Malaysian Peninsula is an excellent base from which to explore the delights of South-east Asia. Its British colony heritage still shines through (notably in the Raffles Hotel, a must for afternoon tea or an evening drink), but its modern façades, as witnessed by the thrusting city centre high-rise developments, plus its mix of Arabian, Hindu and Buddhist influences, give it a unique flavour. And, like Hong Kong, it offers some of the best shopping in the world, both for duty-free luxury items and locally-made arts and crafts, including exotic porcelain, silks and pewterware.

Historic ethnic areas include Little India, Arab Street and Chinatown, and the obvious tourist attractions include the amazing **Discovery Island** of Sentosa, part theme park, part beach resort and part garden wonderland, the 'open' **Zoological gardens**, **Jurong Bird Park**, the Chinese mythological village of **Haw Par Villa** and **Empress Place**. Getting round Singapore is made easy by cheap taxi fares (tipping is not expected), an efficient bus service and the MRT (Mass Rapid Transit) rail system. Crime is also

Bird-singing contests are a feature of Singapore markets

rarely a problem here as the penalties for even petty offences are swingeing.

From Singapore, ships sail either north to Bangkok, the rest of Asia and east to the islands, or north-west to Malaysia and Thailand.

Kuala Lumpur, or KL, is the capital of Malaysia and, from its port of **Port**

 BRIT TIP

The Far East in general, and Singapore in particular, is not the place to have anything to do with drugs. Refuse any appeals to carry or deliver parcels for anyone, no matter how innocent they seem.

Klang, a tour of this huge city is a must. Breathtaking skyscrapers, a host of mosques and temples, bustling markets, including a lively Chinatown section, beautiful gardens and even museums (notably the **Negara Museum**) make it a history-rich destination and a fascinating place to wander, while it is also a shopper's paradise, especially for local crafts. Public transport is also well-run and inexpensive.

Don't miss: The Sultan Abdul Samad Building and KL Railway Station, outstanding examples of its architectural heritage.

Penang is an island resort boasting a magnificent historical centre in **Georgetown**. The seventeenth-century fortress of Fort Cornwallis is worth a visit, while Penang Museum and Art Gallery sets the island's varied history in perspective. **Kota Kinabalu** is a relatively new city of high-rise buildings, a coral-island studded coastline and heavily wooded mountainside, topped by the imposing Mt Kinabalu. The modern mosque and museum are other attractions as are the nearby fishing villages where visitors are always afforded a generous welcome. **Kuching** is the capital of the east Malaysian state of Sarawak. Located on a riverbank, it has an eye-catching waterfront, historic buildings, beautifully landscaped parks and gardens and one of Asia's finest museums, with an excellent collection of local ethnological and archaeological material.

Thailand bills itself as 'the most exotic country in Asia' which is quite a claim considering the competition, but hard to argue against. The island of **Phuket** is a big tourist resort with fine beaches and caves, spectacular reefs and lush vegetation, with thickly forested slopes giving way to tumbling waterfalls and hidden coves. Shopping is its other principal claim to fame, especially silk and pearls. **Don't miss**: The local seafood.

Bali – a wonderful backdrop for Song of Flower

Pattaya is Thailand's 'Riviera', a famous beach resort of excellent water-sports, especially on the offshore coral islands, and vibrant nightlife, while **Chiang Mai** is another popular tourist destination, with its slower pace of life, eye-catching temples and cottage industries, notably umbrellas, silverware, nielloware and silk. But **Bangkok**, with its port of **Laem Chabang**, is Thailand's really unmissable attraction, rich in archaeological treasures, including the fabulous **Emerald Buddha Temple** and the **Grand Palace**. Take a tour along the Chao Phraya River and explore the canals of **Thonburi** for a real close-up of Thailand's modern character, and then head for some more world-class shopping, with Thai silk, rubies, sapphires, silver, ceramics and bronze all out to catch your attention.

Don't miss: The Ancient City, a 1,200-acre open-air museum and Bangkok's Floating Market.

The vast, widespread, volcanic islands of **Indonesia** are Singapore's other near-neighbours and also make a rich cruising experience. The capital **Jakarta**, on the island of Java, is home to 7.5 million people and reflects the history of the country since the arrival of the Dutch in the seventeenth-century. **Old Batavia** is a magnificently restored slice of the city's heritage, which can also be viewed in the Jakarta Museum.

Don't miss: The vast open-air museum of 'Beautiful Indonesia in Miniature Park.'

Surabaya is a sprawling city of some three million with fascinating Old Arab and Chinese quarters, while **Semarang**, Java's provincial capital, boasts many splendid old colonial buildings and **Borododur**, the largest Buddhist shrine in the world. **Bali** is the most familiar to European visitors, a true island paradise in its own right, famous for its beaches and volcanoes. Art and culture also play a large part in Bali's make-up, with Ancient Hinduism replacing Buddhism as the main religion, and her local artisans produce much sought-after carvings of wood and stone, gold and silver jewellery and traditional Balinese paintings. The Balinese people are also noted for their uniquely ritualistic forms of music, folk drama and dance. Your cruise ship should also provide a grandstand seat while sailing around the remains of the volcanic island of **Krakatau**, reportedly site of the biggest explosion in the history of the world (I wasn't there at the time – August 1883), while some of

the smaller vessels also visit the temple-rich island of **Lombok**, where Muslim and Hindu cultures live side by side in a picture-postcard setting of towers, fountains and crumbling palaces, and the great National Park of **Komodo Island**, which boasts the world's biggest 'lizard', the 10-foot Komodo Dragon, and is one of the great wildlife areas of the Far East. Lombok and Komodo are also two of the 17,000 **Spice Islands** of this region,

The colourful Jeepney is the characteristic fun feature of Philippines public transport

scattered between Sumatra and Borneo, which also include the bustling Dutch/Portuguese island of **Timor** and its bustling port **Kupang**, and **Sumbawa**, with its intriguing mountain villages.

Brunei, on the north-west coast of the island of Borneo, surrounded by the east Malaysian states of **Sarawak** and **Sabah**, is a richly-prosperous nation run by the Sultan of Brunei, reputedly the world's richest man. The port of **Muara** serves the capital, **Bandar Seri Begawan**, a bustling city of spotlessly-clean streets and amazing sights like the built-on-stilts water village of Kampong Ayer and the **Royal Regalia Building**, complete with its gold and silver ceremonial armour and the Royal Chariot.

Don't miss: The Omar Ali Saifuddin Mosque, with its lift to the top for a really spectacular over-view of the city. Excellent beaches and unspoiled jungle complete the picture for this unique country.

The Philippines are the other big island group of South-East Asia, no less than 7,017 of them offering idyllic beaches, lush, green mountains and ultra-modern cities (and therefore more great shopping). **Manila** on the biggest island of Luzon is the chief port of call, a sprawling, crowded metropolis with a wealth of sightseeing possibilities. Check out the Walled City of Intramuros, the old Spanish Fort Santiago, the 200-year-old Malacanang Palace, Rizal Park, the Chinese Cemetery, the Pistang Pilipino market and Manila's Chinatown. Other excursions take in **Taal**, a small but active volcano in the middle of a lake, and the coral island of **Corregidor**, scene of some of the most heroic and brutal action of the Second World War. For shopping, embroidered clothes, coral jewellery, wood-carving and hand-made baskets are all local specialities. The rest of the vast archipelago has yet to be fully appreciated and integrated into many cruise schedules, but that is likely to happen before too long as the visitors discover the delights of **Cebu**, the 'Queen City of the South' on Visayas island (fabulous beaches and historical sights, including Fort san Pedro and Magellan's Cross), **Zamboanga City** on Mindanao (with historic Fort Pilar and rare pink-sand beaches) and **Davao** (also on Mindanao, and with great sights like the Buddhist temple of Don Wa, the Davao Museum and some spectacular tropical parklands).

Don't miss: The frequent festivals, processions and boating regattas which are a feature of Filipino life and any trip to the Chocolate Hills of Bohol.

Back on the mainland, **Vietnam** has started to appear on a few cruise schedules as it re-establishes political links with the rest of the world, and it offers a wealth of ancient treasures, historical architecture and friendly, welcoming people, with its principal attraction being **Ho Chi Minh City** (formerly Saigon). The National Museum is the door to 4,000 years of history, the Notre Dame Cathedral is a must-see novelty and the Cholon and Benh Thanh markets can provide hours of shopping interest. The ancient port city of **Danang** is another temple-rich destination, also famous for China Beach, where the American GIs used to relax, the Marble Mountains and the Cham Museum. **Nha Trang** is also a popular port of call, with some truly stunning beaches and terrific seafood to back up the historic elements, which include the seventh-century ruins of Po Nagar, the twelfth-century tower of the Cham Sanctuary and the Pasteur Institute.

Hong Kong officially became part of China on 30 June 1997, and the cruise world is among those waiting to see what changes this will bring to this busiest and most beautiful of ports. Here, the modern and ancient Chinese worlds clash in a riot of sights and sounds, and you could be convinced this is the most crowded place on earth in parts. High-rise tower-blocks spring up almost as fast as the architects can draw them, twisting, narrow streets house a multitude of shopping opportunities (not to mention the huge, purpose-built shopping malls and areas like Nathan Road on the

Kowloon Peninsula), temples and monasteries litter the city and surrounding hills, and Victoria Peak, with its funicular railway, offers a truly outstanding view of the lot. Mix in some superb restaurants, vibrant nightlife and fascinating museums, and Hong Kong quickly becomes a port of call that will make you want to stay for a week or longer (and several cruise lines do, now, offer some attractive add-on stays).

Hong Kong is a magnificent port to sail into

Don't miss: The house-boat village of Aberdeen and a trip to the Portuguese colony of Macau, with its unique blend of Portuguese and Chinese culture.

China is another relative newcomer to the cruise scene map and is quickly becoming one of those destinations which every well-travelled sea-goer has to visit. **Beijing** is a once-in-a-lifetime city of cultural diversity and richness to which no guide book or film can do justice. From the ports of **Xingang** or **Tianjin**, the Chinese capital is two to three hours' journey away, but it is worth every minute (especially if your ship arranges an overnight excursion) to view sights like the awe-inspiring Forbidden City, the splendid Summer Palace and the blue-tiled Temple of Heaven. And that is just the start. The Ming Tombs, Great Wall at Badaling, Beihai Park and the Beijing Waxworks Palace also introduce the foreign visitor to a world which can be completely overwhelming in terms of its cultural experience. The more cosmopolitan city of **Shanghai** is similarly impressive for its wealth of historical sights and new attractions, like the commercial centre of Nanjing Road. Old Town's Y Yuan bazaar and Five-Star Pavilion, Yu Yuan Garden, Long Hua Temple Pagoda and the Jade Buddha all provide a glimpse of the past. The Shanghai Museum of Art and History also delves into more than 7,000 years of Chinese events. **Guanghzou**, or Canton, has been a South China coast trading port for almost 2,000 years and offers the history of the Memorial Garden to the Martyrs, Yuexiu Park, the seventh-century

Huaisheng Mosque and the Dr Sun Yat-Sen Memorial, while students of Buddhism won't want to miss Foshan, a nearby pilgrimage site of temples and pagodas filled with images and carvings of the main Chinese religion. **Nanjing** is one of China's most attractive cities, with its broad, tree-lined streets, excellent history museum and park at Xuanwu Lake that also boasts a zoo and a theatre. The imposing Mausoleum of Dr Sun Yat-Sen is another tourist trap. **Dalian**, the northernmost port, is a unique Chinese-Russian-Japanese mix of architecture and history, with a fine museum of natural history as well as a large seaside park and renowned local craftsmen, who fashion eye-catching crystal animals and pictures from shell fragments.

Don't miss: Beijing.

Japan completes this cruise sweep of the Far East with yet another drastic culture change and more unique sights. Four main islands – Kyushu, Shikoku, Honshu and Hokkaido – make up the bulk of the country, which is intensely mountainous, topped by volcanoes like the picture-perfect Mt Fuji on Honshu island, just south west of Tokyo, with its small, fertile plains, rich forests – and ultra-modern cities. The massive port of **Yokohama** is the gateway to **Tokyo**, but the two form a vast urban sprawl that is both vibrant and orderly (the latter a vital feature of Japanese life). The glittering, neon-lit Ginza district is the hub of its shopping and entertainment activities, but the city's many parks and temples are equally attractive for new visitors.

Don't miss: The Imperial Palace Plaza and its timeless park filled with the local trademark cherry trees.

Nagasaki, on Kyushu island, is Japan's most western-influenced city, and offers the International Cultural Hall, with its museum homage to the awesome destruction and horrors of the 1945 atomic bomb attack, as well as some striking European architecture and picturesque surroundings. The ports of **Kobe** (now extensively rebuilt after the great earthquake of 1995) and **Osaka** offer tours to the historical capital of **Kyoto**, with its Kinkakuji, or Gold Temple, and the Sanjusangendo Temple with its Hall of 1,001 Buddhas. Shoppers here should hunt out the locally-made Satsuma pottery and inlaid jewellery. Osaka also features the sixteenth-century castle and sixth-century Shitennoji Temple. **Okinawa Island** and its port of **Naha** in the extreme south are another blend of ancient traditions and modern western influences, with its motorways and neon-lit skyline mixing freely with sacred temples and an Imperial castle. Here, the shopping bargains include bingata, a woodblock-print cloth, and lacquerware.

AUSTRALASIA

WHO GOES THERE

Abercrombie & Kent, Crystal, Cunard, Orient, P&O, Princess, Radisson Seven Seas, Seabourn

Season: Year-round (November–April most commonly)

The far-flung islands of the South Pacific have been a cruise destination since the days of Captain Cook (well, sort of), and, while no one can claim to be the first to sail them these days, they do provide a significant opportunity to get off the beaten cruise track and explore some of the most truly picturesque corners of the world. And, as you travel down from the likes of Papua New Guinea to Australia and New Zealand, the geographical diversity is also among the most startling you will encounter, including as it does, the volcanic Samoan islands, the tropical splendour of North Australia, the stunning 1,242-mile Great Barrier Reef, the exotic South Pacific Islands of Tahiti, and the almost Norwegian fjord coastline of parts of New Zealand. Island

Crystal Harmony *is a visitor to New Zealand*

life is slow-paced and informal and surprisingly rich in history, with magnificent beaches and the attendant wonders of rich marine life, wonderful deep-sea fishing and some of the best snorkelling and scuba-diving anywhere in the world.

 BRIT TIP

When it comes to the climate here, beware. It is some of the most humid territory in the cruise world. So, when you venture out of the ship's air-conditioned interior, expect temperatures in excess of 100° F and 90 per cent humidity

South Pacific culture is still alive and thriving and islanders will happily exhibit their centuries-old traditions and customs for visitors. Village markets also offer a unique taste of local life, with artisans hard at work at their arts and crafts. The only real drawback is the extra cost and duration of flights to this part of the world. It couldn't be further away and, if you are travelling all that distance for a cruise, you want to make it a significant one in terms of time, hence they are often the most expensive you will find. Having said all that, it is still the least visited of the main cruise areas, and it has the added attraction of being the most untouched commercially, and therefore the most natural. It should also go almost without saying that the beaches are truly stunning and watersports are one of the prime activities.

Papua New Guinea, the largest and most northerly of the islands (unless you count Australia in terms of size), is almost inaccessible to anything other than sea transport, hence cruising scores another big advantage here. Virgin tropical rain-forests, rugged mountains, colourful bird and other wildlife, brilliant tropical beaches and timeless native villages add up to a real scenic wonderland. A tour along the **Sepik River** can take you back hundreds of

BRIT TIP

Surprisingly for this tropical wonderland, the crime rate in Port Moresby is very high and this is NOT the place to go wandering on your own. Ship-organised excursions are essential for visiting even the main sights, and you shouldn't stray far from the main group at places like Paga Hill and Hanuabada.

years to a region almost completely untouched by modern life, while the **Trobriand Islands** are a glimpse of tropical paradise with their thatched huts fringing white coral beaches and people who still insist on ceremonial gift

Sunset in the South Seas

exchanges and traditional music and dance to welcome all visitors. **Port Moresby** is the one sizeable port and city, boasting a lively, modern, high-rise centre, with the attractions of the National Museum and Art Gallery, War Museum, National Arts School (featuring exhibits of the islands' complex and varied tribal lifestyles) and Paga Hill, with a panoramic view of the whole area. The traditional side of life in the area is still evident in the stilt villages of Koki, Hanuabada and Tatana, so don't forget your camera. Cruise ship visitors do NOT require special visas.

From Papua New Guinea almost as far as New Zealand stretch the islands and atolls of the South Pacific – the **Solomon Islands**, Tuvalu, French Polynesia, Vanuatu, Fiji, Samoa, the Cook Islands, New Caledonia and Tonga. In the mountainous, forested Solomons, islanders travel among this cluster of six large islands and a myriad smaller ones by canoe, but the apparent modern idyll covers some deep scars caused by bitter battles in the Second World War. The main island is **Guadalcanal**, which was at the centre of some of the fiercest American-Japanese fighting, and the capital

Honiara contains a sombre War Memorial to the many thousands who died here. Today the **Solomon Islands** are an independent member of the Commonwealth, with a well-developed fishing industry, and the principal attractions of Honiara include Government House, the Botanical gardens and Watapamu, a typical islanders' village. **French Polynesia** consists of some 130 islands spread over 1.5 million square miles of Pacific Ocean, and is subdivided into the five main groups of which **Tahiti** (in the Society Islands) is the main island and **Papeete**, the capital. The majority are steep, volcanic mountains, but one group, the Tuamotus, is mainly composed of low-lying atolls, strung together by often-submerged coral reefs. Papeete is a modern city with government offices, businesses, shops and restaurants. It also boasts the Gauguin Museum and some lovely one-off boutiques and sidewalk cafés along Boulevard Pomare. Organised excursions will take you to visit some of the mountains and waterfalls, or to go fishing, trekking or horse-riding. The recent nuclear tests by the French government – conducted flagrantly in the face of world opinion – were carried out on the tiny atoll of Mururoa and are still a touchy subject with the rightly-indignant Polynesian islanders. Other French Polynesian cruise stops include picture-postcard **Bora Bora** (discovered by Captain Cook in 1777 and probably the epitome of a South Sea island with its almost vertical basalt peaks soaring above a typical turquoise bay and fringed by the inevitable coral reef necklace), **Hiva Oa** (where the artist Paul Gauguin lived and died), **Moorea** (a larger version of Bora Bora), **Raiatea** (with its dense rain-forests) and lush, archaeologically-rich **Huahine** (for the site of Maeva, a fifteenth-century settlement with restored marae, the ancestral shrines of local chiefs). Radisson Seven Seas' new ship *Paul Gauguin* will be based year-round in Tahiti to offer a specialist product in French Polynesia.

Don't miss: The canoe trip down the River Faaroa on Raiatea, where the jungle provides a canopy of ferns, orchids and vanilla.

 BRIT TIP

In Fiji, the bravest souls will surely want to raise a coconut shell full of the local herbal beverage – Yaqona – which is utterly unique in its non-alcoholic potency. The locals claim it is an aphrodisiac.

You have to search to find **Vanuatu** on many ship itineraries (Seabourn and Orient were the only lines in 1996) but it is worth it to get off the beaten track even by the South Pacific's standards at sleepy harbours like **Port Vila** and **Espiritu Santo**, where you are as much of an attraction to the locals as they are to you. On Espiritu Santo, the remains of a huge Allied base, which supported the battle of Guadalcanal in the Second World War, lies rusting in the bush. The 320 islands that make up the **Fiji** archipelago boast more tropically-adorned volcanic mountains overlooking impossibly-blue waters, plus historical sights and the mind-boggling fire-walkers of the Fijian

Cultural Center at **Pacific Harbour** on the main island of **Viti Levu**, who call on a Fijian god to help them withstand the white-hot stones. The capital **Suva** is alive with lush, flowered greenery and flamboyant trees, and the central market is a lively tropical mélange of fish, vegetable and fruit sellers. Albert Park is one of Suva's most attractive areas, with the nearby Government House and the peaceful Thurston gardens.

Don't miss: The Fiji Museum in Thurston gardens for a comprehensive view of Fijian history, including the double-hulled war canoe and replica village.

 BRIT TIP

Contrary to the rugby jokes that did the rounds after Wales lost to Western Samoa in the World Cup – which went something along the lines of 'Wales lost to Western Samoa? Thank goodness they weren't playing the *whole* of Samoa!' – there is no Eastern Samoa. The companion islands are American Samoa to the east, and rugby is not played there.

Western Samoan islanders proudly preserve their age-old Polynesian culture in the face of creeping Westernisation, and most people still live in *fale*, or traditional open-sided thatched houses in coastal villages. Robert Louis Stevenson lived and died here and his grave, atop Mt Vaea on the main island of **Upolu**, is visited by only the most energetic of tourists. Other points of interest in the capital **Apia** include Aggie Grey's Hotel (Aggie Grey was reputedly the model for Bloody Mary in James A Michener's novel *Tales of the South Pacific*), the Congregational Church and the First World War Memorial.

American Samoa comes as something of a culture shock after Western Samoa, with its bustling, brash town of **Pago Pago**. You are suddenly re-introduced to traffic and trash-cans, but there are still opportunities for quiet nature walks, sightseeing and even golf. The **Cook Islands** offer a legendary level of warmth and hospitality, with much of their culture living on in their vibrant song and dance, an opportunity to witness either of which shouldn't be missed. The main island is **Rarotonga** and the capital **Avarua**, where you will find wonderful little craft and produce markets with some outstanding weaving and wood-carving. The beaches, needless to say, are brilliantly white and the interiors tropically lush.

 BRIT TIP

Bartering and tipping are both regarded as something of an insult on the South Pacific Islands. Topless bathing is also a definite NO for the ladies and even shorts may be frowned on.

New Caledonia boasts the second-largest barrier reef in the world, shining emerald and turquoise through the clear waters. The main town of

BRIT TIP

My parents are big fans of the Lone Pine Koala Sanctuary just outside Brisbane for getting to meet the natives – inquisitive kangaroos, cuddly koalas and sad-faced wombats. Watch out for the koalas – they have a grip like a vice!

Noumea is situated on a peninsula with numerous bays and coves providing excellent scuba-diving and snorkelling in the reef-protected lagoons. Also worth a visit are the Botanical Gardens and Zoo near the main town area. Otherwise known as the French Riviera of the South Pacific, Noumea is home to a bewildering variety of restaurants, bistros and chic boutiques selling everything from shell necklaces to incense burners. The **Tonga** archipelago (156 islands spread over 288 square miles) features more strong cultural ties, rich natural beauty and a way of life that is unique to these islands. Tongans are typically fat and friendly and are still ruled by a king, hence the sights of the capital **Nuku'alofa** include the Royal Palace, Royal Chapel and Royal Tombs. The town also has wonderful gardens and a bustling market, while the island group of **Vava'u** offers kayakers the chance to skirt palm-fringed islands and coral reefs and explore marine caves.

A koala at the Lone Pine Koala Sanctuary

After cruising the exotic islands, the ports and cities of **Australia** can seem just a little hum-drum by comparison, despite the country's 23,000 miles of impressive coastline, but it is purely a question of re-setting your culture dial. Here it is all about a vibrant, emerging continent, modern cities, rugged outdoor adventures, watersports and a landscape that changes from dense tropical forest to harsh, unforgiving desert. **Darwin** is the most northerly settlement, a multi-cultural town that has long outgrown its frontier roots to provide such modern-day pursuits as casinos and museums housing Second World War memorabilia. Journey into the outback to see local aboriginal art and wildlife at Kakadu National Park, including the 'jumping crocodiles' on the Adelaide River. **Cairns** is the gateway to the unmissable **Great Barrier Reef** but also offers a cosmopolitan, tropical air with tree-lined streets and a great mixture of indoor and open-air markets for some great shopping. Although it is the scuba-diving capital of the Reef, Cairns also hosts white-water rafting, canoeing and horse-riding. Your cruise ship should also spend at least a day in the vicinity of the Reef, which is the largest living thing on earth. Composed of more than 300 types of coral, it is populated by technicolor fish and rare birds, with the combination of white surf, azure waters and cloudless skies making for an unforgettable experience. **Brisbane** is a thriving young city of sky-scrapers and colonial buildings, with the added attractions of Mt Cootha Botanical Gardens, the Queensland Art Museum, Queen Street Mall and the XXXX Brewery! Just to the south is the Gold Coast and **Surfers Paradise**, a rapidly-expanding section of resort development with great beaches, theme parks and natural attractions like the Currumbin Bird Sanctuary.

 BRIT TIP

When it comes to wine, South Australia can boast some of the most spectacular reds in the world, notably St Hallet's Old Block Shiraz and Rockfords Black Shiraz. Heaven in a bottle.

Sydney is surely the most photogenic port in the world with the unmistakable span of the Harbour Bridge and the outline of the Opera House, and that is just the starting point of this most impressive of cities. The historic area of The Rocks, where restaurants and museums have replaced the warehouses and convict-built streets, Darling Harbour, Sydney Aquarium, the National Maritime Museum and Taronga Zoo will all demand your attention, and that's before you go shopping or try one of the many excellent restaurants (and the local wines, of course). **Hobart**, on Tasmania, is Olde Englande Pacific-style, with handsome Georgian buildings, picturesque cottages and narrow lanes backed by lush, green hills. Here is a modern city with a good feel for its history, and the seaside wharves feature many sandstone warehouses filled with shops and cafes to help you browse away a few hours in relaxed but sophisticated style. **Devonport**, on Tasmania's sleepy north coast, offers the opportunity to visit Cradle Mountain and the Lake St Clair National Park, a World Heritage site of spectacular alpine scenery, dense forests, towering sand dunes and unique flora and fauna, including the famous Tasmanian Devil (no, not the Warner Brothers cartoon, but an equally fierce marsupial carnivore that will take on – and kill – prey up to three times its size). **Melbourne** is Australia's cultural, financial and commercial centre, with a fine display of outdoor cultural sights, including grand, tree-lined avenues, well-preserved Victorian architecture, art museums, gardens, open-air restaurants and the Royal Botanic Gardens, with the world's third oldest zoo. You can visit the State Houses of Parliament, the Museum of Victoria, pan for gold in nearby Ballarat and take a vintage steam train ride through the countryside. **Adelaide** is a small, compact and wonderfully relaxed city at the centre of one of South Australia's greatest wine-producing regions, of the

Barossa Valley. Principal tourist sights include the festival centre, Parliament House, the University of Adelaide and the enclosed Rundle Mall.

Albany, in the historic first colony of Western Australia, displays many original buildings, including the state's oldest house and post office and a memorial to the famous Light Horsemen of the tragic First World War battle of Gallipoli. Finally **Perth**, even further round on the west coast, completes the sweep of Aussie cities with its port of **Fremantle**, where you will find Victorian pubs, hotels and shops, more wine-growing country, the Swan Lager Brewery and Cahunu Park, another good place to see kangaroos and koalas.

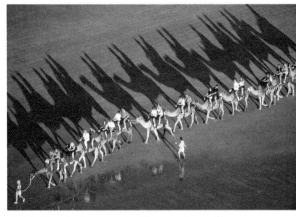

Cable Beach, Broome, in Western Australia

Don't miss: Any excursion which takes you out to the Pinnacles Desert.

If you can imagine Britain with clean cities, Scandinavian scenery, Alaskan wildlife and friendly Pacific manners, then you arrive at **New Zealand**. Wild-sculpted dunes, majestic mountains, wilderness fjords and island-studded bays are just part of the remarkable wealth of attractions on offer, which are rounded out by the opportunity for white-water rafting, jetboat rides, bungee jumping (!), hiking, whale-watching, gold-panning and horse-racing, plus some spectacular ports of call. **Auckland**, or the City of Sails after its yacht-filled harbour, is a city of stunning natural beauty, set as it is over seven extinct volcanic hills and around two bays, combining the best of the old and the new, including some impressive museums brimming with Maori artefacts. Shop at the colourful Victorian Park Market, visit the Underwater World Aquarium, take a ferry across to Devonport harbour and climb Mt Eden for the magnificent view of it all. Shopping bargains include Polynesian crafts in Karangahape Road and knitwear in Queen Street.

Don't miss: Either by tour from Auckland or the nearer, less-frequented port of Tauranga, the Maori homeland of **Rotorua** for its village and craft centre and geothermal springs, with evil-looking bubbling mud pools and geysers.

Christchurch is frequently labelled the most English city outside England (although Canada's Victoria on Vancouver Island could argue the point), a garden metropolis of parks, Gothic architecture and the spired Christchurch Cathedral all set along the meandering River Avon that somehow helps to slow the city pace down to a gentle walk. The capital, **Wellington**, cascades down pine-clad hills to its pretty harbour. Ancient timber homes and early Victorian architecture live comfortably alongside modern tower-blocks. The lively waterfront and main shopping area of Lambton Quay are at the forefront of the tourist attractions, while stairs, lifts and cable car take you from the quay to the top of Mount Victoria for a stunning scenic overview. **Napier** boasts glorious art deco buildings that rival Miami's for authenticity and scenic beauty, with the Marine Parade oceanfront another highlight for its beautifully landscaped gardens and the Nocturnal Wildlife Centre. **Dunedin** offers the feel of Scotland (Dunedin is, in fact, the Gaelic name for Edinburgh) with its Victorian red-brick buildings, mist-draped Larnach Castle and 30-acre oak woodlands of Glenfalloch, plus the panoramic views of Otago harbour. And when it comes to the spectacular coastline, the **Bay of Islands** offers scenery aplenty in its sheltered waters, plus world-record-setting deep-sea fishing and the Bay of Islands Maritime and Historic Park. There is also a quaint cruise around the bay for a close-up of the wildlife, which can include dolphins and penguins, on the old milk-collection steamer called the Fuller's Cream trip. **Milford Sound** is pure fjord country, a valley carved out by glacial ice thousands of years ago, with improbably high cliffs and waterfalls plunging down into the gorge where seals sun themselves and penguins dive through the icy waters. Finally, no cruise around New Zealand would be complete without a look at **Marlborough Sounds**, a maze of inlets and labyrinthine rock formations which offered Captain Cook a haven on one of his Pacific explorations. The pretty town of **Picton** sits at the head of neighbouring Queen Charlotte Sound, and its Dunbar Wharf is home to the last sailing vessel of the old British East India Company, the *Edwin Fox*.

THE INDIAN OCEAN AND AFRICA

WHO GOES THERE

African Safari Club, Cunard, Mediterranean Shipping,
Noble Caledonia, Fred Olsen, Orient, Radisson Seven Seas,
Renaissance, Seabourn, Silversea

Season: Year-round (November–April most commonly)

Considering the vast amounts of tranquil, inviting ocean, the eye-catching exotic ports and islands and the extra attractions of activities like safaris and other wildlife opportunities, it is surprising that the Indian Ocean and its African coast are virtually ignored by the cruise lines in any significant numbers. Even where they do visit, it is quite often just a 'passing through' segment of a longer cruise. Only the specialist, small-scale operator African Safari Club, and their homely ship *Royal Star*, and Mediterranean Shipping out of South Africa currently offer a year-round option. Stretching from the Red Sea in the north to the Cape of Good Hope off Cape Town in South Africa, and eastward through the tropical islands of Madagascar, Mauritius and the Seychelles to India and Sri Lanka, this is a colossal area of untapped cruise potential and just a few ships currently have it virtually to themselves.

The main argument against the region as a mass-market destination is its lack of a-port-a-day capability. The area is not port-intensive by any means, and some of the countries and islands are several days' journey apart. This obviously makes for more relaxed, elegant cruising, but it doesn't generally make for readily packaged one- and two-week itineraries, hence the current lack of real cruise volume. However, the Port Management Association of Eastern and Southern Africa (PMAESA), which was established in 1995, has as its main objective the active promotion of the whole area as a cruise destination, and several lines, notably Orient and Fred Olsen, have all made significant commitments already.

 **BRIT TIP**

In India (and Sri Lanka for that matter) shoppers are expected to haggle over the prices of goods like Kashmir shawls, semi-precious jewellery, carpets and lovely gilded fabrics.

Once again the attractions of the area – apart from virtually guaranteed sunshine and wonderful beaches – are its exotica, the great geographical diversity from deserts to mountains to tropical rain-forest, the fascination of culturally-diverse areas like Buddhist Sri Lanka, Arab-influenced Djibouti, historical Zanzibar and tribal Madagascar, and the spectacular flora and fauna of places like Kenya and South Africa, the latter of which is rapidly becoming a major tourist attraction in its own right.

India can be the start or finish point to an Indian Ocean cruise, with its main port at **Mumbai** (formerly Bombay), a bustling, people-choked city of some 10 million souls that varies from the Western-style skyscrapers at Nariman Point through the history-laden colonial atmosphere around Bombay Fort to the poverty-stricken shanty suburbs where it seems impossible human beings can exist at all.

An organised tour of Mumbai, covering the main sights of the Dhobi Gatt laundries, the Gateway to India, the temples of Elephanta Island, Gandhi's house and museum, the Prince of Wales Museum and the Hanging Gardens, is probably the best way of tackling this congested city for the first time. **Cochin**, in the lush, southern Kerala region, was a Portuguese settlement back in the sixteenth century, but its history goes back much further

Modern Mumbai/Bombay

as the proverbial land of incense and myrrh, a 900-year-old Jewish colony (including a sixteenth-century synagogue), and ages-old local traditions and customs, including the Kanakali, a folk dance involving elaborate hand movements and ritualistic gestures.

Don't miss: The Mattancheri Palace with its fabulous mythological murals.

Colombo, the capital and main port of **Sri Lanka**, is a fascinating mix of colonial and Oriental, with much of the architecture harking back to the days of the Raj, but the sights and sounds of the bazaars, temples and local specialities like the dancing elephants are timelessly original in their local setting. The other principal sights include the Colombo Museum, the ancient shrine at Kelaniya, Victoria Park and the President's Palace. The civil conflict between the government and the breakaway Tamil region remains a serious concern, but the most recent reports I have on the island suggest it is still a friendly, rewarding place to visit providing you heed local tourist advice.

Don't miss: Any all-day excursion to the inland city of Kandy, former royal capital of the Sinhalese kings, and one of the most sacred Buddhist sites with the sixteenth-century Temple of the Tooth.

Sailing west from Colombo brings you to the 2,000 coral islands that make up the **Maldives**, an unspoiled beach paradise featuring rare sea birds, glittering coral reefs and sealife (including giant turtles) and luxuriant vegetation. The main island is **Male**, and idyllic, palm-fringed beaches are taken for granted. Next up are the French-influenced **Seychelles**, and more tropical island splendours. The main island of **Mahe** is quite mountainous, with a pretty, ramshackle town of **Victoria**. It is also home to the giant Aldabran tortoise at the Botanical Gardens and to some fabulous marine life, which can be viewed on a glass-bottomed boat ride at the beach of Beau Vallon or more sedately at the National Marine Park. The island of **Praslin** offers an even richer tapestry of white beaches, dark mountains and verdant forests, with the world-famous Vallé de Mai National Park often compared to the Garden of Eden for its botanical wonders. The third Seychelles port of call is often **La Digue**, a must for all ornithologists as the home of the Black Paradise Flycatcher, one of the most rare and exotic species on the planet. You can rent a bicycle to explore more closely, or tour as the locals do – on the back of an ox-drawn cart.

 BRIT TIP

The increase in tourism on the Seychelles has led to a consequent rise in petty crime, and visitors are advised not to take any valuables with them on beach trips.

The **Comoros Islands** offer yet more perfect, crystal-clear lagoons, lush forests and volcanic peaks, with French-controlled **Mayotte** being the most photogenic for its coral reef bays, while **Moroni** features the Karthala Volcano, a wonderfully pretty harbour and offers magnificent diving off the west coast. The massive Indian Ocean island of **Madagascar**, and its tiny attendant **Nosy Be**, are a naturalist's paradise in much the same way as the Galapagos Isles are in the Pacific. Unique ecosystems, fascinating wildlife like the Madagascan lemurs and fragrant plants like the ever-present frangipani and bright yellow-flowered ylang-ylang make it an unforgettable visual spectacle. On Nosy Be, visit the lemur preserve of **Nosy Comba** to have one of these cute monkey-like animals eat a banana right out of your hand, or just relax a million miles away from everyday cares on the beaches at **Tanikely**. The mixture of African and Indonesian cultures is well exhibited on the main island, but it is best to stick to ship-organised excursions from the main port of **Diego Suarez** as the locals, who tend to speak French rather than English, are notoriously unhelpful.

 BRIT TIP

As in much of tropical South East Asia, the climate in Madagascar can be pretty fierce, especially as the winter season in the northern hemisphere, when many ships make the journey south, coincides with the summer down here. Expect temperatures in the 90s Fahrenheit and enervating humidity levels.

To the east of Madagascar lies the tiny volcanic island of **Reunion**, a rugged, tropical gem that is well worth seeking out in cruise itineraries. Impossibly spectacular scenery, including the lunar-like **Plaine des Sables** around the active volcano cone, French/Creole hospitality, the bustling port of **St Denis** with its colonial flavour and the inevitable sun-soaked beaches make for quite an unexpectedly intense experience. A new cruise terminal should be completed in 1998, making Reunion one of the hottest new destinations to visit.

Mauritius, to the east of Madagascar, is the other island destination of the Indian Ocean, a charming, carefully-controlled tourist environment where no building can rise higher than the indigenous palm trees and visitor numbers are restricted to annual quotas. Consequently, the atmosphere is of tranquil, unspoiled beauty at the same time as delivering a high level of modern comfort. An island tour is a pure delight, starting from the

The mountains of Reunion

harbour of **Port Louis** with its markets and gift boutiques, and taking in the Royal Botanical Gardens, the spectacular beach at Grand Baie and the Casela Bird Park, with dozens of rare species.

Coming to mainland **Africa** provides another fascinating geographical experience. Starting in the north with the country and city of **Djibouti**, at the strategic meeting of the Gulf of Aden and the Red Sea, this poor semi-desert land boasts the world's hottest climate (averaging 86°F and often exceeding 104°F), some impossibly contorted desert rock formations and a mixed Arab-

A stunning beach on Reunion

African culture, plus the French influences of 96 years as a colony. The port city of Djibouti fully highlights this crossroads feel of the Middle East and Africa, especially in its pulsating Arab markets. **Kenya** is at the heart of this region, both for its city and port of **Mombasa** and for the delights of using it as a base to explore the hinterland, with its massive landscapes and rich wildlife. The heavily Arab-influenced Old Town area of Mombasa is a real delight as the winding streets give way to colourful mosques, lively markets and elaborately-carved houses. Shop for woodcarvings, highly-patterned native cloths and soapstone chess sets.

Don't miss: The sixteenth-century Portuguese fortress of Fort Jesus.

Most cruises out of Mombasa will also offer the option of a pre- or post-cruise safari or other journey inland to see the delights of the **Masai Mara** region. The vast low-level forests and grasslands are home to all the major species of African wildlife, including lions, elephants, leopards, buffalo, rhino, impala, wildebeest, zebras and gazelles. **Tanzania** offers more spectacular game parks and other natural wonders, like the stunning 10-mile wide, 2,000-feet deep crater of **Ngorongoro** with its swarming animal populations, Lake Manyara at the entrance to the Great Rift Valley (and the archaeological treasure of Olduvai Gorge), **Manyara Park** with the greatest concentration of elephants in the world and the **Serengeti National Park**, a 5,600-square-mile expanse dotted with rocky outcrops, acacia bushes, forest and small rivers, not to mention the small matter of millions of zebras and wildebeest, plus lions, cheetahs, giraffes, hyenas and other typical African inhabitants. This is THE place for wildlife. The main ports are the city of **Dar Es Salaam** on the mainland, a lively, modern, often chaotic centre, designed mainly to handle cargo, and the island of **Zanzibar**, the most common cruise ship harbour. The latter, the nineteenth-century centre of the Arab slave trade and spice industry, is a real tourist trap, with its crowded bazaars, narrow stone streets and strong-scented spice shops. Other sights include the Arab Fort and Dhow harbour, the ruins of the Maruhubi Palace, the Palace of the Sultans, the site of the notorious slave market (now a small cathedral) and the house where Dr Livingstone lived before setting out on his last expedition into the continent. Almost inevitably, there are some more splendid white-sand beaches, although swimmers are strongly advised to heed the warnings about the fierce currents which make the east coast quite treacherous.

South Africa has long been a cruise-ship destination, but it is only since the end of apartheid and the onset of democratic rule that its possibilities as a tourist destination have been fully appreciated, and the country certainly expects to be enjoying a major holiday boom by the end of the century – so get in first! Having travelled widely in Southern Africa (my family lived there for seven years) I may be a touch biased, but to my mind it is the perfect blend of natural wonders, scenic cities and blissful climate, with the added attraction of more good wildlife-watching opportunities, great beaches and some outstanding wines in the Cape region. The only real worry for its long-term prospects is the increase in crime in the major cities which has already made parts of Johannesburg no-go areas. Cruise-and-stay options should

 **BRIT TIP**

Hikers will find the Cape a real paradise, with 140 trails over the top of Table Mountain alone. The Cape of Good Hope itself offers some rewarding hikes, plus the chance to view the meeting of the two great oceans, the Atlantic and the Indian, and the line of marker buoys that mark the join, stretching into the distance.*

become big business in South Africa, though, centred on the two great ports of **Cape Town** and **Durban**. The former is right up there with Hong Kong, Rio de Janeiro, Sydney and Istanbul as one of the great scenic ports of the world, with its backing of awesome Table Mountain. It is worth getting up early for the sight of sailing into port with that unforgettable backdrop. The city itself will keep you more than fully occupied for a day, with St George's Cathedral, the Victoria and Alfred Waterfront (where new shops and cafés mix with working fishing boats and ships under repair), the seventeenth-century Castle of Good Hope, the beaches of Hout Bay, Clifton Beach and Sea Point Promenade, plus the unmissable chance to take the cable car to the top of Table Mountain for a breathtaking overview of the area (but not on windy days, which are rather frequent). Start to travel to the immediate hinterland and more delights are in store: the awesome scenic route of Chapman's Peak

*Surely you didn't fall for that old gag? Marker Buoys indeed! Everyone knows the meeting of the two oceans is easily spotted because the Atlantic is two feet higher than the Indian.

Drive, the Cape of Good Hope Nature Reserve, the beaches of Fish Hoek, the nautical charm of Simonstown, and the magnificent, mountain-framed scenery and charming picture-postcard Cape Dutch homesteads of the Cape winelands, typified by the historic town of Stellenbosch, the 'Town of Oaks'.

 BRIT TIP

You can watch the tugs and pilot boats buzzing in and out of Durban's Small Craft Basin from the BAT Centre, which consists of a lively restaurant, theatre, and gift shops centred on the arts.

Don't miss: The chance to sample the local wines, and, from October to December, the Cape of Good Hope Nature Reserve when it bursts into vivid bloom as part of the richest floral kingdom in the world.

Durban is the Indian Ocean gateway to South Africa and the largest city in the province of Natal, a lively mix of Zulu, East Indian and European cultures. A quick drive through Durban reveals this heritage in the shape of the Indian Market, Zulu Arts centres and Zulu dancing, as well as the many modern shopping complexes, the Botanical Gardens and the exciting entertainment venues in the harbour, right on the quayside.

Journeying out of Durban brings you to **Natal National Park** and more African wildlife, while the **Valley of a Thousand Hills** is truly spectacular and offers the chance to learn all about Zulu culture at **Assagai Safari Park**. **Port Elizabeth**, the fourth-largest port, is a more elegant, relaxed city than Durban, and can boast a variety of readily-accessible scenic attractions which have earned it the nickname of 'the 10-minute city' (because none of them is more than 10 minutes away). The possibilities include rich bird and floral reserves, early morning and late afternoon game park drives, a snake park, an oceanarium, museums, arts and craft galleries, vintage steam train outings and boat excursions along the pretty coast. **East London** completes the line-up of South Africa's cruise ports and is part of the 'Romantic Coast', a near

 **BRIT TIP**

For all the fact South Africa has some marvellous scenic wonders, its sheer size dictates it also has some pretty boring stretches. Steer clear in particular of the featureless Little Karoo Desert, the vast expanses of Orange Free State's maize fields, and the coast route through the mist-prone Transkei, between East London and Durban, which is like driving through Wales on a wet day.

300-mile stretch of long, unspoiled, safe, clean beaches in resorts like Haga-Haga and Lagoon Valley, tangled dune forests and evergreen nature reserves. The beaches of **Nahoon Reef** and **Eastern Beach** are ideal for surfing, while nature lovers will enjoy the Umtiza Forest, with its unique Umtiza trees filled wirh chattering monkeys, and the **Gonubie Bird Sanctuary**. Back in town, check out Latimer's Landing, a major new waterfront development featuring restaurants, flea markets and gift shops.

Don't miss: Mpongo Park, a 20-minute drive from East London, where you can dine above the resident hippos after a day of watching antelope, rhino and other typical wildlife in action.

ANTARCTICA AND SOUTH AMERICA

WHO GOES THERE

Antarctica: Abercrombie & Kent, Hapag-Lloyd, Noble Caledonia, Orient, Society Expeditions

Season: December–February

South America: Abercrombie & Kent, Costa, Crystal, Cunard, Hapag-Lloyd, Noble Caledonia, Mediterranean Shipping, NCL, Fred Olsen, Princess, Royal Olympic, Seabourn, Silversea, Society Expeditions

Season: September–April

Linking these two rather disparate destination areas together does make some sense as they are both the preserve of specialist operators who often offer unique views of and excursions to the ports of call. South America is also a genuine geographical link to cruising in the incomparable Antarctic Ocean since the main starting points for South Pole voyages are the southernmost ports of Chile and Argentina.

South America is a unique blend of European culture, native heritage and African traditions and rhythms that lives for Carnival time, the chance to dance the night away in exuberant, evocative style. It is a continent of swarming

Abercrombie & Kent explore both Antarctica and the Amazon River in great detail, offering a unique cruise experience

cities, impenetrable jungles and lonely outposts like the Falkland Islands and Straits of Magellan. You can shop in exclusive boutiques in Montevideo and Buenos Aires or native craft markets; dine out on exotically-spiced foods; enjoy fabulous colonial architecture and modern sky-scrapers; and learn about a major ecological system on the verge of breakdown because of the devastation of the rain-forests of the interior. It is a continent that is both exciting and heart-breaking at the same time.

The principal attraction of South America, though, is the **Amazon River**, 3,900 miles long and up to 30 miles wide in places, it can more than cope with the medium-sized cruise ships that aim to explore this region and it positively engulfs the small, expedition ships, which are the only ones to get you a real close-up experience of the Brazilian jungle. The majority offer the Amazon cruise from the port of **Belem** at the mouth of the great river as far as Manaus some 1,000 miles from the Atlantic Ocean, but Abercrombie & Kent and their little adventurer the *Explorer* are notable for journeying some 1,000 miles further up to Iquitos in Peru, providing a far more intimate view of this mind-boggling world of improbable waters and impenetrable forest. Considering much of the time the banks are just distant blurs on the far horizon and what wildlife there may be is practically invisible, it is nevertheless an intensely rewarding cruise as you still get to visit some fascinating ports of call along the way, including the **Breves Narrows**, a labyrinth of narrow channels and one of the most scenic areas with its stilt houses and fishermen in dugout canoes; **Alter do Chao**, the Altar of the Earth, a white sand beach offering great swimming and a small village where you can taste the local drink guarana, made from caffeine-rich seeds; **Santarem**, a trading port full of all manner of floating craft; **Boca de Valeria**, a close-up view of a genuine Amazon village and its people, who all want to be photographed or barter for beaded necklaces and other local curios; **Anavilhanas**, a tiny port on an island archipelago beloved of the great marine biologist Jacques Cousteau for its brilliant sights and abundant wildlife, including river dolphins, turtles, sloths and the scarlet ibis; the **Wedding of the Waters** at Manaus, where the two rivers of the dark-stained Rio Negro and coffee-coloured Solimoes (as the Amazon is known in its upper reaches) meet and are flowing so fast they go side by side for nearly four miles before finally merging; and **Manaus** itself, a duty-free port and sprawling city of some 1.5 million people that was briefly the richest city in the world at the turn of the century because of the rubber boom, and still boasts a nineteenth-century Opera House, art deco Municipal Market, Indian Museum and Natural Science Museum full of all South America's nasty beasties which (hopefully) you never got a close-up of on the river.

 BRIT TIP

Haggling for goods in the craft markets and stalls is expected – and so are pickpockets and other petty thieves in most of Brazil's cities. Take good care of your wallet and handbag, and NEVER take valuables on to a beach, especially in Rio, where crime is a serious problem.

Travelling south along the coast of **Brazil** brings you to other fascinating ports like **Fortaleza**, the country's fifth-largest city, most famous for its lace industry and with a wonderful handicrafts centre in the converted old city jail, the Centro de Turismo, where you can shop for leather, wooden carvings and sand paintings in bottles as well as hand-made lace; **Recife**, an immaculate city with great shopping at the Pernambuco Culture Center, another prison-turned-craft-market, and pretty churches and bridges; **Salvador**, with its historic Baroque-styled Pelourinho District from its colonial days, dozens of churches (nearly 200 in all) and superb public market of Mercado Modelo; **Santos**, the largest port in South America and gateway to the impossibly crowded, smog-laden city of **Sao Paulo**; and, of course, huge, scenic **Rio de Janeiro**, home of the spectacular annual Carnival (the weekend before Ash Wednesday), magnificent museums, world-famous beaches like the Copacabana and Ipanema, the world's largest football stadium, the Maracana (holding in excess of 200,000), sleek, high-rise developments and poverty-ridden shanty-towns huddled on the steepest slopes surrounding the city. The setting, of course, is breathtaking, with the huge Guanabara Bay dotted with rocky, palm-covered islands and surrounded by steep, domed mountains like the famous Sugar Loaf and Corcovado with its giant statue of Christ, and, in keeping with the great crowded city centres of the world these days, notably New York, Tokyo and Cairo, you'll either love it or hate it.

Don't miss: The cable car ride to the top of Sugar Loaf for the stunning view over the city and the bay.

After Rio, the **Uruguayan** capital and main port of **Montevideo** is a positively restful experience. Heavily influenced by European culture, it is a vibrant, modern city full of art deco buildings, heroic statues and elegant monuments, the fascinating Prado District and the Rambla, or riverfront drive.

Don't miss: Any excursion to a local ranch for a demonstration of those traditional gaucho (cowboy) skills and a barbecue feast.

The neighbouring port of **Punte del Este** is the up-market beach resort area for Montevideo, set on a peninsula lined with white-sand beaches, it attracts South America's jet-setters to the calm waters of the west side, the large waves of the east, or just to shop, play golf or go deep-sea fishing.

 BRIT TIP

Buenos Aires offers some tempting European-style shopping on pedestrianised Florida Street, but it is a long walk from the harbour. Taxis are relatively cheap (a 10-minute ride shouldn't cost more than £3–£4), but many take only TWO passengers.

You can't usually visit Montevideo without paying a visit to **Buenos Aires**, the cultural heart and political capital of **Argentina**, a sprawling, sophisticated city of broad avenues, parks and flowers. Sample the fare at one of the many open-air pavement cafés or shop for the immaculate leather goods of Avenida Lavalle, tour the ornate opera house Teatro Colon or, for a real taste of South American experience, visit a local dance parlour to learn the tango. Other famous landmarks are the Casa Rosada, the former presidential palace of Juan and Evita Peron, Evita's Tomb and the Obelisk.

Puerto Madryn is Argentina's other main port, and is usually the gateway to the fabulous wildlife preserve on the Valdes Peninsula, with its collection of birds, the 13,000 or so amusing sea elephants and offshore whale-breeding grounds. The port also boasts some fine seafood restaurants. Those patriotic souls who fancy a visit to the bleak **Falklands Islands** can also do so on a South American itinerary out of Montevideo. Be warned, the wildly dramatic, windswept cliffs, hills and beaches (home to numerous waterfowl and sea-birds) are rarely warm, so you will need to have packed a couple of warm sweaters (a similar effect can be gained much closer to home in the Shetland Isles, and at least they have plenty of whisky there). Still, the wildlife can be quite rewarding, with the tiny Magellan's penguins, black-browed albatross, kelp geese and rare Peal's dolphins all adding up to a naturalist's delight.

Going further south still brings you to the two most southern ports, Chile's **Punta Arenas** and Argentina's **Ushaia**, the southernmost town in the world (population: 20,000 hardy souls). The months of December and January are just about the only time of the year that the vast, rocky wilderness of **Tierra Del Fuego** and its famous point of Cape Horn are anything like hospitable, but again they offer a unique experience, especially for nature-lovers. At Ushaia you can take a catamaran trip to see the teeming wildlife of the Beagle Channel or visit Fagnano Lake with its peat bogs (see, it's the Shetlands again) and beaver dams, and dine in a charming country inn. Punta Arenas is another frontier-like town, where local museums, housed in what used to be mansions, honour the region's cultural and natural history. Dine on unique shellfish and other seafood, and shop for wood and shell carvings in the duty-free zone. The hardiest of sailing aficionados will also want to savour the newest cruise experience being offered by Princess, Seabourn and Silverseas, the chance to sail right round Cape Horn and up into the truly spectacular Chilean Fjords, which make Alaska and Norway look tame by comparison. Sailing between the fishing towns of **Puerto Natales** and **Puerto Montt**, you can enjoy the magnificent sight of the **Torres Del Paine**, where the glaciers are topped by sheer rock spires, and condors soar overhead, and you can do it in supreme comfort and style, soaking up scenery that could be the moon for all its similarity to anywhere else on earth. This, truly, is one of the last great cruise frontiers and will appeal to anyone with a thirst for adventure in their soul.

And talking of frontiers brings me neatly to the last serious cruise area of the world, **Antarctica**.

Whether it is the awe-inspiring natural beauty of one of the world's most forbidding regions, the abundance of stunning wildlife or just the feeling of achievement at having cruised where only a relative handful have gone, the adventure experience of Antarctica is at once exciting, educational and

A WORD FROM THE WISE

Captain Ben Haas, vice-president of Orient Lines and former skipper of their ship, *Marco Polo*, summed it up for me when he explained: 'My first opportunity to cruise Antarctica was unreal. During the months of preparation, a picture formed in my mind of what to expect. But, when the first Antarctic iceberg appeared in our sights, it was quite different from what I had imagined. Massive, brilliant white and blue (and completely flat on top like a magnificent, illuminated condominium); nothing had prepared me for such an awesome sight. The ice has a mesmerising effect (you just cannot get enough of it), in every shape and hue. In Antarctica, the days are so long and wildlife is amazing. During the cruise season, in the window of the short austral summer, the sea is surprisingly calm and the weather is usually bright and sunny. I always wanted to make the long voyage from the Antarctic Peninsula by way of the Ross Ice Shelf to New Zealand, and in the *Marco Polo* I achieved that ambition. For me, one of the most interesting aspects was the lectures from our team of experts, who brought it all to life and took us into the huts where explorers like Shackleton and Scott had wintered. It makes you feel quite small.'

uplifting. Nothing in your normal life will feel quite the same after you have gone ashore by Zodiac landing craft, trodden the ice of the great frozen Southern Continent or looked a giant penguin in the eye. In fact, no pictures or words can really do it justice and the appeal of cruising this icy wilderness will be either instantly obvious or totally off-putting.

 BRIT TIP

Remember this is still an expedition, for all the creature comforts of ships like the *Marco Polo*, and, as such, the route and ports of call are distinctly subject to weather, ice and wildlife conditions and can be changed at short notice. Despite the drawbacks, these are among the most popular cruises anywhere, and it is vital to book EARLY to get on.

Round trips from Ushaia or Punta Arenas, or the grand Antarctic circum-navigation all the way to New Zealand are all on offer.

On the round-trip itineraries expect to visit the likes of **Hope Bay**, with its huge Adelie penguin rookery, **Deception Island**, a volcanic caldera where the bravest souls can swim in the steam-heated waters, spectacular **Paradise Harbour**, dotted with floating icebergs, and the gentoo penguin rookery of **Port Lockroy**, surrounded by spectacular mountains. The circumnavigation route (lasting in excess of 20 days) comes within 736 miles of the South Pole at the American **McMurdo Station**, the largest research facility based on the continent and home to hundreds of scientists, and also takes in **Cape Evans**,

 **BRIT TIP**

Although the vistas are always icy, don't pack as if for sub-zero temperatures (it will usually be around 55°F during the day). Most ships will supply you with the necessary all-weather parka, but do take a lightweight waterproof jacket and over-trousers, comfortable, waterproof boots and plenty of film. Specialist publications also advise taking small gifts for the scientists who show you round their research stations – current magazines, books, fresh fruit and souvenirs from your home town.

Cape Royds and **Cape Adare**, where the stark huts bear witness to the incredible hardships suffered by the first Antarctic explorers. And, in addition to the comical, fearless penguins (which, having no previous experience of Man, are interminably curious), you should also see giant elephant seals, leopard seals, humpback whales and killer whales, as well as countless seabirds. Don't get the idea, however, that you can rush off and trample around this great wilderness unhindered. Groups are carefully supervised to maintain environmental controls, and the local wildlife cannot be interfered with in any way.

Well, that about wraps it up for the whole wide world of cruising. I am often asked where my favourite cruise areas are, but the simple truth is I just enjoy cruising. All the different regions have their attractions and it isn't difficult to get the best out of them by doing your homework and getting stuck in. Whether it is Barbados or Brisbane, Alaska or the Amazon, they all have a rich and rewarding experience to offer. Hopefully, by reading this book you will have gained a better understanding of what it is all about, but there is simply no substitute for first-hand experience. Just get out there and cruise!

(* Papas & Beer – the answer. Ordering a shooter is the recipe for instant mayhem to break out as the resident bartender grabs his unsuspecting 'victim' and, with whistles blowing and crowds cheering, proceeds to empty one of his lethal cocktails forcibly down the poor unfortunate's throat and then lift him or her upside down for a violent shaking to get the maximum alcoholic effect. I kid you not. Ugh!)

＊

CHAPTER SEVEN

Hold The Front Page

(or, the Latest Cruise News)

Once again, the amount of last-minute cruise news is considerable, and here is as much as we can legitimately squeeze in at this stage of the Brit's Guide's production. Cruise line by line, here's the latest hot gossip.

Celebrity: They are doubling their Alaska capacity by sending their newest ship *Mercury* to the US West Coast for the summer season in 1998.

CTC: The popular, budget-priced British-based operator sold their ship, *Southern Cross*, to Festival in 1997, but insist they will be chartering another ship for a full ex-UK 1998 programme. No details were available, however.

Festival: The fast-growing Italian-based line have unveiled a series of 7- and 14-night Baltic and Norwegian Fjord fly-cruises in 1998 sailing out of the German port of Kiel. Also new in 1998 is the Seagulls Club for children, with separate dining and activity programmes. And they have ordered a new, 1,200 passenger ship for 1999.

First Choice: The big British tour operator has confirmed plans for a Med cruise operation in 1998, but no other details were available at press time.

Freighter Cruising: A new, independent magazine, *Freighter Travel Review*, has been launched in Britain to give the full inside track on this lesser-known cruise style, with a full run-down of the many lines and agents who book passengers on cargo ships world-wide. For more information, call them on 01206 503798.

Millenium Cruises: Many lines are already booking those once-in-a-lifetime trips for New Year 2000. Cunard have announced their schedules and are taking provisional bookings, while their prices will be revealed in 1998. Crystal, Fred Olsen, Orient, Radisson Seven Seas, Seabourn, Silversea and Windstar are also taking pre-registrations.

NCL: There seems no end to NCL's current growth as they seek to recapture their pre-eminent position among the big operators. They have revealed a tenth addition to their fleet with the purchase of the splendid MS *Aida* that operates in the German market for Arkona Reisen. NCL will initially lease her back to Arkona in 1998 but work closely on future sales and marketing of this 1996-built vessel – almost a German version of P&O's

Oriana – which takes some 1,200 passengers around the Med and Caribbean. NCL have announced another big step forward with the inclusion of ALL tips (a saving of £35–40 per person on a 7-day cruise). New flights to San Juan increase their capacity on Saturday sailings of *Seaward* and enhance further her British appeal. New itineraries include South America for *Norwegian Crown*, a second ship in Alaska and the 'stretched' *Norwegian Dream* (capacity up to 1,760) débuting in Europe with Baltic and Scandinavian voyages from Dover.

Fred Olsen: In a bid to target a younger market, the usually ex-UK sailings of the largely British passenger carrying Olsen line have been boosted by a series of Barbados fly-cruises in 1998 aboard their *Black Watch*.

P&O: Their classic liner *Victoria* heads for a £4m refit in October that should enhance her appeal.

Princess: They have announced a new Grand Class Gold Butler Service for all suites and mini-suites on Europe-based ships in summer, 1998.

Royal Caribbean: The new 78,000-ton *Vision of the Seas*, due to début in Southampton on May 9, 1998, will become the latest RCI ship to be featured in Europe when she operates her inaugural season out of Barcelona offering 7-night trips around the western Mediterranean. She then features a fascinating transatlantic repositioning cruise in September, taking in the Shetlands, Iceland and Newfoundland.

Royal Olympic: The big Greek line have announced their intention to begin modernising the fleet with three new vessels, in the 600–1,000 berth range, for delivery in 1999, 2000 and 2001. They also have more Greek island cruise-and-stay options in 1998, plus some attractive winter fly-cruises to South America and the Caribbean.

Sun Vista: This new operation (formerly Celebrity's classic cruiser *Meridian*) by Singapore-based Metro Holdings will be featured in several tour operators' cruise brochures in 1998, notably Lunn Poly's Cruise Collection and Kuoni's Cruise and Stay. The *Sun Vista* will offer various 4- and 7-night programmes around Thailand and Malaysia after a $15m refurbishment. Full details have yet to be released, but the style looks not dissimilar to Star Cruise, i.e. a good Western/Oriental mix.

Thomson: Proving their commitment to the cruise business, Thomson have added a fourth ship in 1998, the 25,500-ton *Topaz*, formerly the 1964-built *Regent Sun*, from American firm Cruise Holdings. And, in a bold move to enhance their value-for-money appeal, she will be *fully inclusive* of drinks and tips, have open-seating dining and feature a 24-hour buffet. If the generally spacious style of *Topaz* is updated as well as their other Cruise Holdings ship, *IslandBreeze*, she should be an extremely enticing prospect, with a series of Caribbean itineraries out of Port Canaveral in Florida to the Bahamas and Mexico from May–October. A week's cruise PLUS a week's stay in Orlando leads in at an eye-catching £799. Thomson are enhancing their tie-up with NCL's *Seaward* by booking 45 per cent of her cabins in 1998, and all their holidays now feature the Money Back Guarantee.